Praise for *Untethered*

"I knew Dave Proctor's record-setting run across Canada was hard—
it's a really big country, after all—but I had no idea how hard until I
read *Untethered*. Following his progress as he navigates the physical,
logistical, and personal challenges of his journey makes for a great
read."

—*Alex Hutchinson, New York Times bestselling author of*
***Endure** & contributor to Outside & Runners World*

"Dave embodies the indomitable spirit of the ultrarunner. His adventure
crossing the length of Canada running is inspiring and reveals the
mental fortitude that can be unlocked from us all."

—*Harvey Lewis, World Champion Big's Backyard*
Ultra & Men's Champion Badwater 2014

"Running a long way with Dave is always a pleasure, and sharing every
day of his transcon adventure via this book is a great way to do that
without the sore legs."

—*Robbie Britton, British 24-Hour Men's Champion*

UNTETHERED

THE COMEBACK STORY OF ONE OF THE LONGEST FASTEST RUNS IN HISTORY

DAVE PROCTOR

OUTRUNNER PRESS
Okotoks · Alberta · Canada

Front Cover Photo Credit: Vera Neverkevich Hill

Back Cover Author Photo: Doug Mitchell

This book is dedicated to the three loves of my life: Julia, Sam, and Adele.

When I look at you, I see perfection.

Julia, in you I see a natural leader full of intuition and intelligence.

Sam, your kindness and good heart inspire me to be a better man.

Adele, your spirit and outgoing nature restore
my faith in humanity's future.

You three have made me the luckiest man on the planet and
I am proud every minute of every day to be your father.

All men should strive to learn before they die, what they are running from, and to, and why.

—James Thurber

Contents

Crossing A Continent i

Foreword iii

Introduction v

Chapter 1: Newfoundland.. 1
   First Steps..1
   I Remember This Feeling 7
   Slow Suffocation.. 9
   Acceptance 11
   A Winged Beast.. 14
   Choice... 16
   The Clock Never Stops 19
   Come Hell or High Water..................................21
   A Parting Gift 24

Chapter 2: Outrun Rare 27

Chapter 3: Nova Scotia 53
   Mainland 53
   Dazed and Confused 55
   Boiling Point 58
   The Fracture.. 62

Chapter 4: New Brunswick 66
   This Is This..66
   The Three Amigos...69
   The Vault 72
   Three to Five Percent 76
   Groundhog Day...Again 79

Chapter 5: Quebec..82
   The Language of Love 82
   St. Lawrence Seaway....................................... 85
   Lightning and Rainbows 88
   Salamander, Coyote, Eagle and Dragon 91
   Happy Mistakes 94

Worthy Of My Suffering 98

Chapter 6: Eastern Ontario 102

Go My Own Way 102

Non-Striving 108

A Hard Stretch 111

Developing Tolerance 115

Eating Contest 118

Efficiently Consistent 121

Protest 126

Pick Your Battles 129

Chapter 7: Western Ontario 134

Superior 134

Brothers' Quarrel 137

Tension 141

Amends 143

Two-Stepping with Terry 146

Legends Never Die 150

Highway of Courage 152

Unconscious 155

Like a Dog 160

Like It's 1991 162

Limbic Overdrive 164

Lake of the Woods 167

Chapter 8: Growing Pains 170

Chapter 9: Manitoba 188

The Hundredth Meridian 188

Flashbacks 191

Letting Go in the Prairies 193

Cyborg Status 195

Seven Weeks 198

Chapter 10: Saskatchewan 203

Blinders 203

Piercing Pain 205

Survival Over Reward 208

Shaky Ground 213

Tough Cowboy 215

Alberta-Bound 218

Chapter 11: The Captain's Chair **222**

Chapter 12: Alberta **229**

Time with the Lady 229

Julia, Sam, and Adele 232

Familiar Territory...................................... 236

Home Stretch 239

Enter the Rockies...................................... 242

Chapter 13: British Columbia **247**

God is Great 247

Liquid Courage... 252

Hit and Run... 255

Tokens 258

A Tethered Beast 261

Finding Hope 264

Silence of the Salamander 267

Flight of the Dragon.................................. 271

Chapter 14: The Aftermath............................. **282**

Acknowledgments **295**

Photo Gallery **297**

CROSSING A CONTINENT

*—Lazarus Lake, legendary founder of the fabled
and feared Barkley Marathons*

If there is one question a transcontinental runner gets more than any other, it is: "Why?"

Unfortunately this is also the most difficult question to answer.

Because for the transcon runner it is inconceivable that anyone could *not* want to run across.

As someone who completed a transcontinental crossing myself, the best response I ever came up with is: "Look at the map... there is an ocean on one side, and another ocean on the other side, and untold, unknown adventures in between. How can anyone not want to cross it?"

Naturally, there is an insatiable desire to read accounts of other people's crossings. It is the same journey, experienced in an infinite number of different ways.

The commonalities are many.

Every transcon runner must deal with so many obstacles and

detours. We all face the harsh reality that there are only twenty-four hours in a day, and every minute has to be applied to the run in some form or another. Spending every waking moment outside can be glorious; but there is no respite from clouds of biting insects, pouring rain, high winds, or scorching heat/bitter cold.

Every transcon is a journey to the edge of physical limits. It becomes a test of pain maintenance and nursing an ever-growing number of "minor" injuries and trying to prevent any of them from blossoming into the "major" injury that will end the attempt.

Every transcon is also different. Attempts range from the low budget, solo effort—pushing a cart of supplies and sleeping wherever the runner can lay their head—to the fully supported speed record attempts with dedicated crews and vehicles.

The routes can be as varied as the methods. Every runner will see different sunrises and meet different people. Every trip will have its own adventures.

But, in the end, every transcon comes down to the same thing.

It is a single-minded effort to lay down a continuous string of footprints from one ocean to the other. No matter how well-supported, the run is built on long hours alone under an endless sky. Whether crossing craggy mountain ranges, broad rivers, or endless plains, a transcon is as much an exploration of what is inside the runner as what surrounds them. The trip changes the traveler in ways that are difficult to explain.

This story chronicles one such journey. Like all transcons it is special for many reasons.

It is special because it is an attempt to break a venerable record for crossing North America at its widest traversable point.

It is special because it is redemption for a previous failed attempt.

And it is special because it is a unique journey.

No one made this exact trek ever before, and no one will again.

FOREWORD

—*Pete Kostelnick, Guinness World Record for the fastest*
coast-to-coast run across the United States

The idea of crossing, on foot, a massive landmass stretching thousands of miles is perhaps the most extreme mental and physical undertaking known to today's human.

Once considered a logical necessity of Homo sapiens, these days it attracts some of the most, shall we call it, *intense* personalities. It takes a special kind of wiring to (want to) do it. Most people who have the inkling to attempt something so mundane and endless quickly find out they don't have the physical or mental means to do it.

And then there are others that take that first step.

No matter what rate you move at, covering land on foot acquaints you with that stretch of land in a way that no other forms of transportation can. As the land slowly moves past, you look off to the left and see a tree at least one hundred feet deep in the forest and know that tree will never mean more to anyone else than it does to you as the millions of other trees cheer you along from the sidelines.

As the sun sets, you see a village up ahead just to the right and know there is a stranger there somewhere working the evening shift, who will become your new best friend in a few miles with a warm meal to replenish your soul.

When Dave and I chatted about his desire to run across Canada in record time as we competed in the IAU's 24 Hour World Championship for our respective countries in Belfast in 2017, I was less than a year separated from doing the same across my homeland in the States.

Even though I was his junior in age and in every other way in the sport of ultrarunning, I felt like the older brother, not wanting to ruin the surprise for what my younger brother was in for. Most of it is not glamorous or pretty, but somehow impossible to resist. But I knew he would do it, no matter how many times it would take to get it right. And I also knew he would hate himself if he didn't.

When you know you can break a record like running across one of the biggest countries in the world, a country that touches an ocean on either side, you don't just obsess about it. It becomes your new world, and everything else must fit into that.

For a certain type of ultrarunner, where no cookie jar is ever big enough, and no distance far enough, it is the ultimate road to fulfillment.

Dave's account of his run across Canada is a rare story that will keep you turning each page to see what happens next in his quest for a record, all while seeing the beautifully diverse country of Canada at his side.

Perhaps the best viewpoint to be had, though, is seeing how Dave's mind overcomes significant physical and mental hurdles in ways we can all benefit from in all aspects of life.

Buckle up for a wild ride with the man in the cowboy hat!

INTRODUCTION

I've always thought of myself as an ultramarathoner. Over twenty years, I've run thousands of marathons and hundreds of ultramarathons, pushing my body in ways that even I can't comprehend.

I've set world records, Guinness records, Canadian records, and many course records. But it's not just records that were broken. My concept of limits has been challenged, stretched, taken apart and re-formed countless times. I've surprised myself by reaching new heights, only to be consumed by the search for what's beyond the end of my rope or my well.

The relentless pursuit of 'more' hasn't been easy to understand; and the reward has often not been worth the suffering.

Yet I persist.

This is a tale of my search for meaning, in the only place I thought might have answers: *out there.*

When I ran my first ultramarathon in 2006, I thought the answer lay just inches away, somewhere around the next bend in the trail. Now, hundreds of thousands of kilometres later, I'm still searching.

The goal of running across my great home country of Canada and breaking the Trans Canada speed record has been in my blood for many years; but the attachment to a goal sometimes too large to comprehend is a prickly pear.

The objective—to run across Canada faster than anyone else—is superficially simple: get out there, put one foot in front of the other, and keep repeating until you're done. Yet, the logistics of route planning, packing, lodging, crewing, and simply logging the daily distance again and again and again can take on a nightmarish complexity that scares most athletes away.

The wish to do something gets you out the door. After that, it's about the complex web of reasons behind the relentless striving.

It's also a complicated story because I'm a complicated person living a complicated life.

I feel that somewhere out there is my missing piece, and until I find that piece, I remain incomplete, unfinished, and imperfect.

The answers to the questions "Who am I" and "What is the meaning of life?" have never seemed so elusive. Perhaps the answers lie forever at the end of the metaphorical rainbow, in some unreachable place where folklore is real and heroes are giants amongst giants, accomplishing incomprehensible feats of daring greatness recounted time and time again to audiences young and old.

Perhaps they're hidden in plain sight, right under my feet, and the only way to find them is to get out there and run.

My thoughts as I set out on this monumental undertaking were therefore not about badassery, triumph, praise, or romantic notions of adventure; but about suffering, sacrifice and self-questioning as I searched for the answers I burned for.

Open any world map and you'll notice as I did years ago—because it's impossible to miss—that at just shy of 10 million square kilometres, Canada is the second-largest country in the world.

All I had to do was run across it—faster than anyone before me.

CHAPTER 1: NEWFOUNDLAND

First Steps

DAY 1	COMPLETED	REMAINING
105.2 kms in 11:41:01	105.2 kms	7053.8 kms

The surprisingly hilly landscape of rugged Newfoundland sprawls in all directions from my vantage point alongside the shoulder of the Trans-Canada Highway.

I steadily plod my course facing west atop this 108,860-square kilometre rock, the sixteenth largest island in the world.

This is the starting point for my second attempt to run across Canada. And if all goes well, I'll break the Trans Canada speed record.

I was setting out to endure the longest, fastest run in human history, arrogantly challenging the late, great Al Howie's record set in 1991 when he rocketed across Canada in 72 days, 10 hours, and 23 minutes.

1

The legendary tales of the "Spartan Tartan" with his cascading blond hair and bushy ginger beard, averaging 100 kilometres a day for 72 consecutive days, seemed less daunting last week when I was still sitting on my sofa, bourbon in hand.

My girlfriend of eighteen months, Lana Rae Ledene, had joined me on this grand adventure five hours ago and roughly fifty kilometres east. It was a cold, humid morning when we arrived at the Terry Fox Memorial on the docks of St. John's harbour.

We had rented an Airbnb just a short walk from there where I struggled to sleep in the nights prior. It's not that it wasn't comfortable; it was that this was my second and final attempt to run across Canada, and I knew very well exactly what lay before me over the next seventy-two days.

The anguish and nervous attention to readiness that accompany such an effort can only be understood by the doer. I fought every urge to turtle, to find a reason to not get on with it, to choose comfort over pain. I knew what I was doing, but the nagging voices kept me up at night, and they were relentless.

Lana Rae had agreed to crew me for the first sixteen days and to head up logistics for the entire run. This is no small feat, as the daily management of the crew vehicle, meals, hotel reservations, grocery shopping, on-the-fly troubleshooting, coordinating other crew members' flights, budgeting, and all the miscellaneous everyday surprises can unravel even the most organized person.

But she is no ordinary woman. She exudes confidence, capability, and an attention to detail so sharp that it takes most people off guard.

She had not been feeling her finest for many days now, having come down with a respiratory virus that zapped her energy and left her coughing. Although she strained to stay at a distance to avoid spreading it to me, the comfort and peace every hug or kiss brought drew me back over and over.

Earlier that morning, we had stood at a very different start line from the one I had been at in Victoria four years earlier, on my first attempt to run across Canada.

This time, the event lacked fanfare: no media, only three onlookers, no giant RV wrapped in sponsor logos, no national awareness and fundraising campaign—no promise to shoulder the weight of a community.

It was just me, Lana Rae, our SUV full of supplies, and a desire to go for a very long jog, joined by the award-winning Canadian filmmaker and ultrarunner Vera Neverkevich Hill who's been shooting my family and me for the last three years as part of a feature-length documentary about transcontinental crossings.

My life for the next 67 days was going to be simple: wake up at 4 a.m. and roll into my running clothes, applying skin lube and sunscreen. The crew would make my coffee and Stoked Oats with lots of peanut butter and maple syrup, then start to pack up the hotel room and load everything into the SUV.

While eating, I'd use a Theragun percussive massager, a lacrosse ball, and a massage stick to help break up fibrosis and lactic acid deposits so I could start to move. Next, we'd drive to the pinwheel-marked location where I had stopped on the previous day. I'd put on my UltrAspire vest filled with food and two water bottles, then walk back 50–100 metres from where I had left off to make sure I covered every single inch of Canada.

After turning on my waist light, Garmin InReach live GPS tracker, and Coros GPS watch, I'd start running west. During the first hour of running, I'd eat my second breakfast of two G2G protein bars. From that point, I wouldn't see the crew vehicle again for twenty kilometres. When we met up again, they'd have the SUV's hatch open, ready to refill my pockets with snacks, top off my water, reapply lube, and give me a chance to take a bathroom break, switch to dry clothes, and discard or pick up additional clothing as needed.

I aimed to keep these breaks to no more than eight minutes, and I'd start running as soon as I could. I wouldn't see the vehicle again for another twenty kilometres and the next crew stop. After the first stop, these brief breaks would happen every ten kilometres for the remainder of the day until I reached the planned 105 kilometres.

At the end of the day, with one kilometre remaining, my crew would walk out a calorie-dense protein smoothie. We'd walk the remaining distance, drink and break down the day's happenings. Not even a minute was wasted.

After marking each day's stop location both physically and digitally, we'd get in the SUV and drive to a hotel close by. I'd shower right away while my crew unloaded the vehicle and awaited the food delivery Lana Rae had arranged from a local restaurant.

Meanwhile, I'd spend time rolling, stretching, doing muscle activation work, and massaging. When the food arrived, I'd eat dinner lying on the bed as my Normatech recovery pants squeezed my legs like a boa constrictor, sending freshly oxygenated blood to every muscle fiber.

And every night like clockwork, I'd fall asleep with food in my mouth, too tired to chew.

Lights out by 8 p.m., alarm set for 4 a.m., and guess what? It's Groundhog Day.

Now on the road fifty hilly kilometres east of the harbour, I felt like I've had time to work out all the race day jitters and get into a good running groove.

Yet I'm noticing that my right foot, which caused turmoil all through the lead-up training, was nagging me slightly. I tried to shake it off; after all, it was nothing terrible, and things could have been worse.

No one ever arrives at the starting line for a transcontinental run completely healthy, I told myself.

4

As I ran, I listened to music, talked to Lana Rae and my mother on the phone, and watched our filmmaker Vera maneuvering to get the very best start-day cinematic shots possible for her planned documentary.

By lunchtime, Day 1 would be halfway in the books. Life was good. I'd be running on fresh legs and renewed spirit.

Then I felt it, and my heart sank.

It started as a light tickle in my throat that resembled the feeling one gets when a seed gets caught midway and you can't quite cough it up. The tickle soon turned into a pain, and the pain into a cough.

And then the rain started. As the day turned grey and sodden, so did my spirits. I knew these desperately unwanted symptoms would surely make the already exhausting pre-dawn starts even more daunting.

Running one hundred and five kilometres in under twelve hours on the first day had been the plan. I was fit and experienced, and I knew how to do it without hurting myself. In fact, the effort was just sixty percent of what I could do at full strength, and as long as I stayed roughly in that window, I knew I'd be fine to do it again the next day.

When we arrived at the hotel that evening, though, I was shaking uncontrollably from the bitter rain and cold. I hopped in the hot shower, feeling like I wanted to stay in there forever. I was miserably cold and feared the inevitable conversation with Lana Rae about what to do next.

We'd talked about contingencies, but contingency and reality were two different things.

The look on her face was half-distress and half-shame. I knew she'd feel guilty about even the possibility that I had picked up her respiratory bug, and maybe that's why it took me so long through the day to muster up the courage to tell her about my cough and sore throat.

I've learnt that Lana Rae is quick to accept responsibility for her own stuff. But that self-accountability has a darker side: if she makes a mistake, she feels severely disappointed if no one else feels that way; and she more than makes up for it in how she punishes herself.

We discussed this at length, and I tried my very best to convince her that getting this virus from her was in no way her fault and just random bad luck.

Still feeling terrible, Lana Rae brought up the elephant in the room: Covid-19. We'd been hearing continuously in the news that exercise with Covid-19 was impossible due to the crushing load it puts on the respiratory system. We also knew that in Canada, most notably Newfoundland, the public order was a mandatory five-day quarantine for anyone with any symptom of Covid-19. Failure to abide by these orders opened you up to fines or worse.

We each took a rapid Covid-19 test, and the results read negative. But that didn't mean we were out of the woods.

I was still sick. If I couldn't start each day on time and log the planned distance, Lana Rae knew all too well how much would need to be done to rework the schedule, along with the time and cost of rebooking the next three weeks of hotels and coordinating my six other crew members and their busy schedules.

After a lengthy debate, we decided together that I'd start every morning as planned, but with a couple of adjustments: Lana Rae would make sure she had an endless supply of warm liquids and throat lozenges, and I'd walk the hills to save my lungs. I'd start each day planning to run the entire distance; and if, for whatever reason, the symptoms got too overwhelming, then we'd return to St. John's, enter quarantine in a hotel, and start again when symptoms lifted.

We both agreed that aside from each night's hotel or motel room stay—something we couldn't avoid—running alone on the highway was basically in quarantine anyway. We committed that under no circumstances would I enter a convenience store or public facility, essentially leaving me in quarantine on the Trans-Canada Highway; and Lana Rae would add disinfecting the hotel room to her list of tasks.

Finally, we agreed to keep the run quiet on social media, because if news had gotten out that there was a possible super-spreader running clear across Newfoundland, the court of public opinion would have me hanged from the tallest tree. This was just one of the ways in which this run in no way resembled my previous attempt to cross Canada.

It was with all that in mind that I went to bed that night scared as hell, anxious, shivering in a cold sweat. And to make matters worse, I now had a 102 °F fever.

I Remember This Feeling

DAY 2	COMPLETED	REMAINING
102.6 kms in 12:01:58	207.8 kms	6951.2 kms

We awoke at 4 a.m. the next day and began the routine that would define my life for the rest of the summer.

Knowing we had a long road ahead of us, we both tried to maintain a light-hearted mood and stay upbeat.

Lana Rae's an executive at one of Canada's largest banks, and she's a force of nature, impeccably prepared to rise to every challenge. She's also a perfectionist, and her thoroughness made my life easier. I knew that she had planned out every possible detail before anything could go wrong. However, as wonderful as that is, such an approach has its drawbacks. The more variables in play, the greater the chance something goes awry, and her stress levels would rise. When that happened, her stress became palpable, especially to those closest to her, and it permeated the room.

That second morning I heard quite a few expletives while she got everything ready, and when I approached her, she spun around like a whirlwind, driven by her desire to get everything right for me. She wanted this just as much, if not more, than I did.

Her look said "Go get it, champ!" and as we arrived at the day's starting location, I pressed start on my watch and began running west.

It had been four years since my 2018 attempt, and my body decided to give me a brutal reminder of how ugly and painful the first five thousand steps could be. It felt like shards of glass digging into the skin around my ankles, feet, and knees, and the only remedy for this agony was to keep taking more steps. After the first thousand, it seemed like a few pieces of glass fell away, and with each additional thousand, it felt better and better.

My heart rate climbed noticeably on the hills as my lungs struggled to fight the virus. I dialed back my pace. Despite the cold day and a fever, my extra layers of clothing and gloves helped alleviate the chill. I tried to remind myself about everything that was *right* with my day.

Following my mental checklist, I anticipated all my needs before they could derail me. My legs felt strong, my pace was steady, and the nervous jitters began to fade.

Lana Rae and I cracked jokes at the SUV when I arrived for each break. Cell reception was less than ideal, but whenever I had service, I'd call Lana Rae, friends, and, of course, my family.

The hills in Newfoundland were surprisingly steep, but with a level head and unwavering consistency, the day passed quickly. Before I knew it, I was entering the final 5-kilometre stretch of the day which ended right in front of our hotel for the night.

Slow Suffocation

DAY 3	COMPLETED	REMAINING
105 kms in 12:31:01	312.8 kms	6846.2 kms

We awoke to the alarm at 4:15 a.m., rewarded with extra sleep since the day's run would start as soon as I stepped out of the hotel.

The convenience was top-notch, but to be honest, the motel was super sketchy and had a strong horror movie vibe. There was a pool in a greenhouse, a go-kart track, and lots of creepy clowns scattered around the property. Lana Rae propped a chair against the door as we slept, and I couldn't blame her.

I didn't sleep well. My temperature was 104 °F and my cough was worsening. After completing the day's filming and before leaving for the night, Vera asked me to please call her in the middle of the night if my condition worsened, or God forbid, I ended up in the hospital; since, as she explained, she would need that footage also. It was funny but not funny; and after she left, my mind kept racing with questions and doubts about the safety of proceeding with this run. Vera was right to worry and to bring the matter up, but I thought it would've been better for her to discuss it with Lana Rae in order to spare my already fractured mind and to avoid second-guessing our own decisions.

Running with sunrise peeking over my back, I left the scary clowns in the rearview; but I kept mulling over Vera's comments and grumbling at the seeds of doubt she had planted in my mind. We spoke about it later that morning on the phone, and to my relief, things were easily resolved. Vera is a kind soul who wouldn't hurt a fly; she just needed some guidance about what and what not to mention to the athlete she was filming. She was deeply sorry, and we got on with the day.

As expected, my legs began to ache, a familiar and expected discomfort that I knew all too well. The deep throbbing would accompany my every step for the next two-plus months, whether I liked it or not. At this point, I decided to embrace it and make life easier.

Around 70 kilometres into the day, adding to the ongoing list of ailments, I noticed while eating during a pit stop that my sense of taste and smell had disappeared. When running for thirteen hours a day, I think it's safe to say that a guy can and should eat whatever he pleases, and with very little to look forward to, food was the one delicacy that ignited my spirit. Now, with taste and smell on vacation and the pleasure of guiltless overeating of sweets providing no sensory enjoyment, I felt like God was punishing me for a lifetime of sins.

I finished the day back at the hotel room with loads of comfort food that had lost its appeal. The hills here were crushingly steep, temperatures were cold, it rained half the time, and for the first time, I now had a newfound respect for what I now knew without a doubt was Covid-19. It felt like a damp towel was squeezing my lungs, and my heart rate was ten beats per minute higher than it needed to be. The sensation of suffocation didn't end when the day was over. It continued throughout the night as I slept.

Uncertain about what was going to keep me awake—body aches, the cold sweat, or trouble breathing, I knew this run was going to take everything I had, I just never imagined that an insidious virus would be the thing that could potentially spell my doom out here.

Acceptance

DAY 4	COMPLETED	REMAINING
103.5 kms in 12:28:10	416.3 kms	6742.7 kms

The town of Gander is a national treasure. With a population of just under 12,000, it isn't known for its natural beauty, culture, or business activities, but rather for its heartwarming people.

The 2017 Broadway musical "Come from Away" depicts Gander and its people as one of the most welcoming parts of Canada, and it's well-deserved. The small airport's only runway had at one time accommodated 38 planes, receiving almost seven thousand passengers and crew diverted to the Gander International Airport following the terrorist attacks of September 11, 2001, in the United States.

In the musical, Gander is portrayed as logistically ill-equipped to handle the flood of humanity that descended on the town. Even so, the residents opened their homes and hearts to thousands of strangers, reminding everyone that kindness and love for fellow humans in the darkest of times is the common strand that binds us all.

The people of Gander stepped up in a way that only Newfoundlanders could: with compassion, warm food, and a sense of community that should make us all proud to be Canadian.

Newfoundlanders are a rare breed, and I can't tell you how many times both Lana Rae and I were stopped by locals asking if we needed a hand or just wanted to have a friendly chat. People from this island prioritize community, decency, kindness, and a neighborly approach to everything, way above the wealth, status, possessions, and appearances that mainlanders consider important. Running through Gander made me smile, and when I did, there was always a resident on Main Street waving and smiling back.

By the time I reached Grand Falls-Windsor later that day, an old injury in my upper/mid back was burning like a hellfire out of control. Nine years ago, while carrying my son Sam out from his grandparents' home, my heel had slipped on the bottom step, and I had fallen backward. In a sudden action to protect Sam from impact, I straightened my arms and exposed my bony back to the top concrete step, which crushed my T1 vertebra.

Ever since that day, that old fracture burned when I ran, especially with the extra weight of a running vest. I had to accept this discomfort because I needed the vest to carry fluids, a GPS device, clothes, and food I picked up from the crew vehicle to take with me as I ran.

I'll delve into radical acceptance a bit later; but believe me, it can get worse. For now, I had accepted Covid-19, brutal weather, and back pain I knew was there to stay.

I just kept muttering to myself on repeat, *This is this... this is this... this is this.*

Multi-week races are hard as hell, and the hardest days are usually found in the first ten. This often doesn't make sense to folks unacquainted with very long-distance running, so let me explain.

Since the beginning of time, the human body has been designed as an endurance machine, and the ability to endure requires adaptation. So in a world that places primary value on comfort, with grocery stores containing twenty thousand food items so that you don't need to hunt, gather, grow, or prepare, it's no wonder we have gravitated to complacent, lazy, and idle behaviors.

Left to our devices, we typically accept some things as too difficult or too painful and give up, especially when survival is not on the line and we have plenty of food in the fridge.

Simply put, what's the point?

All other things being equal, humans will always—and I mean *always*—prioritize survival over reward, and comfort over effort. We're genetically programmed that way.

Yet if we can mentally flip that switch, and emphasize reward over survival, we can endure many things.

The trick is to remember that when every one of your senses is screaming at you to stop, Stop, *STOP!*, those voices inside your head are telling you one big, fat lie.

Persist through this self-made physical and mental hell, and somewhere around ten days later your body will have adapted enough to endure the challenges and your soul will be set free. I've even joked with Navy SEALs that Hell Week just ain't long enough.

The other reason the first ten days suck so much is that cognitive memory has a runway. If you were asked what you had for dinner last night, you could easily recall what was on your plate. If then asked what you had for dinner last Sunday, it might take you a while—but after recalling where you were, what you did, and with whom you ate, you could most likely remember what you ate. Much longer, and it gets harder and harder to remember.

Put bluntly, suffering is temporary, and after a while we either adjust to it, remember it as less than it was, or forget about it entirely. The mind no longer remembers what it was like to be anything other than in the moment.

That's what it's like to be Forrest Gump, and that's how I felt. I finished the day when my watch read 103 kilometres; and despite the aching legs and the respiratory struggles, I was pumped about my day's efforts.

Sometimes, however, that feeling can be premature, the result of endorphins or something else masking what your mind is really going through; and this was only Day 5.

Hours later, I awoke suddenly and without warning, frustrated and angry at my short, fitful, and unproductive attempt at sleep.

I turned my head to read the alarm clock. It was 2 a.m.. We were in some dingy roadside motel in northern Newfoundland, and I was annoyed because I knew the alarm would sound in two hours. Anxiety got the better of me, spinning my mind like a Ferris wheel so badly that even a healthy dose of the sleep aid zopiclone couldn't touch it.

I decided that if I couldn't sleep, then I should at least be doing something productive. Maybe I could bank some time during the difficult day that was to come; perhaps I could catch up on badly needed sleep the next night.

I turned to Lana Rae, who was fast asleep, waking her up to suggest that we get up and start running now.

She answered sharply, "Dave, go to sleep. The alarm is set for four." Her tone said she meant business and that the topic was not up for debate. Somehow, I managed to nod off for an hour or so, but it wasn't restful.

A Winged Beast

DAY 5	COMPLETED	REMAINING
105.1 kms in 12:16:35	521.3 kms	6637.7 kms

When the alarm sounded a short while later, it announced the excruciatingly early start to a very long, hard day on the road.

I dragged ass getting ready, already painting a dreary mental picture of what the day would look like.

Even though I'm doing the running, I always say "we"—and

yesterday we finished atop a tall climb, so today I was gifted with a long descent and a chance to wake up my legs.

Before long, they were ready, but the rest of me was not. To say that the morning was a challenge would be an understatement. With my head drooping and feet dragging on the rocky asphalt between steps, I shuffled slowly and mindlessly from hilltop to hilltop.

Running without sleep is not just physically a strain. It can easily scramble the mind into catastrophizing the little things that a fully rational mindset could easily process, plan for, and dismiss.

Given the slightest chance, tiredness magnifies self-doubt, which seeps into your deepest, most vulnerable inner fears; and left unquestioned, rapidly spreads until it feels like truth. It can burn your self-confidence like a powerful acid.

But it was also a perfectly natural reaction to my situation. Any reasonable person who looks down the highway at 6,000+ kilometres and feels confident is delusional. You simply can't know what the days are going to bring.

So instead of looking at how far I needed to go, I tried to remind myself how far I'd already come.

With seventeen years of ultrarunning experience under my belt, numerous national running records, many race wins and course records, and countless times when I found grit I didn't know I had, I reached into my mind and tried to find the "me" that had done all those things.

It was at that point that my gaze was drawn up and westward toward the most beautiful thing a broken runner can envision.

Perched upon a distant mountain top stood a majestic, black, fire-breathing dragon.

I'll tell you now that he represents something very powerful: a source of strength when I'm at my weakest. He is my confidence when I have none and a vision of myself when I'm at my best.

Seeing him perched looking down upon me reminded me what I was capable of, and I really needed that today.

Today, despite the raw, rocky, start, I had managed to summon the dragon. For now, I'd just have to keep running and see where the adventure took me.

Tomorrow, I might not be so lucky.

By the end of the day, my violent cough had stripped my vocal cords raw and I had lost my voice. My respiratory system was failing hour to hour, and I knew that my lack of voice was the least of my concerns.

Lana Rae started a new nightly routine of putting Vicks VapoRub in a pot of boiling water and draping a towel over my head as I took deep painful breaths into my lungs. As crushing as it was, it really did the trick. It broke up and eventually eliminated the huge volumes of congestion and mucus that were robbing me of both strength and sanity.

Choice

DAY 6	COMPLETED	REMAINING
101.2 kms in 12:29:20	622.5 kms	6536.5 kms

4 a.m. and I am lying in bed, still awake, not at all fully rested.

A tidal wave of cold sweat has left me soaked all night long and robbed me of sleep, comfort, and even the ability to breathe comfortably. I guess this is what Covid-19 looks like.

Choice is a funny thing. Being 500+ kilometres in already and feeling like garbage stirs up obvious questions.

What am I doing out here? What was I thinking? Why don't you just stop?

I could choose to quit, but I don't want to.

I don't need to, I tell myself.

My mind tells me I've been through worse, but my body protests in violent disagreement.

I ate my oatmeal that morning knee-deep in questions, most of which were just circular thoughts that didn't get me out there and running. With no voice, I was subject to the rounds of non-stop judgements and bias in my own head.

Emilio, my salamander—I'll get to him in more detail in a moment—would just not shut up! The incessant chatter of the defeatist voices echoed endlessly in my head as I lifted the spoon to my mouth, which I opened just enough to whisper the word *"Worth."*

Lana Rae and I made our way out to the start point at the usual 5 a.m. time.

Now, long before this run, I once sat at my kitchen table with a pencil and paper, drawing a sailboat being blown through a gusty, turbulent storm, crashing violently into massive oncoming waves. The captain and crew are capable, and the ship is built to sustain damage, but it's no easy task to make progress.

Dominating that storm is a massive, malevolent thundercloud. The cloud had a face, and from its mouth blew gale force winds. This cloud I labeled "Legacy."

The wind that Legacy blew met two gigantic sails; and alongside the sails I wrote the words "pain" and "suffering."

Finally, I drew the ship's mast: a strong, stout pole jutting from the deck. I wrote the word "Worth" next to the mast. If my Legacy was strong and my (self) Worth held without snapping, the sailboat would shoot swiftly across the sea of Pain and Suffering, through the storm and into calmer waters.

The two non-negotiables were the scale of my Legacy and the depth of Pain and Suffering.

The question then and now remained the same: should I set sail, when I knew what the sea would be like, or stay docked in the harbour and hope for better conditions that might never come.

It always came down to choice: What do I choose to do?

I chose this storm because my goal, my life, my hopes, and my dreams were worth it. I was worth it.

So before hitting start on my watch and taking my first step that day, I whispered again to myself: *"Worth."*

Dave, you are worth any level of suffering that may come your way.

The rain continued throughout the entire morning. As my posture started to slump and I started to imagine the boat ripped into shreds of fabric and driftwood, I would find myself straightening up and repeating the word.

This happened over and over until the silly repetitive nature of doing this started to actually feel empowering.

At times, I'd laugh at myself for how corny this practice was; but nevertheless, every time I'd straighten up and pick up my pace.

As crazy as it sounds, this newfound control surged life into my pain-wracked body. I felt alive, like I was taking the bull by the horns! Nothing was happening to me; I controlled *everything*.

Lana Rae looked surprised when this coughing, miserable rag doll of a man arrived at the crew vehicle with a big smile on his face, but she saw the joy in my eyes.

The skies opened up for the rest of the day, as if signaling a change. I finished the day a different man than the one who started it.

I still didn't have an appetite, and I struggled to eat enough in the hotel room; but my change in mood stirred up a much different mood in Lana Rae. She took my back and we fell instantly into the soundest sleep I'd had in days.

The Clock Never Stops

DAY 7	COMPLETED	REMAINING
100.1 kms in 12:14:06	722.6 kms	6436.4 kms

I awoke the next day after a magically deep sleep, and the world seemed good again. It's amazing what a good night's sleep will do for body, mind, and spirit.

A friend told me that I was running into what he believes is the most beautiful part of the province; and boy, was he ever right. I spent the first half of the day running in the cold rain, but the views alongside Grand Lake were a welcome distraction.

Yet my cough persisted, and the struggle to breathe kept my voice a distant memory.

To protect my voice and breathing, Lana Rae had implemented a rule that limited the amount of time I spent talking with her, Vera, and friends and family on the phone. She contacted my mother and others to reassure them that I was all right, but that I wouldn't be holding conversations anytime soon.

Partway through the day I started to get the runs, and Lana Rae and I quickly realized that it must have been the well water from the last motel. We improvised a plan to drink only canned iced tea and soda pop until we could get to the next town to buy bottled water. The frequency of ditch-side bathroom breaks and the lubricating routine to limit chafing ate up a large chunk of the day and shortened the amount of time I had for self-care at the end of the day.

The effort required to balance running and non-running time during a major undertaking like this surprises most people.

Breaking a speed record is always a race against the clock, and it never stops. If I'm not running, I'm eating. If I'm not eating, I'm sleeping. Anything that eats into the time to accomplish one of those tasks lessens the time and focus for the other two tasks.

There are only 24 hours in a day, so deciding what comes first and last is a fluid, day-by-day negotiation between my crew and me. In this case, not shitting myself on the side of the busy Trans-Canada Highway was critical, so time spent to tend to that was top priority. Other things had to be either put off or cast aside.

Passing through Deer Lake, the valley opened up and the skies cleared, framing columns of mountains to the north and south with a large alpine lake on the right. During one of my many bathroom breaks, I struggled to descend the extremely steep embankment of the ditch to a place with some privacy. The Newfoundland ditches were so steep that it would be impossible for a motorist to spot a desperate runner taking a squat to relieve himself.

After struggling for minutes to climb back out from one impossible pitch, I was bent over at such an angle that my phone fell out from the front vest pocket and slid back to the spot I'd just left.

Aside from the obvious disappointment of realizing that I'd need to go down again to retrieve it, I was more alarmed at what it was on course to slide into. To my joy and amazement, the phone stopped mere inches from the very spot where I just taken a giant dump. I should have been angry that I had to double back to get it, but I felt blessed instead that a complete disaster had been averted.

Feeling lucky, I climbed back up onto the street and continued running, resuming my fast-enough-but-not-too-taxing pace.

Not too long afterwards, as I approached Corner Brook, I couldn't help but compare the rugged beauty of this landscape to the Canadian Rockies where I live. By now I was hungry, and not wanting to put myself into a dicey situation again, decided to eat as much as would agree with my stomach. It turned out to be quite a bit, but I couldn't taste any of it.

I continued through the valley until I approached the base of a ski hill, where the highway shot straight up. Lana Rae alerted me that the hill would continue for seven kilometres and summit when I reached Corner Brook, so I took an extra banana loaf with me and said a prayer as the climb started.

The transport trucks climbing the same hill seemed to struggle even more than I did, and I felt proud of myself as I slowly passed one truck—until I remembered that it was carrying a much heavier load than I was.

The snow along the ditch became deeper, and atop the climb alongside the beautiful town of Corner Brook, I could have sworn it was Christmas. The snowy alpine terrain was a winter wonderland with sprawling views of the land below.

It's a privilege to suffer in places this beautiful. I felt a deep gratitude, and a renewed awareness of the rareness of the opportunity and how lucky I really was to be here.

Eventually I met up with Lana Rae and the crew vehicle. Looking ahead, I expected an equally long descent, but instead, the west coast of Newfoundland had me running a very long, straight plateau. It was a stunning, rewarding, and beautiful way to close out the day.

Come Hell or High Water

DAY 8	COMPLETED	REMAINING
100 kms in 12:31:05	822.7 kms	6336.3 kms

I'm not sure what woke me first—the alarm or the resounding waterfall of rain on the Airbnb and its parking lot. I clumsily shuffled through my bags, stacking the required layers to keep me both warm and dry enough. But my efforts lasted only minutes as the monsoon outside thoroughly soaked all those layers.

What made matters worse were the swirling winds that drove the rain both sideways and back up, completely negating the advantage of rain gear. There I was, on the tail-end of Covid-19, still no voice, a relentless cough, soaking wet and cold as hell, with no break in the clouds in sight.

I soldiered on, alone with my thoughts, heading southwest on the quiet highway.

I had seen quite a few moose alongside the highway, and on this stretch stood a tall, flexible fence intended to block them from entering the road. Sadly, a solitary giant moose with a huge rack had found himself stuck on the wrong side of the fence, vulnerable to the cars speeding by.

Afraid of being followed, the moose would sprint away from me in the ditch, pausing to turn to see if I was still "chasing" him. In a panicked attempt to flee, he took to leaning his gigantic hooves up on the fence in an attempt to push it down and escape. The fence would bend around 45°, but not enough to allow him to jump over it. This continued for the better part of twenty minutes.

All that time, I wondered when the moose would realize he was ten times my size and that he could easily turn the tables and become predator instead of prey. The fence that was supposed to protect the moose *and* motorists from each other was now putting all of us in great danger.

I tried feverishly to call Lana Rae and ask her to circle back to my location, but as usual in Newfoundland, there was no cell coverage. After what seemed like an eternity, the wildlife fence came to an end, and I saw the massive beast lope off through a field and under the canopy of trees. Good thing, too, because as I continued to check my cellphone, there was still no signal.

I came upon Lana Rae and the crew vehicle at the next scheduled interval, soaking wet and shivering, and desperately crawled into the front seat to strip off my soaked clothes. I could feel the cold in my bones. Lana Rae had cranked the SUV's heater to give me a moment of reprieve, and as wonderful as it felt, it also brought on terrible coughing fits that ignited a pain deep in my lungs, chest, and back.

After a while, the world was good again. I felt like I had a new lease on life as I left the vehicle with warm clothes, dry shoes, a full belly, and a dry jacket.

But that feeling didn't last for long.

To my surprise, the gusty downpour returned and very quickly transformed into what seemed like a Category 5 hurricane. My warm layers turned into my worst possible nightmare within minutes.

I needed help, but as before, when I looked down at my phone in a Ziploc bag, it showed no bars. I feared hypothermia, partly because it was something that has taken me down hard in past races. Without cell coverage, though, I had no way to call for support. I could only pray that Lana Rae or Vera would drive back, anticipating that I might need help.

After forty minutes of bitter cold and biting wind, and soaked to the bone, I crested a hill and my phone shot up from no bars to four. "I need help," I muttered, and what I heard was, "I'm on my way." As soon as Lana Rae appeared, I leapt into the front seat, shaking like a leaf, and stripped naked as fast as I could. Lana had already prepared warm noodle soup, and as I ate the soup it warmed my soul and my body.

Finally, the rain stopped, and remarkably, the remainder of the back forty kilometres were actually enjoyable.

As we wrapped things up and headed for our lodging, I could tell that the day's stress had understandably affected Lana Rae's mood. The lengthy drive to the nearest restaurant, mistakes in our order, and delays in getting our food pushed her over the edge, tipping her temper into choice curse words.

Her need to find control and order amongst all the chaos ran head-on into my need to reach my desired end-of-day Zen state of calm, cool, relaxed, and unbothered.

Despite my lack of voice, we knew we had to talk about it. We spent the rest of the evening discussing how much we both wanted to show up for the other and how we both needed to adapt some of our default behaviors so we could achieve our common goal.

It wasn't fun, but it made me better at understanding her needs amidst the chaos, and helped her channel her frustrations in a way that protected the flow of calm I fought so hard to achieve at the end of each day.

We fell asleep spooning, me as usual the "little" spoon, comforting and replenishing each other for the days to come.

A Parting Gift

DAY 9	COMPLETED	REMAINING
88.3 kms in 11:07:57	911 kms	6248 kms

Day 9 was the only day in Newfoundland that I didn't run more than 100 kilometres, due to the very real restriction of finishing the day at the Port aux Basques ferry terminal, 88 kilometres in. My goal going into this speed-record attempt was to complete this island in nine days, and assuming the rest of the day went well, that was exactly what I would do.

I had known that Newfoundland was going to kick the shit out of me. And having fought Covid-19 for just over a week, I had a new appreciation for the term *struggle*. Nonetheless, I was extremely happy and proud, knowing I could cross the first of nine provinces off my list on the way to sunny Victoria, British Columbia.

Well aware that this was going to be my only decreased mileage day on the entire run, I spent my day hydrating, eating, and spending extra time on much-needed body care including self-massage, muscle activation, and stretching. An injury that had ailed me coming into this run was now glowing brighter with every passing day. The tibialis posterior muscle on the inside of my calf needed more and more attention to calm shortening due to tendinopathy, and the plantar fasciitis was worsening, if not tearing.

I spent the better part of the day with improved cell coverage, and used this rare opportunity to call my children, parents, family, and friends, checking in to catch up on all the hot gossip. My stories of the unreal winds along the southwest corner of the island did not disappoint.

The good news was that the headwind I had faced for 80% percent of this trip had now miraculously appeared at my back on the way out of Newfoundland, as if the gods had granted an easy retreat from this wild and rugged land. Lana Rae's take was a lot more down-to-earth. She took it as a message from the island to "get the hell out...and here's a healthy push off to send you on your way."

I arrived at the ferry terminal in Port aux Basques with plenty of time to grab a bite, talk to locals, and board the boat for the overnight crossing at 7 p.m. After boarding, Lana Rae, Vera and I settled into our cabin for the night, and as the ferry departed, the rhythmic rocking of the ocean rewarded me with the best night's rest yet.

As I lay there, proud that I had run 912 kilometres in nine days—averaging 101 kilometres per day—my thoughts turned to the fact that I still had over 6,250 kilometres remaining, with only 63 days left to break this impossible record.

I remained sorely aware that on such events, the clock never stops.

By all rights, I should have been feeling small, overwhelmed, intimidated, and outright paralyzed with fear.

But as I looked out my tiny cabin window, all I saw was that beautiful, giant two-winged creature circling in the distance, and my fears and insecurities slipped away.

CHAPTER 2: OUTRUN RARE

As we left Newfoundland, my memories kept drifting back to 2018.

Four years earlier, I had been sitting in the rear of a giant motorhome with "Outrun Rare" logos and a ten-foot-tall photo of Dave plastered on all sides, as my wife Sharon and my buddy Wayne Gaudet drove us towards the legendary start line of Al Howie's record-setting Trans Canada run in 1991—Mile Zero in Victoria, British Columbia.

The path that led me to Victoria had been full of twists and turns.

My now 14-year-old son had been recently diagnosed with relapsing encephalopathy with cerebellar ataxia, an extremely rare disease that took a painstaking seven years to accurately diagnose and had no definitive treatment and an uncertain prognosis.

As we learned more and more about our son's condition, we felt more and more abandoned by the Canadian medical system, the only system in the developed world without a rare disease strategy.

I was desperate to create the change we so badly wanted to see— to find a way to raise awareness and funds to help fight rare diseases, both for Sam and other medically vulnerable groups.

So when I set the Guinness world record in 2016 for the longest 24-hour treadmill run, I saw a once-in-a-lifetime chance to harness my love for running to fuel a national awareness and fundraising campaign for rare diseases.

And so my plan to break Al Howie's legendary 1991 Trans Canada run record—72 days, 10 hours, and 23 minutes—began to take shape. I set a goal of 66 days for my attempt, which would beat the record by six days.

I had previously set a Guinness world record for the furthest distance run in 24 hours, raising almost $100,000 for rare mitochondrial diseases as part of MitoCanada's MitoTreadmill challenge in 2016. So it was an obvious choice to dedicate this new run to supporting the Rare Disease Foundation.

Thus was born Outrun Rare, my 2018 attempt to break Al's record.

I set a fundraising goal of $1 million and worked feverishly to create publicity through media appearances, a corporate sponsorship with Staples, events along the run route and much more.

Now, two years later, my plans were coming to life.

Less than 24 hours earlier I had been full of excitement—yet a sudden turn of events had filled me with dread and panic.

Just one day prior, I had hopped off a motorbike at an Outrun Rare sponsor's photo shoot when a sudden searing pain shot through my lower back, down my right leg and into my heel.

I spent the rest of the evening rolling on a lacrosse ball, hoping that all I had experienced was a soft tissue impingement and not what I secretly feared: a herniated disc.

Each slight bump on the road that morning sent an alarming and visceral jolt through my entire body.

I couldn't tell which was worse: the unbearable pain or the inner voice that accompanied it.

Bump. Dave, why even start, you know this'll end ugly and quickly.

Bump. You were such an idiot putting this whole run at risk getting on that bike.

Bump. You plan to run nine million steps, but you struggle with even one.

Bump. You are the only person in the world that knows the simple truth that this run across Canada will fail before it even begins.

I had made a promise that I, Dave Proctor, was going to ignite change by showing an entire nation how a father would go to hell and back for his child.

Unfortunately, I was already physically in hell and the run hadn't even started.

Outrun Rare, conceived in love and honour, now felt like a noose. The expectations I had set felt like shackles.

I was now a prisoner of my own promises, unable to escape them, unable to deliver on them.

I felt that I had no choice: I *had* to run. This thing was bigger than me, and the wind was filling the sails of that boat, moving it with or without me. This was, after all, only partly a personal goal. The bulk of it, I told myself, was about making lives better.

And yet, I was profoundly disappointed in myself.

The motorhome ground to a halt at the Mile Zero sign, next to the memorial to Terry Fox, the Canadian national hero whose grit and determination to run across Canada to fund cancer research despite the loss of a leg is to this very day unparalleled.

Did I really belong here? Who dares set foot amongst the gods?! Who was I kidding?!

I jerked awake from my half-asleep state and with the help of our communications director and friend Stephanie Gillis-Paulgaard eased my already-broken body down the steps of the rig and towards the many uneven steps that led to the famous Steve

Fonyo Beach where I would start my run.

Every jarring step stabbed my equally broken heart. I had imagined this moment countless times, and in my imaginings, the aroma of hope, gratitude, and strength had blessed the day.

The hordes of spectators and media were just as I had pictured them in my dreams, but now that they were here, I feared they'd notice just how physically unsuited I was to the task.

My internal disappointment stank like rotting fish and filled the day with negativity.

As Sharon and I stood near the water, she played a video on an iPad of our three kids, Julia, Sam, and Adele, wishing me luck and telling me they loved me and believed in me.

A surge of motivation swept over me, and I bent down to dip my cowboy hat in the water to signal the start of this run. Once the clock started, it wouldn't stop until I dipped my hat in St. John's Harbour, over 7,000 kilometres eastward at the edge of the Atlantic.

The show was on.

I made it back up the stairs, and with a group of local runners, headed towards Swartz Bay to catch the one-hour ferry to the mainland.

Funnily enough, the farther I got from Victoria, the better my back felt, filling me with delighted relief and desperate hope that the problem might simply work itself out.

I clutched at the possibility that running might just be the very best thing for my troubles, because I had a hell of a lot of running to do over the next 72 days.

I arrived at the ferry terminal with time to spare before my scheduled departure, and had a few minutes to share the great news about my back with my team.

And then I sat down for the ferry ride. Almost immediately, alarming pain shot down my leg, and excruciating vise-like pain seized the joints of my lower back, bringing me to tears.

It was at that point that I learnt something that would torture me for the remainder of the run: every time I stopped running, even for a minute, I'd feel the worst pain I've ever felt in my life.

Radical acceptance of such helplessness circled in my mind, combined with the feeling of not having a choice. It was a jagged little pill to swallow and made only worse by the knowledge that this was just Day 1 of seventy-two.

Keep running, Dave, I told myself. *It's your only chance at finishing.*

The remainder of the day was filled with sponsor engagements, getting lost on the very confusing Langley roads, and eventually the need to run an additional twenty-five kilometres due to poor mapping and pressure to stay on schedule and meet sponsor and fundraising commitments.

I should have been excited, but I wasn't. Instead, it was all just a blur that blew past while my back kept screaming at me.

Welcome to the shit show, Dave. And guess who's the ringleader!

Days 2 and 3 were spent on relentless climbs in the Canadian Rockies. The punishing Coquihalla Highway, with thirty-five kilometres of sustained ascents, was made even more brutal by non-stop rain and bumper-to-bumper big rigs slamming walls of filthy, gravel-filled water squarely into my face, one after another.

The most therapeutic and satisfying thing was to curse and scream at the trucks as they passed. But the attempt at release only made matters worse.

Anger turned into sadness, eventually despair, and at night, the pain in my back consumed me.

I lay on my belly, back arched, up on my elbows in the only position that wouldn't send me to tears. Any shift in body position, deep breath, or turn of head would tighten the stranglehold on my sacrum and a jolt of lightning would shoot down my right leg.

I fought the desire to use sleep aids, but was forced to give in and take zopiclone. This pain was unreal, but four hours of zombie sleep beat two hours or fewer of fitful, pain-wracked, and jagged real sleep.

Finally, on Day 5, I had the pleasure of running with my good friend Greg Courtice west of Salmon Arm, at the start of a very busy Canada Day weekend.

I could go on and on about Greg's wonderful qualities, but his most endearing attribute is his incredible emotional intelligence. I've never known anyone else who can weed so effectively through all the crap people dish out and connect with them at a deep level.

As we ran, we spent the morning talking about all things Trans Canada.

Around noon the rain picked up, and things got a little spicy.

I remember being grumpy, irritated, and downright miserable when Greg said, "Dave, I've been listening to you for the last many hours, and I've always looked up to you and thought you were an exceptional runner because you are an exceptional person. Now I don't know what is going on, but I can say with certainty that this guy I'm running with isn't the Dave I know and love. And to be honest I don't think this guy can run across Canada."

That was a kick in the balls.

Right away, I got defensive. I let him know with no uncertainty that I wasn't happy. We continued running with Greg now trailing me by many car lengths.

How dare he attack me like this? Who the hell is he to act so self-righteous? Doesn't he understand my pain and the weight of all this?

As the steady stream of traffic whizzed by, my internal chatter grew louder and louder—until things broke. My internal voice shut down and I tried to find a place of stillness where I could look within.

What if Greg was right? What if my current path was headed in one direction only: straight off this highway and out of this run?

I couldn't do much about my physical state, I thought, but if I've learnt anything in the last fifteen years of running ultramarathons, it was that this sport is 100% in your head.

The mental anguish that flooded me right now was all self-imposed.

The only way to flip the switch and have any chance of completing this run was to make a decision.

Was I in it, or not?

I stopped running and turned around.

"What do you suggest I do instead?"

The remaining conversation is a blur even now. But what I do remember is giving Greg a long hug and falling asleep in his arms. He is truly a good and patient friend.

Not long after, Wayne circled back, and I finished the day thirty-five kilometres short of my planned distance. We all spent the night in a hotel, and I was told that I slept for ten hours and snored the whole night through.

The next morning, when I rode out to the previous day's stop, something felt different, and better. Maybe it was just the sleep, but I really believe that as I slept, my subconscious worked tirelessly to take on board the fresh perspective Greg had awakened in me.

Either way, I was running better and feeling more confident with every step.

Routine is absolutely everything on a transcontinental run, and finding an effective routine early in the run is integral to your success. Almost immediately, we landed on a pattern of crew stops at the 20, 40, 50, 60, 70, 80, 85, 90, 95, 100, and 105-kilometre marks.

My crew and I were both very happy with this plan. We were able to iron out the food and hydration frequency and volume fairly easily, and evening campground stays and meal prep worked smoothly as well—a true blessing for all of us.

On the other hand, dealing with the huge number of runners who wanted to join me for portions of the run was rapidly turning into a three-ring circus that tested Wayne and Sharon's patience.

We had simple safety rules for these runners, but most people didn't even read them, just winging it instead. The rules were simple: for example, I decide when we cross a busy roadway or overpass, we don't provide food or water from our supply, and we can't give runners a lift back to their cars. Everyone also had to sign a liability waiver.

We also had a rule that no one should run ahead of me. Transcontinental runs are typically slower than marathon pace, yet when someone drops in for just part of the show, with fresh legs and excitement, it's difficult for them to hold back.

To make it across the entire continent, I needed to believe that I could. Feeling slow was the exact opposite of what I needed to feel. When putting in so much effort, having someone run slightly ahead of me sometimes made me feel small and weak.

Wayne and Sharon tried to rein these runners in, but it kept happening. I learnt early to guard against letting this derail me, but with nothing better to do than run and think all day, I still found it challenging.

As we finished Day 5 of the 2018 run, Sharon found an acupuncturist in Revelstoke, BC, willing to stay late and help me out. After a lengthy intake process concerning my pain and biomechanics, she poked me with what felt like hundreds of needles and left me lying there with relaxing music. I don't quite know what came over me, but I felt a wave of uncontrollable sadness, and sobbed uncontrollably as Sharon held my hand.

On Day 6, bracing myself to tackle the long thirty-five kilometre climb up Rogers Pass, I was caught pleasantly off guard when I noticed that my pace was quickening and my heart rate dropping.

Wayne ran with me for a while, shouting motivational speeches at the "sissy hills." He resembled nothing so much as Captain Dan screaming at the raging storm in the movie Forrest Gump. True, he made me laugh, but his antics also deepened the love I already felt for my friend. I knew he originally expected something very different from this run, maybe a more stoic Dave, perhaps a more stable Dave—but either way, in typical Wayne fashion, when life offered him lemons, he made lemonade.

At the top of Rogers Pass, I got a call from Stephanie with incredibly good news that fueled a fast descent down the east side of the pass: our Outrun Rare fundraising page was going gangbusters—in fact, we had already surpassed the $100,000 mark. At that rate, our $1,000,000 fundraising goal would be extremely achievable.

Topping that, she informed me that the media was banging down the door to talk to me, new sponsors were reaching out to support us, and Outrun Rare merchandise at Staples locations all across Canada was flying off the shelves, adding even more to our fundraising total.

Where the mind goes, the body follows; and as far as my body was concerned, it looked like brighter days ahead. Over the next many days, despite extreme back pain, my body felt stronger and stronger as I found my groove again. The better my body felt, the more my mind followed suit. I started sleeping better at night and my mood improved. It's an incredible feeling when your mind lets go of the idea of comfort and replaces it with acceptance.

That said, the constant need to eat began to be a bit of a drag. My daily menu included a constant supply of foods like banana bread, cinnamon buns, muffins, cookies, penny candy and liquorice, potato chips, Boost meal replacement drinks, beef jerky, burgers, wraps, sandwiches, all kinds of fruit, and crackers.

My mouth, tongue, and throat were lined with canker sores thanks to the enormous amount of sugar and salt shoveled into my body hourly. Salty snacks and sports drinks would nearly bring tears to my eyes.

In an environment where it's imperative to eat and drink all day to keep up with the mounting deficit of calories, electrolytes, and hydration, this growing discomfort was quickly moving from annoying to downright incapacitating.

At the next crew vehicle stop, Wayne, Sharon, and Stephanie quickly got to work debating solutions to my oral dilemma. Hours later, Stephanie pulled up to me on the outskirts of Canmore with benzocaine gel for my mouth sores. The rest of the day I busied myself applying it to the target areas for relief, but that got tedious quickly, so I started swigging the benzocaine gel, swishing it around my entire mouth for a minute, then spitting it out. Amazingly, this broad coverage eased most of the pain.

Yet pain relief had a downside—with my mouth numbed by the gel, I kept biting my tongue because I couldn't differentiate between food and my own body.

Because I was under pressure to slam down calories, I routinely didn't chew my food well enough before swallowing—especially the one pound of bacon that I was consuming everyday for calories, protein and salt.

That left me choking on long strings of bacon fat, having to pull them from the back of my throat and fling them into the grassy ditch by the road. Gross and annoying, but a necessity to continue forward.

Day 10 ended between Canmore and Calgary, near Wayne's home in Exshaw, so we bunked there for a sound night's sleep.

However, the next morning, Wayne himself was in a foul mood. I decided to give him some space. I assumed that the short stay was probably frustrating him, since a guy like Wayne could easily busy himself with household duties knowing he'd be away for the next two months.

In fact, we later discovered unexpected drama behind his mood: he had mistakenly dropped the single RV key behind the dumpster while tossing the trash, and spent the rest of the night frantically searching everywhere, only to find it at 3 a.m. after getting zero sleep. That key stayed on a lanyard around his neck for the rest of the trip.

Running up Scott Lake Hill, many friends from my home city of Calgary joined me, including Ryan Kershaw, Blaine Penny, and a big group from the Bow Valley Harriers Running Club. Catching up was a joy as we ran eastbound on the Trans-Canada Highway, and the Calgary Fire Department provided a fire truck escort through the very busy 16th Avenue roadway.

The growing group of runners behind me, along with our logo- and photo-covered RV and two fire trucks made me feel very special and celebrated.

After so many lonely, grinding kilometres, often with nothing but my thoughts to accompany me, I soaked up the feeling of being joined now by dozens of excited runners in "Outrun Rare orange" with honking drivers, people holding posters on the roadside, and cameras everywhere.

I won't lie, it gave me an extra kick to my step as I took this all in. And as if that weren't enough, my kids Julia, Sam, and Adele now joined Sharon and me in a larger RV for the remainder of the run to St. John's. The kids took turns dropping energy bars and packaged foods from the RV's side windows as it slowly proceeded, for us runners to pick up and eat as we ran.

Imagine the kids' excitement looking out the windows of the RV with a fire truck in front, their dad running behind, followed by another fire truck, with all of the fanfare and cars honking!

Watching my kids' excitement, surrounded on all sides by all this energy, pretty much eradicated my excruciating back pain.

I felt like a cross between Superman and a rock star on the red carpet. The sun beat down, and the temperatures rose, but I didn't care. It was the ultimate send-off as we headed east to tackle the rest of the country.

Somewhere east of Calgary, I glanced at my watch. Time was getting tight to finish off the day's 100+ kilometres day and circle back to a big Staples fundraising event in southeast Calgary. We made a joint decision to cut the day short in Chestermere to arrive on time at Staples.

The excitement of the day had distracted me from the back pain that I'd grown to expect, but now traveling in the back of the RV with friends, every bump and turn in the road became a blunt reality check.

As we pulled into the parking lot, I gazed out upon the hundreds of supporters wearing orange Outrun Rare t-shirts and cowboy hats, which had become my trademark over the years.

Hardly able to stand, and needing help to get out of the RV, I could fake being okay only as long as I didn't stand up, sit down or move!

I hadn't realized the grim reality of my situation until then. I had stayed tight-lipped about my back pain, not wanting to shed doubt upon any aspect of the event or slow the fundraising effort.

Like a bad B-movie actor, I painfully raised myself from the bed in the RV and squeezed together a weak semblance of a smile as I hobbled to the door and swung it open to reveal hundreds of cheering fans.

The presence of friends and family comforted me, but the experience of making my way through the crowd, shaking hands, and seeing people realize just how much pain I was in was excruciating. I hoped perhaps they'd give me a pass, and just chalk it up to the physical demands of the run.

Standing under an Outrun Rare canopy tent, I did my very best to give a rousing speech, then rushed off to the Foothills Medical Centre to participate in a cardiovascular MRI study led by Dr. James White.

This study was a unique opportunity to see how my heart and its tissues responded to the extreme demands of pushing my body hard for more than twelve hours a day, since most cardiovascular research has historically been performed on unhealthy and failing hearts. A study like this could give the medical community data that offered a glimpse of the potential of the human body to adapt when stresses were high.

Next, my brother Dan, who was also doing a tremendous amount of work as project manager for the race, loaded me in his tiny Toyota Yaris to drive me across town to the hospital. If running 100 kilometres/day wasn't hard enough, if riding in an RV that amplified every bump and jolt wasn't hard enough, if speaking and shaking hands at an event where I could barely stand wasn't hard enough— then traveling in Dan's miniature car to lie in an MRI chamber for an hour only to arrive back at the RB at midnight for a 4 a.m. start and a full day's run was definitely hard enough!

It was clear even to me that I jammed more into this day than I could chew—and I could see that if the run had any chance of succeeding, I needed to establish much better boundaries around my time. Driving back from the hospital, Dan and I had a heart-to-heart, and like a good big brother, he gave me wise advice on the subject that calmed my nerves.

As we continued across Alberta, the days were filled with friends who joined me, and daily media interviews conducted while running.

Every night we parked the two RV's side by side in small-town campgrounds, with Wayne and Trish in one and Sharon, the kids and me in the other.

Twelve-year-old Julia, nine-year-old Sam and seven-year-old Adele were at first enthusiastic and upbeat about the adventure, but reality quickly set in when they realized that most of their time would be spent cooped up in an RV in rural Canada with not much to do aside from pick on one another. One evening I was awakened three times by Adele screaming bloody murder because she heard a mosquito buzzing around her.

Needless to say, the 4 a.m. wake-up the next morning was terrible.

A few days after the MRI, my phone rang with news from Dr. White. His interest in this run was obvious by the numerous nerdy questions he asked about how I was feeling and how things were going. I could tell there was an edge of excitement in his tone the way he started explaining the immediate findings of the images taken a few days back.

After the typical medical preamble, he got down to brass tacks and into the topic of blood volume measures. He started by reminding me that prior to my run and during training the MRI's taken showed that my right ventricle was pumping 8.2 litres of blood per minute at rest, which was extremely high. The average Canadian pumps 4 liters per minute.

Then, he went on to tell me that my right ventricle was now delivering a whopping 14.4 litres of blood per minute, possibly the highest recorded number in history. He added that these were just a few of many metrics that they were now combing through to make sense of the heart of an extreme athlete, and that the findings were as remarkable as he had hoped.

The next morning's run into Medicine Hat started into a heavy headwind. This was highly unusual: the winds typically travel west to east, and they're usually calmest at 5 a.m. My buddy Myron Tetrault was returning to run with me for the day. He did his best to run in front of me to break the headwind—one of the few times I wanted someone to run in front of me!—but he's just as skinny as I am and the wind cut right around him.

The wind and 35 °C heat gained viciousness throughout the morning, delaying our arrival at the scheduled 2 p.m. Staples event and guiltily reminding me that many eager supporters awaited us, that Staples had put lots of effort into organizing the event, and that many expectations, as always, were riding on my shoulders.

As we made our way to Staples on the east end of town, the force of the headwind escalated. I leaned so hard into the wind that I must have looked like a cartoon character. When we arrived, staff and volunteers were hustling to secure tents, tables, and supplies from being blown away.

I said a few words and, after thanking the organizers and wishing my best to numerous rare disease families in attendance, I gathered ten to fifteen local runners that had come to run with me, and we took off. The 100-kilometre sustained winds quickly wore the local runners down and within thirty minutes, I was running alone again.

I telephoned Wayne and told him that the winds were getting the best of me. We discussed slowing my pace and even stopping until the wind settled in the evening, and eventually settled on having him and Trish drive at ten kilometres/hour just ahead of me to break the wind.

Wind is a tricky bastard, though.

Now with the RV at arm's reach ahead and the wind cut significantly, I struggled with the heat from the RV's exhaust. Mother Nature took the decision out of our hands when she shifted the wind to northerly, and Wayne took off down the road to set up the next aid stop.

Shortly after Wayne left, Myron and Catherine pulled up again; and having had some rest, Myron was ready to run some more miles with me. For my part, I was happy to have a distraction from my fight with nature. The gusting sidewinds forced us to lean at a ridiculously sharp angle just to stay upright—and every so often the wind would abruptly stop, requiring constant vigilance and fast thinking to avoid face-planting.

After fifteen kilometres of that bullshit, Myron understandably called Catherine for a ride.

The exhaustion of battling the wind all day was setting in, and then something caught my eye to the north: a funnel cloud.

I immediately called Wayne and asked him if he had seen it. He told me to look over my shoulder and I realized that his RV was trailing just behind me, ready to pick me up if it got close or picked up intensity. Knowing that he was already thinking about what to do calmed me, but I was mesmerized by the magnificent, malevolent storm manifesting to the north.

If Mother Nature has taught me anything, it's that there is a surprise around every corner. While I was fixated on the skies to the north, a wicked hailstorm rolled in from the south and showered chaos down upon me. Thank God for my cowboy hat which helped deflect the golf-ball-sized ice chunks whizzing down from the heavens.

Wayne sped in front of me and slammed on the brakes in a driving move I'd seen before only in the movies. I sheltered at the RV's table, catching my breath and questioning my life choices as the hail thundered down on the roof and the RV rocked side to side in the gale-force winds. Trish fed me hot soup as Wayne cackled wildly, almost enjoying this strange and bizarre adventure.

I knew it was hopeless to talk Wayne into letting me stop early; but I also just couldn't imagine stepping out of that RV door to battle that godforsaken wind and hail for another twenty kilometres.

Then the RV stopped rocking and we all looked at one another in confusion. Wayne walked to the door and started laughing like a madman.

"Get your ass out here, Proctor," he said. "God is on your side, young man. Your 100 kilometre/hour side wind just shifted to a 100 km/hour tailwind."

All I needed to do for the rest of the day was lift my knees. The wind did the rest of the work, and boy, did I ever run fast. I finished that day ten kilometres farther than I had scheduled, and it felt good for my soul to get through such an ugly day with such a great finish.

The next several days in Saskatchewan I found my stride again. Despite the incessant back pain, the fitness I was building each had offset it, and for the first time I really started believing that I could fight through it and get this run *done.*

In the early days, I had scheduled specific distances to correspond with campground locations and Staples events. However, I found the lack of predictability too stressful and we eventually settled on completing 105 kilometres a day, wherever that left us. For whatever reason, this regularity really eased my nerves.

Wayne and Trish would drop me off in the morning where I had finished the day before, and they'd meet me again at the 20, 40, 50, 60, 70, 80, 85, 90, 95, 100, and 105-kilometre points with food and beverage, the same pattern that I used on my second attempt.

We had found a good daily rhythm. Wayne adapted to my need to see all my food and drink options laid out, rather than just being told what was available.

Meanwhile, Sharon and the kids in the second RV would sleep in and get rolling in the late morning. She was stressed from maintaining employment back home, managing the kids and keeping them occupied, and constantly moving from one campground to the next while grocery shopping, cooking all meals, and coordinating opportunities for Outrun Rare activities.

In essence, she was a single parent. The exceedingly heightened workload, paired with being on the road while I was fully focused elsewhere and too tired to help at night, turned into stress that was evident when I returned to the RV at the end of each day's run.

One evening upon getting back to the campground, I noticed Sharon walking in circles around the RV with the kids crying inside. After many minutes of trying my best to calm her down I saw a spark of alarm in her eyes. "Your dinner! I forgot to make dinner!"

She broke down crying and together we got dinner organized and decided to order in more, rather than cooking. Later that night we debated the idea of her and the kids breaking off from the run and going home early, that maybe we had collectively bitten off more than we could chew. Sharon was adamant that it was just a tough day and that there would be brighter days ahead.

At the same time, having the kids waking up in the middle of the night screaming and crying about bugs was getting old. My back pain was getting so severe that it took many hours to fall asleep, even with my nightly dose of zopiclone. Being awakened just hours later by a screaming seven-year-old and finally drifting off just before the alarm sounded again was starting to—scratch that—*was* grating on my nerves.

But they were kids! What could anyone do? The thought that there really weren't any good choices robbed me of what little sleep and calm I still had at the start of each day.

As we neared Moose Jaw and a scheduled Staples event, two gentlemen joined me for 50 kilometres and as always I enjoyed talking about all things running, life and politics...just talking.

Arriving at 10 a.m. on the nose, I was expecting to see tents and people cheering. But our lines had gotten crossed and we discovered that they were setting things up for noon. Wayne and I debated waiting around for a couple hours, but if I kept running, I'd have made quite a bit of progress in two hours and still be close enough to town to circle back. That idea seemed much more appealing, so I grabbed a Tim Horton's breakfast sandwich and continued running. I didn't love the idea of driving back to the event, but these were commitments I had made and I wanted to honour them.

Over the next couple days, it became obvious that Wayne and I were getting on one another's nerves. I can come across as bossy when my mind is narrowly focused on doing just one thing and doing it right. Or perhaps the sheer size of our joint undertaking was finally weighing on Wayne; or perhaps it was just that two dudes spending this much time together was bound to cause friction even among the best of friends.

Regardless, at each day's end we'd each migrate to our own RV and shut the blinds. The toll it was taking on both of us would have ruined a weaker friendship or made simple acquaintances into enemies. But the next morning, like clockwork, we'd wake up friendly again and jump right back into our respective roles, with Wayne as the boss, me as the athlete, and most importantly both of us still strong, lifelong friends.

Running through the manicured beauty of Saskatchewan's farmlands had a calming effect. The morning's sunrise was unmatched; and combined with soft winds blowing through the wheat and canola fields, the whole experience felt like a living poem of timeless peace.

I could almost forget about the relentless agony that gnawed at my deteriorating body—until we reached the outskirts of Regina, where a lengthy construction zone jarred me back to reality and crusted mud, large stones, and an uneven running surface sent jolts of pain up my spine and down the backs of my legs.

My pace slowed, my limp became more pronounced, and I could feel my face clenching, revealing the agony that every cell of my body felt.

The slightest change of terrain or uncertainty about what was ahead of me tipped me over the edge from being okay with things to being highly unreasonable.

If this were the case for the remaining 5000 kilometres, I thought, *you might as well just kill me.* We scheduled a massage therapist to come by the house I was staying at that night, but it hardly made a dent in the pain.

As we approached the Manitoba border, my back pain dramatically worsened—so much so that my pace slowed to a crawl, my gait was jagged and bent, and I completely lost my appetite. The pain zapped all feelings of hunger to the point that the thought of food made my stomach turn.

My head and shoulders slumped forward, tipping my cowboy hat forward so crazily that I resembled a tattered scarecrow whose flimsy body had been pecked away by birds. My pee breaks became strangely frequent despite pulling back on hydration volume.

One day, just 150 kilometres west of Winnipeg, I was wrapping up my day when I could feel one of my water bottles leaking down my leg. The water was warm, which didn't shock me since water does heat up as I run. But when I checked the water bottle, I was surprised to discover that it was full and dry.

A couple hours later I noticed the feeling again. I immediately stopped and looked down.

Holy shit. I was urinating on myself and had no sensation of even doing it.

The rest of the day can only be described as ugly, and after 105 kilometres, it finally came mercifully to a close. I crawled into the RV, laid down on my stomach, ate what I could, cried and went to sleep.

I knew something serious was probably going on, and the next morning, I talked with my physiotherapist Tyson Plesuk, sports doctor David Nabeta, and chiropractor Greg Morris to figure out why I was peeing myself.

They all were concerned that it might be the early stages of a syndrome called "cauda equina," where the nerve roots in the lumbar spine are compressed, cutting off sensation and movement. The symptoms include urinary and/or fecal incontinence, urinary retention, numbness in the groin and upper thighs, weakness or paralysis in the legs, and sciatica, and I had several of these symptoms.

They warned me that having run 2,500 kilometres with a pre-existing disc herniation increased the risk of cauda equina, and emphasized that I needed to stop and get it checked out immediately, since left untreated, cauda equina could be irreversible and leave me wearing adult diapers the rest of my life.

As a young man with three kids and a lot of running left to do, the news was difficult to hear, but even harder to believe.

Not me! I thought. *Not now!*

I'd been surging towards the goal of breaking the Trans Canada record my entire life, and I didn't know if I'd ever get the chance to do it again.

Then there was Outrun Rare. Every day I was out running on the highway, more funds were raised. I knew we were creating massive awareness—but at what cost, if I continued?

I also knew that the moment that I told Sharon, she'd put a stop to the run immediately. So, I bought myself some time by keeping the news to myself, hoping maybe, just maybe, the symptoms would vanish, and my form would correct itself and this scare would soon be a faded memory.

Then again, maybe not.

With the pain worsening and my pace slowing by the day as we approached Winnipeg, the typical 100+ kilometre days dropped to 80, then 60.

This death spiral was evident to everyone but me as my hope remained bright that a return to normal would occur. Random urinary incontinence was still happening, but it wasn't getting worse, which somehow gave me a glimmer of hope that brighter days might lie ahead.

Being an eternal optimist has its downside. Running through Winnipeg with local runners chatting about all things running, life and so forth gave me a real boost; and for the first time that week, I didn't see my daily mileage drop. Instead, I saw a significant improvement in both pace and distance over the previous day. After a restless sleep, Wayne drove me out to the next day's start point.

A sinking feeling that something wasn't right filled every recess of my mind as I reluctantly strode towards the sunrise. Something just didn't feel quite right. The searing pain in my back and down my leg was particularly bad that morning and it felt like my already-limited hip mobility was locking up.

Not long into the day's run, I noticed a strange sensation that to this day I still don't know how to describe. It felt like an awkward pressure followed by an overwhelming sense of shame.

I stopped, turned, and looked back at the road, hoping I wouldn't see what I thought I'd see. But there it was. I had just shit myself!

Raising every alarm bell that my already catastrophic symptoms had worsened, I had now lost control of my bowel function. I stopped in my tracks, trying to reason with myself about what had just happened, when I was seized with overwhelming fear and sadness that left me crying uncontrollably.

What do I do? Should I kick that in the ditch?

Who do I tell? I can't stop. Should I stop? What next?

Every rational and irrational question came rocketing through my mind. Every one of my thoughts felt like an entrapping chess move that limited choices and amplified consequences across the board.

The more I shuffled through the possible plays, the more it became abundantly clear that there was only one reasonable way forward. I walked on the highway for the next hour almost enjoying the calm, purity and serenity before the shit went down (pun intended).

I knew that sharing with the team what had been happening would start an avalanche of concern, planning, and action that would occupy every moment of my being. Unlike the run, there would be no glory, no sense of accomplishment, and no celebration after the suffering: just defeat.

Knowing the first conversation would be the hardest, I started with a call to our communications director Stephanie as I walked along the road shoulder.

It's best that she knows first, I thought. *It all has to flow downhill from there, so you might as well start there and get it over with.*

As the director of a PR and communications firm that specializes in crisis management and communications, I figured Steph most likely would already have backup plans to support the backup plans, so I trusted her most with the news. I also liked the way she always handled hard conversations with care and compassion.

Her response was exactly what I needed and instantly cut my anxiety by at least half. After hearing the story, her voice felt like a hug, and she laid out a carefully detailed plan. We would communicate this news in ways that minimized the fundraising impact while preserving my family's privacy. Both her delivery and professional planning eliminated my anxiety by at least half.

The second person I called was Sharon, then my brother Dan. After that, I talked to Wayne and Trish during one of the day's pit stops. The further I made it down the list and the more calls I made, the calmer I felt.

Not once did I hear the stern disappointment and frustration that I expected. The clearly disappointing news was met with love, care, and compassion for my own personal wellbeing. The overwhelming message was to stop, get medical care and to look after myself.

That night, after posting a slow and short day, Sharon, Wayne and Trish, Stephanie, Dan and I jumped on a call and had a powwow to discuss next steps.

Everyone agreed that the days of the run were numbered, and we all voted to call it quits. Out of respect, they gave me the floor at the end to speak to what was discussed and ultimately have the final say.

Through tears, I told them that I just didn't know how to quit; but if Sharon and the others refused to let me run tomorrow, I'd respect and abide by that.

Knowing and understanding the situation was one thing, but not giving it one more effort tomorrow—as long as there was even a sliver of a possibility that everything might be better—was something I just couldn't bring myself to do.

I begged them to allow me one final effort the next day, and if all didn't go swimmingly then I would bow to fate and call off the run.

In the end I was looking for compromise and in true loving form they gifted that to me. *Go ahead and give it one more try*, their acquiescence seemed to say, *but then we need to close the casket.*

The next morning felt like a young child's funeral. It's not that I've ever been to one, but I felt the loss of the dream as profoundly as if it were the loss of one of my own children.

What was left of my dream quietly echoed in the morning's breeze. Wayne and Trish tried their very best to be positive and optimistic, but they are poor actors and their compassion for my situation was apparent. They were giving me time to grieve.

Off I strode down the gravel road that paralleled the highway, gazing up at that beautiful sunrise that I knew would be my last from the highway. Maybe I just needed one last day out there to take in the beauty of the Trans-Canada Highway, to remember it as it had been for so many days. I wanted to gaze out to the vast lands one last time and see the farmers tending to their fields. I wanted to see the familiar Canadian Pacific railway train whiz by, blowing its horn.

But mostly, I think I wanted to go out on my own terms.

As much as I had painted this initiative as a rare disease campaign, I had also nourished a personal dream to cross Canada faster than anyone had ever done it. In the lead-up, I had endured brutal runs in blizzards, stress fractures, and had broken my body and mind down only to build them back up again.

I had given up time with family and stayed up countless nights fantasizing about the experience. And here I was, shovel in hand, at what felt like my own child's funeral. It broke my heart.

There is strange beauty in suffering that only a run like this can highlight, pairing purpose and effort. In a world of comfort and ease, we gravitate toward voluntary pain in hopes of feeling more human and more alive, paradoxically finding comfort in the discomfort.

In moments like this, I'd rather suffer physically than accept the inevitable psychological suffering that would begin the moment I announced that my final step had been taken.

Deep down in my heart was a burning pain that would be hard to extinguish, and I didn't know if I could.

Off to my left past the billboard announcing the geographic center of Canada, the parked RV awaited. When I reached it, I looked Sharon, Wayne and Trish in the eye and finally said the words I had never wished to say: "Let's call it a wrap."

I hit the Staples button we had glued next to the RV's door, the one that said "That was easy" when you pressed it.

The comic relief was sorely needed, and we all had a good laugh.

The next morning, we made a video announcing that I had stopped running and that the Outrun Rare race was officially over.

I thanked everyone for supporting rare disease research and helping drive the message that rare disease families in Canada deserve better support and encouraged them to visit our website and log miles to complete the rest of the unfinished journey to St. John's, still 4,500 kilometres away—a unique opportunity for people across Canada to show that rare lives really do matter, and that by supporting our cause, they could pick up the torch, take matters into their own hands, and make change happen.

I can see now that Outrun Rare was a success despite my failure to complete the run. Over the next month people all over Canada and beyond logged a whopping 41,000 kilometres, enough to circumnavigate Planet Earth and far more than the 4,500 kilometres originally needed to complete the original distance.

We raised more than $320,000 and created massive awareness about the plight of families with rare diseases. After all, that's what the run had been about.

And yet, as I stood on a lonely road in the middle of the second-largest country in the world, all I could think about was taking a shovel and digging the deepest hole I could, one big enough to hide in for a long while.

CHAPTER 3: NOVA SCOTIA

Mainland

DAY 10	COMPLETED	REMAINING
105.5 kms in 12:04:17	1016.5 kms	6142.6 kms

The overnight ferry from Port aux Basques, NL to North Sydney, NS had a silver lining in the form of a thirty-minute time zone difference, which continued to benefit us as we traveled west, ultimately gaining 4-1/2 hours of time. Those precious hours gained meant catching up on much-needed sleep. The downside was our arrival time in Nova Scotia: 8 a.m., much later than my usual 5 a.m. start. But that was fine; a late start meant a late finish, and I'd head straight to sleep.

As I stepped off the ferry, the lush greenery of the mainland contrasted starkly with the rocky cliffs of Newfoundland. Cape Breton Island now awaited, with breathtaking views and possible sightings of the Gulf of St. Lawrence's majestic migratory whales, a sight I'd eagerly anticipated.

Though my fever had settled, an unrelenting cough and rib pain persisted, despite my constant consumption of cough lozenges. The day's journey led me over a narrow bridge and up a steep five-kilometre climb. At the summit, I beheld some of Canada's most spectacular views, overlooking Goose Cove and St. Ann's along the legendary Cabot Trail.

Newfoundland now lay behind me.

It was at that moment that the magnitude of my undertaking truly hit me.

I stood at the eastern edge of the second-largest country on Earth, contemplating the vastness of my journey to Victoria—over 7,000 kilometres. I had put 1,000 kilometres behind me, but the bulk of it remained.

The sheer size of it all suddenly made my heart race; and I had to consciously choose wonder over fear, embracing curiosity and a can-do attitude despite what remained undone.

Throughout the day, Lana Rae and I shared our reflections on the incredible shared experience we'd been gifted. Remembering her story of a beautiful old white church she had passed on the highway, I knelt outside and offered a prayer when I reached it. I'm not what you'd call a religious person, but there's something out there that you just feel, and I've always felt a kind of connection with the divine as an omnipresent energy.

As I stood up, no lightning struck, so I took it as a sign that things were okay between me and the universe, at least for now.

Maybe this was going to be a good run after all.

As the sun set behind the hills, Lana Rae and I concluded our day near a lake somewhere between Whycocomagh and Baddeck. As I approached the SUV, I was suddenly overcome by violent coughing and excruciating pain in my left lower back that radiated around my ribcage. I dropped to my knees, clutching my side, gasping for breath, and wincing in agony. The coughing persisted, intensifying the torment.

I felt like I must have jinxed myself, and after the coughing stopped and the agonizing ordeal finally subsided, Lana Rae chuckled, thinking I was exaggerating to entertain her or seek attention. This sudden switch from pain to amusement infuriated me. How could anyone—especially my love—find my agony even remotely funny?

I remained on my knees and brushed her arm away as she tried to help me up. Dammit, that hurt! How could she not see that?

During our drive to the hotel, she denied laughing; but I couldn't let go of the memory of her laughter echoing in my head. That night, as I lay on a lacrosse ball desperately trying to release the muscles causing my ribcage to twist, Lana Rae's amusement continued to haunt me. My back hurt so badly that I neglected the pain in my ankle and foot even though I knew it would only worsen.

I guess I was just going to have to find out one day at a time how the run would go. I did everything I could to summon patience. Meanwhile, Lana Rae provided a prescription muscle relaxant to help the pain, and I fell into a deep sleep.

Dazed and Confused

DAY 11	COMPLETED	REMAINING
105.1 kms in 12:32:39	1121.6 kms	6037.4 kms

I awoke at 4 a.m., enveloped in thick mental fog.

Finding the motivation to swing my wobbly legs out of bed was challenging. I vacillated between silently acknowledging that I should get up (but wondering why) and not caring at all.

As I slowly climbed out of bed, rotating my back, I felt immense relief as I discovered that most of the discomfort was gone, thanks to some combination of the prior evening's muscle release work and the muscle relaxants.

Time dragged, and it felt like an eternity to finish breakfast and coffee. Lana Rae urged me to hurry, but I had no sense of urgency or motivation, which was quite unlike me. I had never struggled with motivation. Self-doubt, maybe, but if I knew I was supposed to be doing something, I'd always stay a step ahead, taking action.

Could it be that I was still high as a kite? I thought about that. Then again, without the muscle relaxants, I wouldn't have been getting up at all.

Lana Rae dragged me out of the hotel room, then when we got to the day's starting point, literally kicked me out of the vehicle. Recognizing my still-foggy state, she adopted a taskmaster persona, instructing me in a tone impossible to disobey to start moving.

For the first time on the run, I began my day walking. Slumped and apathetic, I continued moving only due to Lana Rae's relentless yelling from the window as she drove slowly by on the opposite shoulder, telling me to get my ass in gear. After what felt like an eternity, I started running just to quiet the barrage being hurled my way.

As relationship books about "love languages" remind us, we all tend to motivate friends and family the way we'd like to be motivated, rather than adapting to the other person's preference. While the approach might not have been my first choice, I knew Lana Rae loved me and wanted the best for me. Dragging my limp body along this road was the last place I wanted to be; and yet, her actions managed to clear my fog enough to get my pace to an acceptable level.

That was good, because the rest of the morning was a struggle up a motivational mountain that seemed steeper than ever. Lesson learned: don't run high.

After what seemed like the longest five hours ever, I crossed the Canso Causeway linking Cape Breton Island to the rest of Nova Scotia, and the fog in my mind finally lifted. I'd expected something magnificent after hearing about this causeway all my life, but it turned out to be a simple road extension of less than a kilometre.

Oh well. Tick it off the list. Now it's behind me.

Unfortunately, I was quickly discovering that the mental fog had been masking an enormously taxing pain in my right foot. Last night, I'd pushed it aside to tend to my back pain. Now, as the foot pain intensified, my attitude soured again. The ache just wouldn't go away.

The pain in my back and ribs was also still present, but I'm a firm believer that the brain can only notice so many stimuli, and right now, my foot took center stage.

In that morning's mental haze, I had also made the error of failing to generously lube my nether regions. Now a painful early-stage blister was forming just where I didn't want one. And as if that weren't enough, I clung to the lingering irritation I'd felt about Lana Rae's laughter yesterday like a thorn in my side. It was a real challenge to mindfully let go, and I made myself do deep breathing exercises as I ran, imagining clouds drifting by in the sky, knowing that holding onto anger would not serve me.

As I approached the crew vehicle at day's end, I noticed Lana Rae had the vehicle's engine idling again. For someone who had been stressed about budget and record-high fuel costs, it seemed like an unnecessary waste of resources. I didn't say anything, but Lana Rae sensed my frustration. Our minds were in different places at the moment; that much was apparent, and a lot was said without a word being spoken.

As we wrapped up the day, circling back to the hotel, we quietly ate our meal and went to bed.

Boiling Point

DAY 12	COMPLETED	REMAINING
105.5 kms in 12:26:56	1227.1 kms	5931.9 kms

Day 12 began outside Iron Mines, Nova Scotia, with the usual 4 a.m. wake-up, putting on the running gear I'd laid out the night before, and lubing and putting on sunscreen while Lana Rae made oats and coffee and loaded the vehicle so we could make it to the day's starting point by 5 a.m.

Today, however, I struggled, eating up precious minutes to loosen the tissue around my ankle and foot with the Theragun.

Getting up had felt particularly awkward. Lana Rae and I had left many things unsaid the night before; and I knew her well enough to tell that when she goes silent, a storm's brewing. Lana Rae had sought support from our sports psychologist Erin Zelinski throughout the trip to help avoid any tendencies to take over or railroad, and to help control her temper. While her attention to logistical details was a godsend, unchecked perfectionism can come across as bossy and controlling, which neither of us wanted, especially under these circumstances.

Nevertheless, the morning rolled on as usual, with the sunrise at my back, and I felt myself sliding back into a place of familiarity. The first forty kilometres passed with the typical initial ache followed by settling into the day's routine. The morning's solitude was a welcome relief after the negative energy of the past couple of days.

I noticed that my Altra Rivera shoes, nearing the end of their lifespan, were starting to give out after the relentless distance and unforgiving tarmac. At the forty-kilometre mark, Lana Rae pulled over onto a side road, allowing me to sit for a moment, eat some fruit, and prepare my vest for the next ten kilometres. Since the skies were clear, we thought applying more sunscreen was a good idea, but Lana Rae's liberal application of it to my legs and arms irked me.

I voiced my displeasure, questioning the volume used and suggesting that if we were concerned about sticking to our budget, we should consider conserving it.

Lana Rae's response was sharp. She told me to stay in my own lane and stop telling her what to do. She emphasized the importance of skin cancer prevention, arguing that the additional sunscreen cost was a small price to pay. This escalated into a heated argument, and I brought up the issue of the idling vehicle from the day before, along with her laughter during my coughing fit.

It became evident that she wanted to have a serious discussion to get her point across.

Well, engaging with Lana Rae in an argument is a daunting task on a normal day. She becomes tactical and logical when angry and is well and thoroughly able to take apart the most well-founded counterpoints. Add strong feelings and you have an unwinnable war.

I fought back initially, but my arguments were swiftly countered with questions that weakened my position. The more I lost ground, the more my emotions took over, and this culminated in a shouting match—in the middle of nowhere, five thousand kilometres from home—along with frayed nerves and expressions of disgust written all over our faces. I stormed away from the crew vehicle, walking a couple of hundred feet down the road, and found a grassy patch in the ditch to sit and collect my thoughts, because I didn't want to run in such a state.

As I glanced back at the SUV, I noticed Lana Rae watching me with a furious expression on her face, as if to say, *Jesus, Dave, you're already injured and behind schedule; we don't have time for this.* Perhaps she was just waiting for me to get up and start running. I don't know, but the longer I waited, the more I realized I was wrong in my attempts to control her behavior. I was also frustrated with myself for raising these concerns at a terrible time, knowing it would lead to the kind of argument we just had.

After about ten minutes, Lana Rae walked down the shoulder of the road and told me to stop moping, man up, and get running, emphasizing that she didn't want to be the reason I failed out here.

I told her that I would start when I was ready, and that I needed a moment to calm myself. This seemed to exasperate her further, and she stormed back to the SUV.

Shortly after, I got up, brushed the dead grass off my shorts, put on an upbeat song, and began running west. For the rest of the day, we hardly spoke, which gave us ample time to reflect on our thoughts and recognize where we had both been right, or most likely, wrong.

I tend to internalize more than anyone I've met, and my internal chatter and relentless quest for self-improvement can be both productive and paralyzing. Doubtless that was a factor.

In a world where dominance is crucial, the harsh internal confirmation of stupidity, wrongness, and unworthiness was like a cannonball to my metaphorical ship, something that even the most seaworthy vessel could not stand, even in good weather. For many hours, I walked the tightrope of internal mental chatter, challenging self-belief and questioning the invincible image of myself I had constructed.

I ran west along the shoulder of the highway, my mind lost in thought as traffic approached. As I approached an overpass, I noticed a vehicle slowly driving down the on-ramp and decided to tuck in behind the guardrail to allow them passage. To my frustration, the vehicle also stopped. I hesitated, waiting again for them to pass; but once again, they stopped as soon as I stepped out from behind the guardrail. Exasperated, I jumped back behind the guardrail to let them pass, but they stopped once more.

I waved my arm in the air, trying very hard to unambiguously give them the go-ahead. *Please just get going,* I thought, *before one of us gets killed.*

Then the vehicle approached slowly and I saw the passenger window lowering. A sweet elderly woman with a beautiful smile informed me that she was Joel Campbell's mom and had come to find me to bring cookies. Joel, a dear friend from Calgary, had mentioned that his parents lived in the area, wanted to meet me along the highway.

These wonderful people had gone out of their way to help me.

I felt embarrassed. I felt I had probably come across as rude during our earlier awkward exchange and sensed their embarrassment as well. I thanked them profusely, and after some small talk, I took a couple of raspberry cookies for the road, one in each hand, and they departed.

Later, I called my friend Joel to share the funny story, and we both laughed. It was clear that the apple didn't fall far from the tree: Mr. and Mrs. Campbell were truly lovely people.

At the next vehicle stop, I shared this amusing story with Lana Rae, and we finally both had a good and long-overdue laugh. I hugged her and apologized.

She did the same, and we used this event to reset and remind each other of our deep love and commitment. After all, we were in this *together.*

The day's constant, stiff headwind intensified in the afternoon, delivering punishing gusts during the final four hours; and each step felt ten times harder as I leaned into it to maintain balance. At times the wind would push one leg into a position parallel to the previous step, essentially nullifying the effort of that stride.

In moments like these, I find myself again consciously going to an emotionally safe place where I feel in control of my environment. There, I sometimes find myself sitting at my parents' house in High River, Alberta, where they still lived in the same house I grew up in. I sit at the round kitchen table, with my dad across from me, smiling warmly as we sip coffee. My mom is to my right in the kitchen, making pancakes and bacon, the TV on in the background, broadcasting a Blue Jays game.

It was there that I went as the wind picked up. In that moment, I felt happy, loved, valued, comfortable, and, most importantly, safe.

I finished the day with my GPS watch showing another 105 kilometres logged. I climbed into the SUV and rode the ten kilometres to Truro, relieved to be done with a challenging day.

The Fracture

DAY 13	COMPLETED	REMAINING
105.1 kms in 12:11:52	1332.2 kms	5826.8 kms

Lana Rae and I awoke in the hotel knowing it would be our last full day together before Wayne took over crew duties. Last night, we held each other tightly, cherishing the connected feeling, fully aware that we wouldn't see each other for a while. It made me all the more grateful we had resolved our previous differences with love and respect.

Today also marked a remarkable worsening of my symptoms and inflammation in my right foot and ankle as I took my initial steps of the day. As I encountered a local running group under an overpass just outside Truro, the pain seemed to go away for a while. Running together in the pouring rain, we discussed everything related to running, and they asked thoughtful questions about my journey so far.

Ten kilometres later, they turned off the highway, leaving me alone once again with my thoughts—a place I'd by now learnt could be a slice of bliss and gratitude or my own private hell. I called Lana Rae to tell her how much I hated being alone in the rain, especially as I tackled the hills approaching the toll station. Our talk ranged from yesterday's argument to how things were progressing to—most importantly—how much we'd soon miss each other.

Meanwhile, we had come up with a plan for Lana Rae to drive the 25-hour journey from Calgary to Ottawa, replace the rental vehicle with her personal Nissan Pathfinder, and then fly home, as the rental fee hikes were becoming even steeper than the hills I'd ascended. We agreed that it was a good idea, and I thanked her in advance for her willingness to make the grueling drive. She humorously mentioned that if I could run it, the least she could do was drive it.

At the top of the hill near the toll booth, the rain stopped, replaced by the densest fog I had ever seen. I became alarmed when I could barely see my hand as I waved it in front of my face. If I struggled that much to see my own hand, how would approaching drivers be able to see me even with bright blinking lights?

Lana Rae stayed on the phone, worried about my safety, but it also gave me someone to discuss my worsening foot pain with. The pain that had initially been localized to my foot had now spread throughout my entire foot and up my ankle. In just a few hours, it felt like the range of motion in my ankle had rapidly decreased, leading me to adapt my foot's striking pattern to alleviate the pain.

During the final three hours of the day, I was fortunate to be joined by a couple of local runners who wanted to share some miles, and I was relieved to have the distraction from the constant foot and ankle pain. As soon as they joined me, though, the rain returned, this time in buckets. These two kind, considerate souls soldiered with me through the downpour, and we chatted about a wide range of topics, during which I learnt quite a bit about the region.

Then, as is always the case with folks who come out to join me and don't intend on laying out 7,000 kilometres, they were gone.

I completed another 105 kilometres that day, ending right at the Nova Scotia/New Brunswick border. I had crossed all of Nova Scotia in just four days; and I couldn't have been happier about the achievement.

After wrapping up the day's run, Lana Rae drove us forty kilometres west to Moncton, to where Wayne waited at the hotel. As excited as I was to see my friend, I was equally saddened by Lana Rae's departure. Despite our ups and downs during this trip, it was an honour to accept the struggle, and I had never felt so close and connected to a person in my life.

It helped some that my old pal Wayne greeted me with a warm embrace. We hugged tightly, both excited about the journey that lay ahead. His concern was evident, however, as he witnessed me limping into the hotel room where our Mexican food delivery order awaited.

For a while, we shared beer, conversation, and memories.

As I lay on the bed and eating dinner, it became apparent that something in my foot's situation had shifted. There was a new, deep throbbing in my right foot, kind of like a toothache. The inflammation had spread up my ankle, and the muscles stabilizing my ankle and foot were tensing in a way that demanded attention. The relentless torture I had piled on the whole assembly while tending to my back had taken a serious toll that I'd consciously ignored. Now the chickens were coming home to roost, and I realized that the battle was just beginning. I'd need to fight harder than ever now to complete this monumental run.

One thing I've learnt is that if it looks like a dog and smells like a dog, then most likely, it's a dog. This looked and smelled like a bone fracture. And I had just under 6,000 kilometres left to run on it.

CHAPTER 4: NEW BRUNSWICK

This Is This

DAY 14	COMPLETED	REMAINING
105.1 kms in 12:21:17	1437.2 kms	5721.8 kms

I awoke in Moncton, New Brunswick, ready as we could be to tackle the third of nine Canadian provinces. That morning, however, the pressure of putting even a little weight down on my right foot made me decide to hop across the room on my left to reach the desk where Lana and Wayne had prepared my oatmeal.

The Theragun worked well to break up the tightness and get my ankle and foot moving again. While it hummed across my lower limbs and feet, I watched as Lana Rae showed Wayne the details of our morning routine. For Lana Rae, this had become second nature; but at 4 a.m., Wayne was working hard to take it all in without forgetting some detail and screwing things up later, busily taking notes and asking probing questions about one detail or another.

This would be the first of five crew transitions. New crew members would fly or drive in, relieving the existing ones so they could get back to their lives. In advance of the run, we had all discussed at length the details of handling crew transitions smoothly and the importance in maintaining continuity and flow. First impressions suggested that so far, this was going very well, and these two highly functioning people were working extremely well together.

Lana Rae and Wayne drove me east to my starting location for the day as the blustery wind tore at the sides of the vehicle. We knew the day would be that way, and it added to the first thirty minutes of hell as I waited for my foot and ankle to loosen up. Trying to intentionally toe off was an effective way to quicken the breakup of sinewy tissue, but it only worked so fast.

Meanwhile, the incredible sidewind that came from the south off the Bay of Fundy knocked me around, sometimes even into the ditch. Dressing appropriately was a challenge, as at times the wind was bitterly cold, then all of a sudden it would stop, and I'd feel over-warm and overdressed.

Not long after, the hills came, lined with trees of the boreal forest: rows of yellow birch, balsam fir, red spruce, and maples that made up the canvas of my world for the remainder of the province. The variety of shapes and fragrances was a welcome change and something I won't soon forget. It was a welcome change.

Making my way through this tapestry, I had the pleasure of connecting on the phone with my sports psychologist, Erin Zelinsky. The two of us connected every week for an hour. The calls provided great solace for me, as I knew that I was never too far away from support and a backstop when it came to overcoming various mental stumbling blocks during the run.

After filling Erin in on the latest, I mentioned my foot pain and how I believed it was a fracture.

She asked me about the pain and what I thought about it, trying to determine if the injury were actually severe enough to cause lasting harm. Then she asked me something very interesting: whether I could accept it.

At first, I was a bit taken aback and said that of course I'd rather not feel like this at all!

She then shared a very simple truth that will resonate with me until the day I die:

This is this.

What she meant was that if something troubles you, it doesn't need to be good, it doesn't need to be bad, it just needs to be. The moment you can accept your current state for what it is is the moment you let go of the obsession that it needs to be different.

There's true peace in this state of acceptance: peace in all things, easy or hard, good or bad.

Erin then reminded me of some reading she had prescribed me nine months earlier, where Jon Kabat-Zinn had written in his book Full Catastrophe Living about mindfulness and the concept of acceptance as a key to managing stress. Moreover, she spoke of his teachings in a way that was simple to follow along and made complete sense.

There's a saying that pain is inevitable, but suffering is a choice, one that comes from the desire for things to be as they cannot be. The only solution to suffering is acceptance. To accept the sensation in my foot and ankle for what it was and not desire it to be any different put me back in control.

It's amazing how the answers to the big, ugly problems in life can often be as simple as thinking about them differently. I left that phone call a different man: standing taller, more confident, and wanting to tackle the entirety of the country one step at a time.

My chat with Erin was just what the doctor ordered. During the remainder of the day, I noticed that Lana Rae and Wayne worked especially well together. Wayne brought a vociferous cheerleader energy to the project that was very welcome and complemented Lana Rae's detail-focused logistical mindset. I enjoyed his jovial approach, and I think Lana Rae did too.

As I reached 105 km and the end of the day, we circled back 65 kilometres to the hotel in Moncton where we had stayed the previous night. During the drive, I received a call from Vera, the filmmaker. She had tested positive for Covid-19 and was not feeling well; moreover, she would keep her distance from us for the next week to limit the spread. I felt guilty knowing that I had probably given it to her.

My ankle-impaired running pace and the lengthy drive back to the hotel made for a later night than we would've liked. When we settled in for dinner, Lana Rae was visibly bothered, and I asked what was wrong. She reminded me that this was her last night with me and told me that she was frustrated by the fact that she had a work email to get out and laundry to do still, and that this wasn't what she envisioned our last night looking like.

I fought to stay awake as Lana Rae shared her feelings. I wanted to be there; but she noticed my drooping eyelids and told me to go to bed. I asked her to wake me when she was ready for bed. Hours later, she quietly crawled in. I stirred, rolled over, and we held each other close, quietly sobbing and already missing each other, finally falling asleep in each other's arms.

The Three Amigos

DAY 15	COMPLETED	REMAINING
107.3 kms in 12:32:56	1544.5 kms	5614.5 kms

For someone who doesn't cry, Lana Rae shed lots of tears that morning. We knew that it wouldn't be long until we saw each other again since she'd be driving from Calgary to Ottawa to bring her Pathfinder out. But Ottawa felt so far away.

We both started seeing the run not as *my* project but rather *our* project, one interrupted by work commitments and life circumstances. Taking two months for us to *both* slowly travel the country wasn't in the cards. Something had to give. That's why Wayne was here.

But Wayne wasn't Lana Rae.

Lana Rae and I said a tearful goodbye in the parking lot before getting into the SUV with Wayne. I waved one final time and she was gone.

Without my guardian angel along for the trip, it didn't take long for trouble to find Wayne and me. We got lost and exited on the wrong off ramp just two minutes later. Ever since Wayne had crewed me four years ago during my last transcontinental attempt, I knew he didn't like using Google Maps and would rather follow signs to navigate the streets. Now I did my best to stay quiet.

Wayne is a dear friend of mine, and since he's 25 years my senior, I've always seen Wayne as a bit of a father figure. We met seventeen years ago during my first ultramarathon in Lethbridge. I "blew up" halfway through the run and didn't have a good result, whereas Wayne ended up winning the race in excellent fashion. During the first 15 kilometres, I'd picked Wayne's brain as he shared cool stories of running really long distances. He doesn't remember that exchange, but it's one I'll never forget.

About eight years following that race, we became good friends, often racing and sharing a beer together. Wayne's most noticeable qualities was his charm, but his bright smile, good looks, and radio voice could light up any room. His interest in others and ability to talk to anyone at any time about anything made him one smooth operator. Moreover, his grit and determination catapulted his running to a level where, when others struggled, he always found a way to transcend the pain and muscle on. Now at the age of 67, he still finds himself atop the podium, teaching the younger runners that toughness is learnt over decades not years.

Despite the throbbing foot pain and getting lost, the first forty kilometres clicked by. The two of us automatically fell into a routine, picking up from where we'd left off in 2018. Later in the day, another friend of ours named Myron was set to arrive in Fredericton. He planned to find his way out to the highway to pair up with Wayne. I was really looking forward to it as both Myron and Wayne's personalities gelled well together.

But at the 52-kilometre point, I was a bit confused. I was supposed to see Myron a couple kilometres back, so I gave him a ring.

Myron said that he thought I said that I wanted to see him on the 20, 40, and 60, not the 20, 40, 50, and 60.

No harm, no foul, I told him, as I had more than enough fluid and fuel on me and that I'd see him in eight kilometres.

Now 65 kilometres into the day, I looked ahead and saw a familiar face exiting a cab and wearing a white cowboy hat.

Myron!

We hugged it out and it was obvious that he brought energy and excitement. We ran together, talking a mile a minute, trying to tell one another everything and not realizing that we have another nine days to fill in the silence.

Myron and I had friends for years after meeting at a Bow Valley Harriers group run. Aside from an extensive ultrarunning and Ironman resume, Myron is the smartest, most polite, and most congenial man I know. A loving father of four adult children, he's a Lawyer-turned-businessman who knows everyone and is a wiz at fostering relationships. His depth of knowledge, curiosity, and keen risk assessment skills have paid dividends for him. But maybe his most endearing quality, and the one I like most, is his integrity. He's the kind of person where he wears his ethics as a badge of honour in a world full of conmen and wishy-washy types just looking for a fast buck and a quick exit.

Myron mentioned that he hoped to get in fifty kilometres a day with me for a while, even though his anterior shin was tight and sore. It lifted my heart to be running with him, and I hoped for my own sake that his shin held up.

Myron and Wayne took turns running with me the rest of the day as we passed through Fredericton, finishing our day northwest of the province's capital. We extended the run an extra two kilometres as our maps showed that there was a Dairy Queen just ahead and I had a hankering for a large vanilla milkshake.

Bunking in for the night in the hotel we drank beer, ate chicken and ribs, and bantered on about how the run was going. It was nice having some bro time; and even though I already sorely missed Lana Rae, we toasted ourselves at the "three amigos", and I fell asleep with chicken and ribs in my mouth.

The Vault

DAY 16	COMPLETED	REMAINING
104.8 kms in 12:14:33	1649.3 kms	5509.7 kms

The 4 a.m. wakeups weren't getting any easier, but at least by now they were becoming routine. I rose out of bed slowly, this time not from a lack of motivation but from a lack of mobility. What's more, it discombobulated me at first that Lana Rae wasn't there.

But I'm getting ahead of myself.

Every day before I exit the crew vehicle and start the run, I go through a little mental exercise that I call "the vault."

Let's say you went for a run one morning, ate a banana before heading out, and wore your brand-new New Balance shoes in the rain. If you weren't happy with how the run went, you might blame the banana you ate, the fact that you wore new shoes, or the fact that it was wet and cold.

It's easy to blame externalities when things don't go well. It absolves you from responsibility for your own outcomes.

But it's mostly a cop-out. It wasn't your fault. Nothing you can do, right?

Wrong. Instead, take an honest look at your *internal* environment: the way you are thinking, feeling, your ideas, and behaviors. Keep what serves you well, and put the rest aside.

Before I step onto the road every morning, I ask myself which thoughts, feelings, ideas, and behaviors I want to take with me today. I step into the vault with just those things, and leave everything else in the vehicle.

As the car door closes, it shuts away negative thoughts and feelings.

Instead, I'm secure in this impenetrable vault with healthy thoughts, feelings, ideas, and behaviors such as an immense belief in myself, obnoxious positivity, self worth, patience, gratitude, and love for everyone and everything.

It makes the extremely difficult seem manageable.

And I've locked out the things that most certainly don't serve me well: self doubt, panic, acknowledgment of pain, stresses I can't do anything about, catastrophizing, and self-criticism.

Honestly, negative mental mapping has resulted in 99% percent of all of my poor athletic performances. My vault constructs a one-foot steel wall between those thoughts and me.

So as I set foot on pavement that morning, I ran with just the thoughts I needed, leaving everything else in the SUV.

I spent most of the day alternating running with Myron and Wayne, both of whom brought much-needed relief from the monotony of plodding down the highway shoulder. Wayne told me stories of business endeavours and family life, passing along valuable wisdom without realizing it. We talked about past athletic achievements, politics, and more; and I savoured the time to dig a bit deeper into getting to know my friends.

Wayne brought his larger-than-life personality out onto the road, filling up every second of discussion time with whimsical tales and wisdom about love, life, family, running, and the pursuit of happiness.

I'm not good at asking for advice, so instead, I tried to listen more carefully. In my mind, it was the ultimate sign of trust and respect to listen to his stories. While talking about running, I'd remind myself that while we were both parents, Wayne also had experience as a grandfather and a vast store of knowledge, experience, and understanding to share.

The fact that both Wayne and Myron had spent our respective lives competing in endurance sports also meant they knew when to talk about what, when to push, and when to just run quietly alongside while I popped in earbuds and tuned out the world.

Having the boys out crewing this section couldn't be going any better.

My pace stayed consistently between 5:45 min/km and 6:15 min/km, and my heart rate between 120 and 132, which was absolutely spot on. Work, but not too much work. Sustainable. Perfect, really.

Even better was the volume of food I was eating. During Covid-19, I'd lost my sense of taste and a good bit of my appetite, and everything had tasted the same. Now, I was even surprising myself with my hunger and desire to take in food all day as I ran.

The fears of taste fatigue and an inability to take on 9000 calories a day that I had nursed before starting the run in St. Johns seemed like a distant memory.

Nevertheless, I started a routine of eating every fifteen minutes as I ran, to make sure I was getting enough calories. This intimidated me at first, but now into my third province, I found myself hungry only ten minutes after eating. My metabolism was burning like a jet engine, and I was content stoking the flames. It was nice to be hungry again, hitting my stride, and in a good mood.

Nearing the end of the day around Woodstock, I felt for the first time an abdominal pain, and a panic came over me. Looking down at my belly, it looked as if I were six months pregnant, and I could feel a pressure steadily building minute by minute. It was more than uncomfortable.

Even Wayne made a jackass comment about my Buddha belly.

Thankfully, the desire to wolf down everything in sight went away, and for the final hour of running, I ate nothing but ginger chews in hopes of calming my aggravated tummy.

As I left my vault and climbed in the SUV at the end of the day, fear, worry, and that dreaded foot pain all came to the surface at once.

What if this is something new? Will I be able to adapt my diet, aid stop frequency, or running style? Will this interfere with my sleep? Hopefully this isn't the first sign of some unseen challenge to finishing the run that is only now beginning to rear its ugly head. And if so, what then?

I rode in silence to the hotel with Wayne and Myron as the pain in my abdomen worsened and I crouched forward into a seated fetal position.

That's when I let out the loudest, longest fart in human history, possibly tearing a hole in the seat cushion!

I tried to hide my relief as well as I could.

That's when the boys let out a vociferous celebration, both laughing and clapping, showing their true friendship. Instead of understandable disgust, they were thrilled that I was no longer in gastrointestinal discomfort. The farting continued all night without one mention of disapproval.

Having gotten business out of the way, and daring to tempt fate yet again, we filled our bellies with pizza and beer and talked about chicks and sports.

I was falling into a good groove out here, and it was a full team effort.

Three to Five Percent

DAY 17	COMPLETED	REMAINING
105.8 kms in 12:42:41	1755.1 kms	5403.9 kms

Beep beep beep beep beep beep!

It's 4 a.m. and the start of Day 17. Rolling slowly out of bed, I limped over to the sink to brush my teeth. As I looked in the mirror, I saw that I had lost weight, my skin looked weathered, and with no time to shave, my beard was filling in.

I slowly made my way to the desk to eat my oats and coffee while using the Theragun to loosen everything up again. To my relief, aside from the foot and ankle, my legs and hips felt okay. As always, I felt the burning ache of an old vertebral fracture in my upper back, but I knew that unresolved injury would be a constant throughout the run and was unlikely to flare up. My legs had fallen into a healthy groove, and felt good.

As I was eating and Theragunning, I came across a Facebook Messenger chat that troubled me. Earlier in the week, a stranger had sent me an article about the stretch of highway we were approaching, saying it was very unsafe. And he wasn't talking about oncoming traffic, either. According to the article, many women had gone missing after approaching a "distressed" traveler's broken-down car. I had passed along the article to Lana Rae and Vera and had given the original poster a thumbs-up emoji indicating my acknowledgment of his point.

My apparently ambiguous response, however, triggered a lengthy response from this stranger, insisting that a thumbs-up wasn't a worthy response, then criticizing me, calling me names and questioning my human decency.

It shouldn't have bothered me, but for some strange reason, it did.

I started internalizing what he had said, asking myself if I really was that guy. During the run it was common to receive many posts and messages every day, most of the time encouraging or at least supportive. While I often couldn't respond to all of them, I try my best to respond to my closest circle: most importantly, my kids, immediate family and friends.

Riding to the day's start point, I brought the message up to Myron and Wayne, and they had a good chuckle about it and gave me some good advice to not let it bother me. They were right, so I did my best to let it go, remembering my favorite quote, from Teddy Roosevelt's famous April 23, 1910 speech, "Citizenship in a Republic," better known as "The Man in the Arena."

> "It is not the critic who counts; not the man who points out how the strong man stumbles, or where the doer of deeds could have done them better. The credit belongs to the man who is actually in the arena, whose face is marred by dust and sweat and blood; who strives valiantly; who errs, and comes short again and again, because there is no effort without error and shortcoming; but who does actually strive to do the deeds; who knows the great enthusiasms, the great

devotions; who spends himself in a worthy cause; who at the best knows in the end the triumph of high achievement, and who at the worst, if he fails, at least fails while daring greatly, so that his place shall never be with those cold and timid souls who know neither victory nor defeat."

In short, my buddies were reminding me that the O.P. was a troll, and as such, best ignored.

Overall, this day's run was one of joy. Every day, Myron ran a minimum of fifty kilometres with me, and today was no exception. We ran what seemed like the same endless, narrow highway lined with lush native trees, the occasional lake, and equally endless hills. I knew we'd be ending our day at the relative high point of New Brunswick, where a slope would soon take me into Quebec and along the flat and fast St. Lawrence Seaway.

Somewhere in the middle of it all, my pace picked up slightly as my legs continued to feel good and the last of the lingering viral symptoms cleared. Near the end of the day, I connected via telephone with Erin, my sports psychologist. It was good timing, since I was still circling back to the troll's message, unable to shake his attack. She reminded me that three to five percent of the world's population are mentally unwell, and it's exactly those people who are getting into fights with strangers on Facebook.

We discussed strategies for deflecting their problems so that they didn't become my problems. She asked me what percentage of all of the comments were negative in nature, and I told her it was less than one percent. "Great," she said. "This is well below the average of people who are mentally struggling, so you must be doing something right out there."

That was something that I just hadn't thought about, and I've learnt to be profoundly grateful that I have somebody like Erin in my corner, setting me straight when my head tries to send me off-course.

As usual, I left the phone call feeling like a million bucks and capable of sticking to the plan I had created.

It was thus that at the end of the day, three satisfied men found themselves hanging out in a dingy motel, drinking craft beer, and eating a giant bowl of seafood spaghetti. We turned on the Blue Jays game, but I was so tired I didn't make it past the third inning.

I was out here with my friends, uncomfortable as hell and living my dream.

Groundhog Day...Again

DAY 18	COMPLETED	REMAINING
104.4 kms in 12:27:35	1859.5 kms	5299.5 kms

The alarm reported the date as June 1, eighteen days after starting the run.

The morning felt like every other morning so far. I woke up, put on my clothes, lubed up for the day, ate breakfast and Theragunned while Wayne loaded up the SUV. We drove back twenty kilometres to the starting point, allowing Myron to get a couple more hours of shuteye while Wayne dropped me off where I had stopped the day before and took the first shift.

I climbed out of the SUV, hit start on my GPS watch, started my Garmin InReach, and started running. A few minutes later, I called Lana Rae to wake her up. Since we couldn't actually have coffee together every morning like we normally did, this was our virtual get-together over coffee. I listened longingly to her groggy voice as she crawled out of bed to pour herself a cup before making her way back to bed. We talked for about an hour before I transitioned to my routine of listening to classical music until I met Wayne and Myron at the twenty-kilometre mark.

Like clockwork, the combination of strong coffee and the rhythm of the run brought on the need for a bathroom break. Wayne would park and position the car at an angle so I could open the two passenger-side doors to use it like a portable toilet, with all my essentials in the front seat. I'd eat and drink quickly to not waste time and be on my way after stuffing my vest with food and fresh sports drink bottles. At this point, I'd listen to a podcast, an audiobook, or talk with Wayne or Myron if they were running with me.

Later in the day, I'd see them again at the forty-kilometre mark and repeat the routine, this time reapplying sunscreen. Then I'd see them again at fifty, sixty, seventy, eighty, ninety, one hundred, and finish off the day at one hundred and five kilometres. The boys would hand me a high-fat protein smoothie when I had one kilometre to go, and we'd walk the last ten minutes of the day together while drinking the creamy concoction.

Every day was like this, and there was peace in the certainty and continuity of it all. We never went out to restaurants and did our best to limit surprises. Energy and time management were my priorities, and I felt like I was winning at that game. The fact that this was day eighteen of seventy-two sank in, leaving me with a feeling of reverence for something so magnificently huge that I felt I *had* to get it right.

As the day wound to a close, I found myself running through the breathtaking streets of Edmundston, NB. We were all in great spirits, exploring the old culture and architecture, knowing that early in the coming morning, we'd cross into the province of Quebec, and for the first time during this run, I veered off the Trans-Canada Highway and onto Highway 120 to take an alternate route into Quebec, since it's illegal there to run on the Trans-Canada Highway.

Highway 120 is a stunning, heavily treed roadway with small town charm and a wide, paved shoulder, and it was a nice finishing chute for the day, which ended twenty kilometres west of Edmundston.

The boys might have gotten a bit too liberal with the whipped cream in my smoothie on the final kilometre, as I found my guts tied up in knots for the rest of the night. Too much fat at once can do that. But there was no way I was going to punish them by letting rip with another Big Nasty in the SUV.

This time, I kept my discomfort to myself.

I had other things to focus on anyway.

Early into tomorrow's run, I would pass into Quebec, checking off New Brunswick and all of Atlantic Canada. What felt even better was knowing that pushing on into the center of my giant undertaking, I'd overcome Covid-19 and found a way to look past my fractured foot, still feeling insanely confident about completing this run across the country.

CHAPTER 5: QUEBEC

The Language of Love

DAY 19	COMPLETED	REMAINING
105.9 kms in 12:29:37	1965.4 kms	5193.6 kms

Wayne's back and hips were bothering him as we drove the twenty kilometres to our starting point. He had slept awkwardly, waking up with back pain that traveled down his leg. He tried his best to disguise it. After some verbal arm wrestling, he agreed to let me look at it later that night, as my decades of work as a massage therapist might come in handy.

The morning weather was ideal: 5 °C temperature, still, and an overnight rain that had just ended. I looked forward to getting off the busy Trans-Canada Highway after eighteen days and experiencing the back roads of old Quebec through smaller villages.

It wouldn't be long until we crossed into Quebec and all the signs would be in French. As a Canadian, I'm embarrassed to admit that my French is amateur at best. I stopped learning or using it when I was thirteen.

Fortunately, Myron spoke fluent French and was eager to put his *compétences linguistiques* to work. Wayne, on the other hand, despite having the last name Gaudet, spoke just as little French as I did. What he didn't say in French, however, he managed to communicate with his beautiful blue eyes and devastatingly handsome smile. Wayne spoke the language of love, which at least half the population understood without his saying a word.

Sixteen kilometres into the day, running alongside Myron, I crossed into Quebec, right on track to break the Trans Canadian speed record by six days, but I also knew how much distance remained.

The rugged, old-world beauty along Highway 289 was breathtaking. Giant trees overhung the old winding roadway with very little traffic, allowing the songbirds an audience. I knew that I was at a relatively high elevation, and the roadway would continue a gradual descent north to the St. Lawrence Seaway, which we should be approaching by the end of the day.

I decided to enjoy the downhill for a while.

Myron and Wayne took turns running with me throughout the day. I felt bad for Wayne as he looked pretty stiff, but he persisted, explaining that getting out and running was loosening his back. After eating a much smaller amount for dinner last night out of an abundance of caution regarding intestinal distress, I did my best to increase my caloric intake throughout the morning to avoid losing weight. Accordingly, Myron and Wayne took turns stopping at small-town bakeries for delicious treats to promote my appetite.

Two-thirds into the day, Myron and I ran alongside a huge lake through a beautiful small town named Pohenegamook. We noticed flags and signage featuring what looked like a large dragon.

Curious, they looked it up and found out that the large dragon had a name: Ponik. Ponik had been sighted more than a thousand times in Lake Pohenegamook going back as far as 1873, when a lumberjack named Louis Berube saw a huge creature poke out of the water and then dive back in. Witnesses describe it as having two or three humps and measuring thirty-five to sixty feet long with a horse-shaped head, a barrel-like neck, and a sail across its entire spine.

With my phone out, I kept my eyes peeled for a view of this creature, but no such luck. Given the importance of dragons during this run, I took this as a potentially good omen. The downward slope of the highway increased, and the smell of fresh water, which I was sure was the St. Lawrence Seaway, strengthened.

A good omen indeed. *Thanks, Ponik.*

For some reason, in my mind I landmarked reaching the Seaway as a major milestone, which heightened my excitement. I also knew that after all the climbs of Newfoundland, Nova Scotia, and New Brunswick, the flat, easy running alongside the St. Lawrence was a welcome relief. I was happy to hear that the hotel we were staying at was at the exact one hundred and five-kilometre mark into the day, meaning that I could run right out from the hotel room tomorrow morning.

Hunkering down for the evening, we ordered chicken and ribs and ate our fill.

Now at the end of the day, and after some coaxing and initial outright refusals, I talked Wayne into letting me look at his hip, but even as he gave in, he still protested.

I told him that if he was able to look after me for sixteen hours a day, the least I could do was help him out for fifteen minutes. Digging my elbow into his posterior hip, it was obvious his piriformis and gluteus medius were in lockdown, and it was a simple release.

Standing up off the bed, he noticed immediate relief, and we shared a beer in celebration.

St. Lawrence Seaway

DAY 20	COMPLETED	REMAINING
105.3 kms in 12:06:59	2070.7 kms	5088.3 kms

Day 20 was wonderful for many reasons.

First of all, we had crossed into a new time zone on the previous day, giving us an extra hour of sleep, which we used to its fullest.

Second, Wayne woke up in a good mood, singing and dancing around the hotel room while getting ready for the day. It was obvious that the massage had helped his hip pain. If I hadn't known better, I'd swear he'd gotten lucky last night, but I knew that didn't happen.

Last, we knew the St. Lawrence Seaway was just down the road, where we would run right into it, turn left on highway 132, and remain for the next couple of days paralleling the wonderfully flat St. Lawrence Seaway. Vera was very excited, as this was a pivotal location of the run, and she wanted to film the transition in all its glory.

For only the second time in the last twenty days, we departed right from the hotel room door. We then headed north towards the Seaway. Myron started the day with me, excited to experience the iconic Left Turn to follow the St. Lawrence that I'd been so jazzed about. I marveled at his consistency and strength, as this was his sixth day running fifty kilometres in a row, making it the highest weekly mileage of his impressive career.

As we ran, I noticed he had a slight limp, but I didn't mention it partly because *he* didn't. Only six kilometres after starting, with a giant body of water ahead of us and Vera's drone flying high above us, we turned left onto Highway 132, connecting us to well over a week of flat, beautiful roads. Looking across the St. Lawrence Seaway, I could see hills in the distance.

The St. Lawrence Seaway is made up of a system of locks and channels that permit vessels to travel from the Atlantic Ocean to the Great Lakes of North America. This great system connects the Atlantic Ocean with cities as far west as Duluth, Minnesota via Lake Superior. More notably, the St. Lawrence had been the main entry point for European settlers dating back to 1608, when Samuel de Champlain established a settlement at Donnacona, later called Quebec City. At this point, the Seaway is extremely wide, full of whales, oil tankers, and cargo ships. But as it draws inland approaching Montreal, it steadily narrows to the size of a river.

Here, though, the Seaway was massive, almost twenty kilometres across, and dominated the landscape wherever the road got close to see it.

Running southwest down Highway 132, we passed through stunning old villages like Kamouraska and Saint-Jean-Port-Jolie that seemed to be frozen in time. These historic places were full of old-world charm, with stone streets paving the ancient downtowns, leading to giant stone cathedrals in the town center.

I felt privileged to experience this part of Canada, a part that western Canadians like me don't often get to see. Old homesteads lined the roadway and landscapes glowed with colourful native flowers and mature trees. I enjoyed seeing the worn barns and stables that betold the towns' legacy of hard-working, honest agricultural work. I could just image early settlers fishing along the Seaway, then using it to ship crops harvested from long, narrow plots of land neighboring the shore.

Later in the day as we ran together, Myron mentioned that his shin had been aching all day and that it was starting to feel inflamed. Knowing he had a 24-hour race coming up, we agreed caution made sense—with so much mileage already banked, more bad than good would come from continuing.

Meanwhile, at the next pit stop, Wayne was holding a bag and had a childlike, giddy look on his face. He told me to close my eyes, reach into the bag, and "rip off a chunk."

With a look of confusion on my face, trustingly I did what I was told, tearing a large chunk off the warm, crusty loaf inside. I stuffed it in my mouth and without pause, the angels from heaven sang down upon me. I'm not trying to exaggerate here. I know it was just bread, but it was quite possibly the greatest bread I've ever tasted.

Wayne told me that he had visited an old bakery in the town we just passed through; and though he struggled to communicate with the elderly ladies working there, after flirting for a bit he thought he might have ordered buns. Instead, he said, they gave him this loaf. It was too much effort to make the switch, so he just paid and walked out.

"What a wonderful mistake!" I yelped.

It didn't take long before the loaf was done and dusted, but...what I wouldn't have done for some maple butter.

Since Wayne was in a great mood and Myron needed some rest, I finished the day running with Wayne. He seemed like a brand-new man. He ran with no limp whatsoever and a beaming smile full of optimism.

As we wrapped up the day and headed back to the motel, Myron ran out to grab sushi for dinner and I went to work on Wayne's hip again. Myron must have struggled greatly at the restaurant, as it took him ninety minutes to return. He was visibly upset, both apologizing and angry about the messed-up order.

But it was still food, and it was good. We ate, and then I worked on Myron's leg a bit more before hitting the hay.

Lightning and Rainbows

DAY 21	COMPLETED	REMAINING
105.3 kms in 12:47:25	2176 kms	4983 kms

Twenty-one days into the run, the itch from not shaving my beard was driving me nuts. It was long enough to notice, but not long enough to lie smoothly on my face.

Meanwhile, Myron made a big deal about our having covered three weeks of running 100+ kilometre days as we drove out to the start point, as he and Wayne discussed the flow state that I always seemed to find.

Drawing comparisons between 2018 and now, Wayne exclaimed that "You've got this in the bag as long as you can find a way to keep this going."

I thought he was right. What Wayne and Myron called my "bubble of flow" was a state of complete focus, in the zone, a place where activity feels effortless and all distractions and barriers vanish.

Right now, I wasn't in that bubble yet. I was thinking about the weather. The morning sun was enjoyable now, but forecasts suggested things could get hairy later. Nevertheless, I got going and slipped into my usual groove. While I appreciated the constant companionship and support of the other two amigos, it was nice running in solitude for a while as I caught up on the phone with Lana Rae, my kids, and my mom and dad. That was another nice thing about Quebec: it had better cell reception than Newfoundland.

Three hours into the day, I was joined by Olivier and Andrew from Quebec City. This was my first time meeting Olivier, although we had spoken many times on video calls leading up to the run. Olivier is a good friend of Myron's and selflessly agreed to help us with mapping through Quebec. Aside from his regional knowledge, Olivier also works for the Canadian Navy building maps for a living, so we knew we were in capable hands. His diligence was apparent, now bettered by his joyful conversation and zest for life.

We ran west down the St. Lawrence, exchanging ideas and getting a lesson on the grand history of the St. Lawrence Seaway and its adjacent villages. I could have spoken to these gentlemen for days, but thirty kilometres after joining, their ride showed up and they needed to get back to their busy lives.

I was now alone again on the highway with a giant, dark rain cloud approaching. On the outskirts of Levis, the wall of water caught up with me and was quickly upon me. The lack of sidewalks through this old city, combined with the already swollen puddles, made for a very sketchy section of road.

In moments like these, visibility is critical. It's too easy to get hit by a motorist who can't see you. That's why it was vitally important to wear my blinking UltrAspire waist light. Drivers have a hard enough time seeing through their wiper-swept windshields, making a pedestrian an easy target. A blinking strobe light garners a lot of needed attention.

Two runners and two lights garner even more attention.

Wayne accompanied me for a portion of the run as the rain came to a sudden stop; but the break in the clouds revealed that there was an even darker, more sinister-looking cloud approaching in the distance. Wayne remained at my side as we hurried along a section of road that would connect us to a bridge with a pedestrian walkway. If we could reach that in time, it would take us across the St. Lawrence and into Quebec City.

The Quebec Bridge has been in operation for over one hundred years. This riveted steel truss structure runs nine hundred and eighty-seven meters, making it the longest cantilever bridge span in the world.

Today, it sure felt like it. Wayne and I held our hats tight to our heads to prevent them from being swept away by the gusts. I knew I'd be glad to be off that exposed expanse and amongst the city's buildings where maybe we'd get some kind of relief from the wind.

But reaching the city presented its own problems.

One of my strengths was shutting off my brain and flowing down a boring roadway, but this was obviously not an option here. Upon clearing the river, Wayne and I paused long enough to review the expert maps that Olivier had designed. Navigating through these large, unfamiliar cities was a point of stress for me, as the possibility of something going wrong always demanded my heightened attention.

With lightning and thunder starting, we made our way down the residential streets of the provincial capital. Approaching a scheduled pit stop at the vehicle, Wayne stopped running with me and jumped into the SUV, leaving me alone. One minute later, hell came down around me in the form of dense sheets of rain. The sheer amount of water was punishing, and despite my cowboy hat and rain slicker, I was drenched within seconds.

As if the stress weren't enough.

Wayne and Myron circled back to see if I was okay, and seeing my thumbs-up, they proceeded further down the road. Not long after that, I heard a loud thud, followed by another, as large golf ball-sized hail cascaded down around me. Frantically, I found refuge under a tree in the front yard of a residential property. Waving at the family inside who were watching me from their living room window, I saw Wayne and Myron speed past to check on my welfare.

Minutes later, the storm stopped, and I waved goodbye to the kind family, thanked them for the coverage, and proceeded forward. As quickly as the storm came, it went, leaving behind a sunny, hot sky full of arching rainbows.

Just another day out on the highway in the middle of Canada.

Once I got to the stopping point, the Three Amigos finished the day with my favorite Quebec dinner of chicken and ribs.

I ate two full racks.

Salamander, Coyote, Eagle and Dragon

DAY 22	COMPLETED	REMAINING
104.6 kms in 12:29:09	2280.6 kms	4878.4 kms

My morning got off to a rough start due to a poor night's sleep. For no known reason, I was up all throughout the night, tossing and turning, staring at the back of my eyelids. 4 a.m. came early and by 5, I was dressed and the SUV was loaded, but I still wasn't quite awake.

I called Lana Rae and chatted the first two hours of the day. She was making the long drive from Calgary to Hawkesbury, Ontario, to replace the expensive rental SUV with her personal Nissan Pathfinder.

I've never felt myself so drawn to anybody as I am to her. We could talk on the phone for days and never run out of things to say. She was telling me about a podcast she was listening to, some work stuff, and the juggling act of logistics when it came to the run. It was an absolute pleasure waking up to such a woman and my mood improved.

Twenty kilometres into the day, Myron got out and ran with me. His shin was still bothering him, but he wanted to see how it felt to run on it. We had a great conversation, but his limp was apparent, and after twenty more kilometres, he rightly decided to call it quits. The rest of the day I spent on the north side of the St. Lawrence in the warmest weather so far. Temperatures reached

24 °C, and I was very happy with my decision to start on May 15th to avoid the brutal humid heat that July and August brought to Quebec and Ontario. Sure, it was a bit cold to start within Newfoundland, but reasonable temperatures in Quebec were worth it.

I ran today, as I had every day so far, with the metaphorical "four animals" with me. They would share every step, every hill, and all the weather. They would see what I saw, and they would feel what I felt. You've already met one of them, the Dragon. But since these four have been a constant on my mental state in this extensive journey, let me introduce them.

The Salamander

My salamander is by far the most prolific and dominant of all four. He is a slimy little guy who is pasted to the front, left side of my brain under my skull. He wiggles slightly with his feet and licks my brain with his gross tongue. Worst of all, he whispers in my ear messages of doubt: "you aren't enough," "people don't like you," and "you should give up." His defeatist words are so loud because of his proximity to my ear...and he never stops! He is the only one of the four who has a name, and that's important because of the deep, intimate relationship we have with each other. His name is Emilio. I've found that the more I tell him to shut up, the louder he gets. Instead, it's best to distract myself. It's best to focus my attention up into the sky ahead of me, noticing the large eagle soaring high above my head.

The Eagle

This eagle is a stoic presence and calmness that leaves me feeling in control and centered. His wisdom and symbolic delayed gratification leave me wondering what he can see from his vantage point that I can't see from down here. I'd rather follow his guidance than listen to the pathetic, slithery voice in my ear.

The Coyote

At any point, I can look down into the ditch and see my coyote. If I don't see him, I'll notice the trees or bushes rustling, and I know he isn't far. The coyote bites when you least expect it, taking chunks of flesh from my legs, leaving a bloody trail. As bad as his bites hurt, I've come to understand that I'm more afraid of his bite than the bite actually hurts. Anticipation of the next bite has paralyzed me in the past. I've spent a lot of time kicking and screaming at him, at times even throwing rocks to shoo him, but every attempt is futile. I remind myself that I've taken thousands of bites but never been taken down. It helps some of the time. It's also important to note that the Coyote doesn't make eye contact because he does not respect me. Instead, he keeps his eyes on something else. The giant, black, fire-breathing dragon in the sky.

The Dragon

This enormous, vastly powerful, winged lizard flies in the distance, epitomizing strength, confidence, power, ability, and persistence. He circles in a figure-8 at times, screeching, always reminding me that he's there. The coyote cowers, deathly afraid of him.

Strangely, I am not afraid: I know that ultimately the dragon is me. Deep down, I am strong, confident, powerful, capable, and persistent.

The distance between the dragon and myself is space I myself create because I am uncomfortable and perhaps frightened, not *of* him, but of *becoming* him. His presence is a reminder of who I really am, even if I can't fully accept it at the moment.

If, at the end of this run, I look up in the sky and see no dragon, it will be because I have become him, and he now embodies me: I have self-actualized, fully realizing my own potential.

When times get tough, as they always do, I tether myself to the giant winged beast. I envision a sturdy rope that extends from my chest, winding across the road and soaring up into the sky, where my dragon assists my progression. Here, I can find reprieve and assistance when I need it most.

Let's face it, when you are a fire-breathing dragon, you certainly don't listen to a tiny, pathetic salamander.

I made up these four animals eight to ten years ago to make sense of the "voices" in my head, after learning that in books like Winnie the Pooh, the creation of characters helps children identify emotions, thoughts, and feelings and come to terms with them. Why *not* apply that to self-doubt, belief, stoicism, pain, and actualization?

So for the remainder of the day, I ran with them, and there they were in all their glory. They were around all day yesterday and if I were a betting man, I bet you they'd show up again tomorrow.

It's important to accept that while all those animals are a part of you, it's important to choose the animal you most want to embody, and in your life's journey, look to model its behavior.

I rounded out the day running through downtown Trois-Rivières, finding these old cities quite confusing to navigate, partly because they were designed for horse-and-buggy traffic, but also because all the signs were in French. We found a place where we could actually order, chowed down on fried chicken and pizza, and had a laugh over a cold beer. We were most certainly on a roll, right on pace for the seventy-two-day speed record, and one-third of the way across the second-largest country in the world.

Happy Mistakes

DAY 23	COMPLETED	REMAINING
105.3 kms in 12:41:43	2385.9 kms	4773.1 kms

I awoke to the alarmingly metallic taste of zopiclone. I'd been using it to get to sleep when my foot pain got intolerable, and I feared that if I stopped taking them now, I wouldn't be able to fall asleep. What's worse, I've had anxiety-related sleep issues all my life; and knowing how important it was in my current situation to get a full night's sleep, I didn't want to rock the boat. I planned to rely on those little blue pills as long as necessary, even if getting off them following the run was difficult.

I licked my lips and tried to make the taste go away.

At 25 °C, today was supposed to be the warmest and most humid day so far. This was also the point where my route veered off the major roads of Quebec and zigzagged north of Montreal to avoid the confusion, traffic, parking difficulties, and stop-start nature of running in a major city.

On the other hand, running out in the country meant dealing with a lot more road camber.

Highways are usually sloped, or cambered, anywhere from one to three degrees to allow water to run off during rain and snowstorms. Now, that tiny bit of slant was bothering me. What was more alarming was that I could tell something had changed in my right ankle and foot.

Consistently running in the same direction on the shoulder of the highway facing traffic had taken a toll. For the last twenty-three days and 2400 kilometres, my left foot has been landing three to nine millimetres lower than my right. My left hip was thus similarly lower, creating a painful scoliotic bend in my spine.

I always ran facing traffic, principally for safety and visibility. I'd rather see an approaching vehicle whose driver was distracted by their phone as it crossed the thin white line. Knowing it was coming, I could jump into the ditch.

The alternative was running on the other side of the road with traffic at my back. But I didn't trust that the drivers of vehicles approaching from behind could see me as they rounded a bend or crested a hill. I'd have no warning that they were coming, and some transcontinental runners had been killed in the past in similar conditions.

Up until now, I'd chosen safety over comfort, but now that our course took us along less-frequented roads, I felt I could afford the relief of occupying the other shoulder. My back sorely (pun intended) needed it.

As I ran on the right shoulder, however, it was terrifying hearing vehicles approaching from the rear. Having to relinquish visibility of their exact locations had me holding my breath on approach, bracing for possible impact, and finally breathing a sigh of relief as each one passed.

Nevertheless, as tense and frustrating as this was, I was ecstatic to feel the relief in my foot and hips. I felt like a whole new man as my pace increased and the effort eased. I had also been getting used to the flat roads of Quebec. The Canadian Shield, a vast plateau of Precambrian rock that forms the ancient core of the North American continent, was soon approaching, so I had a good bit more flatness to look forward to.

Keeping an ear on traffic at my back, I spent the day talking to Lana Rae on the phone as she drove across Ontario to meet me. She continually brought up how endless this drive felt and how she couldn't believe I was actually *running* all the way across it.

Around sixty kilometres into the day, at a pit stop in a small town with Wayne and Myron, I noticed two cyclists towing an overloaded baby carriage. Like me, one of the young men was wearing a cowboy hat.

We introduced ourselves, and it turned out they were from Quebec City and cycling across Canada to Victoria, hoping to get in sixty-five kilometres a day. We talked as we progressed west, sharing stories about what we'd encountered. As far as I could understand, they were just two great guys looking to find themselves out there on the Trans-Canada Highway; in other words, a lot like me.

After a while, I resumed my regular pace, but before dropping them I wished them the very best.

During our conversation, my phone started going off as messages began pouring in. At the time, distracted by the deep conversation with two fellow transconners, I ignored the constant buzzing.

Meanwhile, teammates and friends who had helped organize the run had noticed that my GPS track was off the planned route that Olivier had mapped out.

It dawned on me that I had probably missed the turn for Highway 158.

I got out my phone and immediately pulled up Google Maps to locate a back road that returned me to the 158 without adding too many miles. To my good fortune, a turnoff was ahead in 800 meters.

That's when my phone rang. Wayne and Myron were beside themselves suggesting I stop. I told them I'd already located a suitable roadway to get me back on track. A couple minutes after the turn, the boys came barreling down the road behind me, and we confirmed on a voice call how I'd get back.

It's almost an enjoyable thing getting lost out here, though. Sometimes the little unanticipated journeys show you a part of Canada you'd never see; and sometimes, synchronicity strikes. God sometimes changes his plans on the fly and the result is meaningful coincidence. It just so happened that a farm dog came running out from his yard, and I took the time to pet him. Staying on course would have meant that I'd miss out on the exchange.

We ended our day after 105 kilometres, in a tiny village north of Montreal; and when I got into the SUV, Wayne expressed his frustration that Lana Rae couldn't find accommodation for the night any closer than a forty-five-minute drive away.

I told him that if there had been anything closer, she would have found it, and to stick to the plan, since looking for nonexistent alternatives would just eat up what little sleep time we had. The long commute was a sunk cost, and we just needed to accept it and be as organized as we could.

Arriving at the ratty hotel, we ordered chicken from the neighbourhood restaurant and quickly hit the hay, as 3:45 a.m. was going to come pretty damned quickly.

Worthy Of My Suffering

DAY 24	COMPLETED	REMAINING
105.1 kms in 12:17:04	2491.1 kms	4667.9 kms

After an abbreviated sleep, we all woke up considerably less fresh and less feisty than usual.

Following the long drive back east to the day's starting point, I was met at 5 a.m. by my friend Helene Dumais. Helene is an incredible ultramarathoner and local legend who was the first woman to finish the Infinitus 888-kilometre race, which has to be completed in just ten days. Now, twenty-four days into this grit-fest, I was happy to share some time with such a woman, and maybe even learn a few new ways to "HTFU," or harden the fuck up, as ultrarunners say.

Helene and I spent the morning sharing war stories and exchanging ideas on the world of endurance and how the notions of mental strength and confidence were woven into the fabric of the sport. One thing I've noticed over seventeen years of ultrarunning is that the most accomplished ultrarunners are deep thinkers and very stoic. Mindfulness and endurance are concepts that the very best of them seem to have mastered more than any other group of people.

It rained on and off the entire morning. As we ran, I contemplated the two monumental things that were going to happen at the completion of the day.

The first was that I would finish today's 105-kilometre run close to the Ontario border, closing out my fourth province of nine. The second, and most important, was that Lana Rae would be arriving today after driving 3500 kilometres from Okotoks, Alberta, to Hawksberry, Ontario. Since her flight home from Fredericton nine days ago, we hadn't seen each other, and to say I missed her out here would have been an understatement.

The emotion surrounding these landmark checkpoints is curiously dynamic and a bit hard to explain. In a very simple world where progression is everything, being reminded that my accumulated effort had actually gotten me somewhere, and that continued effort would likely do the same, made it all worth it.

I don't obsess over landmarks, quite the opposite, in fact. But the opportunity to celebrate them nonetheless makes enduring monumental undertakings much easier.

My right foot and ankle were particularly painful today as I shifted my weight onto my other leg. Strangely, I took this as a badge of honour. I'd expected that running seven-thousand-plus kilometres wouldn't be easy, and that it'd be impossible to escape it unscathed. In fact, one would have to expect numerous injuries and the need to suffer through quite a bit of agony.

The important thing is what you do with that agony.

That morning, running in the rain with my foot on fire, I thought of a passage from my favorite book, Viktor E. Frankl's *Man's Search for Meaning*. In it, he wrote that "There is only one thing I dread; not to be worthy of my sufferings."

Frankl, a Jewish-Austrian psychiatrist, founded the practice of logotherapy, a process that posits the meaning of life as the central human motivational force. He discusses at length the extreme measures Nazi concentration camp survivors were subjected to during World War Two, and how they found meaning in their suffering.

He also argues that when a man feels the extent of his suffering exceeds his personal worthiness to endure it, he will find himself unable to do so. Frankl's book mentions stories of inmates dying shortly after situational worth was called into question or hope was lost.

Not that I'm saying there's any comparison in the scale of suffering. But one *must* believe in getting through to the other side. Without that, there's nothing to do but give up.

I would have quit long ago if I hadn't felt worth what I had gone through and had yet to endure in seventy-two days of running.

Worth, I tell myself.

An overwhelming sense of self-worth must be at the forefront of all feeling. All the aches, the pains, despair, hurt, and suffering that each of us endures in our own private struggles are worth experiencing because we are worthwhile.

So as my right foot throbs with each of the 125,000 steps I take each day, I smile, knowing I'm enough.

Approaching the crew vehicle sixty kilometres into the day, I looked up to see a familiar and very beautiful face: Lana Rae! Breaking into a sprint, I caught her by surprise, hugging and kissing her from behind.

Wayne asked, "Why don't I get a welcome like that?"

I laughed, knowing that there was only one person who was going to get that kind of greeting.

It was wonderful feeling Lana Rae again in my arms. With very little comfort out here, my heart aches for moments like these, and I stood for a moment soaking it in.

She was finally here!

Meanwhile, Lana Rae, Myron, and Wayne busied themselves

moving all the contents of the rental SUV into Lana Rae's Pathfinder to use for the remainder of the trip.

The cost of the rental plus mileage had been bleeding us dry out here, especially with skyrocketing fuel prices. We planned that Wayne and Myron would drop off the rental at the airport the following afternoon when they flew home from Ottawa. But for now, I felt lucky to have a three-person crew.

The remainder of the day went smoothly. A local cyclist drove up from Montreal to ride with me for a while, and the rain continued on and off, causing me to have to juggle gear to fit whatever came out of the sky on any given moment.

At the end of the day, I crossed the Ottawa river into Hawkesbury, Ontario.

One more province checked off!

Wayne and Myron now planned to go out for dinner and beers, then get a separate hotel room in order to give Lana Rae and me some privacy.

When we got to the room, Lana Rae wanted to review maps with me as she worked on tomorrow's approach into Ottawa. After agreeing that she had indeed picked the best route, we ate dinner and spent the rest of the night in one another's arms.

It was magical holding my love in my arms, and I felt like the strongest, most loved man in the world. I fell asleep with a smile on my face and a renewed confidence.

Which was good, because the hardest, longest province stood before me, and that journey started tomorrow.

CHAPTER 6: EASTERN ONTARIO

Go My Own Way

DAY 25	COMPLETED	REMAINING
107.2 kms in 13:32:25	2598.3 kms	4560.7 kms

We awoke the next morning in the same intertwined position we had fallen asleep in.

On a typical run day, the greatest agony is found in the first steps out of bed on the way to the washroom, where each slight movement sends a thunderous jolt of pain into the deep recesses of my soul. Only spending each night next to my love made my body pains barely tolerable.

As I sat on the toilet catching up with communications, I noticed my buddy and crew member for the prairie provinces had sent me a message. He felt that the proposed route Lana Rae had built for me, which kept me off the Trans-Canada Highway into Ottawa, wasn't an ideal route. Instead, he suggested a route with fewer turns that used the wider shoulder of the Trans-Canada into Ottawa instead.

When I exited the bathroom, I told Lana Rae I'd decided on a different route.

Confusion shifted to anger ask I explained that Joel had suggested the alternative route. She launched into a list of all the reasons for sticking to the original route, telling me that she felt dismissed, hated doing this mapping in the first place, and would not be doing any of it from this point forward.

I tried to explain that the reason I felt compelled to follow Joel's route was that it had far fewer turns, and after running through Quebec the last week with endless lefts and rights and actually ending up lost at one point, I just wanted a mental reprieve from having to watch where I was going all the time.

We loaded the vehicle under a cloud of tension.

This would also be my last day running with the boys. It had been an absolute pleasure sharing this epic experience and seeing this special tract of Canada with my hombres. Their energy, expertise, and friendship will live on in my mind until my last breath. Wayne had said over and over that the Dave of 2018 and the Dave of now were distinctly different. His belief that I'd matured a lot in the last four years and his conviction that I'd get to Victoria in time were immensely reassuring.

I already missed the boys, but knowing my brother Danny Boy was flying in tomorrow to take their place had me excited.

About twenty kilometres in, I took a right turn onto the off-ramp for the Trans-Canada Highway. A giant sign alongside the off-ramp read:

PEDESTRIAN TRAFFIC PROHIBITED

Confused, I gave Lana Rae a shout. After telling her about the sign, she suggested turning around to find an alternate route. Possibly too relaxed and willing to roll with the punches, I told her that I wanted to keep going; let's see what happens.

Well, wouldn't you know it?

Five short kilometres later, a police officer with flashing lights pulled over in front of me. He popped out of his cruiser and immediately told me that running along any 400-series highway in Ontario was prohibited.

I tried to play dumb, saying I didn't notice the sign. I asked him if he could look past this and let me proceed. He said he couldn't and suggested he give me a ride to the next overpass so that I could run on a separate road.

"I definitely can't," I exclaimed, as I went on telling him about my Trans Canada speed record attempt. If I took a ride or proceeded forward using any means aside from running or walking, this entire run would be for naught. I told him that I started in St. John's only 25 days ago, and filled him in on my daily mileage.

He wasn't antagonistic, saying, "Holy shit, man! I totally get it and I'd love to help you out, but the laws are the laws, and I can't let you continue for one more step on this highway."

Looking to the north, I noticed a gravel road paralleling the highway only 400 meters away. As I pointed at the five-foot-tall wire fence next to the road, I asked him if I could crawl under the fence and get to that road

"Absolutely," he said, "but I need to wait here and see you exit this road."

I thanked him for his time and made my way to the fence line.

What I didn't see from the roadway was the mud and muck that surrounded the fence at the low point of the ditch. With my broken body, taking a deep sigh, I dropped to my hands and knees and began an army crawl. Arriving on the side, I looked up to wave at the kind officer.

He waved back and yelled, "Good luck on your journey."

Now running on a gravel road I didn't plan to be on, I checked Google Maps to locate a reasonable route. After that, with my tail between my legs, I called Lana Rae. "You were right," I said. "I just got punted from the highway and I'm now on a gravel side road running west."

"I told you so!" Lana Rae barked.

"Yes, you did," I said, "and I'm sorry, but right now isn't the time to mull on this. I'm messaging the group and calling Olivier to beg for help to construct a new map because I was planning on running 400-series highways all the way to North Bay."

The silence over the phone was deafening. When Lana Rae goes quiet, it's time to take cover.

"Honey," I said, "I've got to let you go so I can call Olivier."

"I'm so mad and frustrated right now," she replied. Then all I heard was a click.

I had officially kicked the hornet's nest, but I didn't have time to sort it out at the moment.

I messaged the team on my Facebook Messenger group and filled everyone in on what had just transpired, zeroing in on Olivier for support.

Fifteen minutes later, he responded. Another ten minutes later, he forwarded a proposed route that only tacked on an extra five kilometres over the next three days.

What a genius—and what a guy to drop what he was doing and build a map to help out someone he'd just met earlier that year.. As thanks, I promised to name my next-born child after him— but may have forgotten to mention my vasectomy!

Some time later, Wayne called, drawing on his former career as an attorney to validate that pedestrian travel along the 400-series highways in Ontario was in fact prohibited.

I spent the rest of the day on side gravel roads running parallel to the Trans Canada highway. On one road there was a sign that said:

ROAD CLOSED AHEAD

The alternative would have been to tack on an extra four kilometres looping onto the roads around it, something I wasn't really in the mood to undertake at the moment, as it was just more miles and it piled onto the fact that I had already made *one* questionable decision on the route that day.

Deciding to test my luck, I proceeded while the two crew vehicles looped the four kilometres around. In the worst-case scenario, I figured I'd need to leave the roadway and venture through the farm field where the closure was. Instead, I ran into a construction site where the road had been dug up to access water pipes below. The foreman granted me passage and the fellas cheered me on and wished me well.

I caught up with Wayne and Myron; but every time I'd reach the vehicle, Lana Rae would park a distance from the two of them. Trying to keep things light, I'd say "Love you, Lana Rae", but in return I'd receive no response, or "I love you back" accompanied by the look of a thousand daggers.

I thought it was a good idea to pave things over, so I swallowed my pride and gave her a call. I heard a hundred "I told you so"s, and with each one, I told her that she had been right. As her tone tempered, I mentioned that the frustration didn't accomplish anything out here, and that it'd be best if she could accept my apology and we could move on. I also reminded her that she had planned to fly out from Ottawa early in the morning and that these hours would be the last we'd spend together until I reached Alberta in thirty days.

This made sense to her, and we kissed and made up. We spent the rest of the day on the phone with one another with smiles on our faces, and I was grateful.

Plan the run. Run the plan, they say. But don't fall in love with your plan.

Before starting this run, I *knew* that things would repeatedly go pear-shaped fast. Attachment to written-in-stone plans on runs like this is a death wish. Keeping emotional distance from plan A assures a flawless transition to a plan B or C if necessary.

Prior to the start in St. Johns, I'd always seen maps as a working, living document that, in its purest form, was meant to change as the run progressed. To help me through this, I would repeat to myself that life is complicated, to not take myself too seriously, and to shrug off criticism and over-analysis.

Predicting that things like today's mess-up would inherently happen left me with a sense of assurance and calm, knowing that one way or another, the show would go on.

That was especially when I knew that the blunder could have easily been remedied by better planning instead of assuming I could run on the Trans-Canada after exiting Quebec.

Don't get me wrong: it was a hard lesson to learn. But letting go of attachment and certainty and going with the flow made the lesson easier to take.

Around seventy kilometres into the day, he and Myron met me on the side of the road for a tearful farewell. I could tell by the look in their eyes that they enjoyed their time out here, and that they also believed in me and felt confident that I would get to Victoria in time. They shared a few last nuggets of wisdom and drove off to the Ottawa airport. I am so very lucky to have such wonderful friends in my life.

The rest of my day was on narrow roads with rush hour traffic forcing me further into the ditch, angering my foot further; but to my relief, the last thirty minutes of the day entering southeast Ottawa traversed a park on a wide grassy trail.

The problem, however (there is *always* a problem) was that nearly a quarter of the trees were downed from a tornado that had raged through Ottawa just days ago. Climbing over fallen trees would have been fine if it weren't for the hordes of mosquitoes marking me as their target. If I looked back, I'd see a giant cloud of them, yet somehow when I stopped to leap over a tree, they'd be on me, leaving me swatting and flailing. Exiting the trail onto the road with only 3 kilometres remaining was actually a welcome feeling.

At the end of the day, I marked the spot where I left off and we made our way to a hotel near the Ottawa airport, where Dan, who had flown in just hours ago, planned to meet us.

Tonight, Lana Rae would walk my brother Dan through the motions of the crewing regimen that we have dialed in the past three and a half weeks. When Dan and I left the hotel the next morning, I wouldn't see Lana Rae again for another month, so we enjoyed one another while we still had time.

It was great seeing my oldest friend and brother again. Once we met up, Lana Rae walked him through everything as I went through my post-run routine of self-release and eating dinner in my compression pants.

Then as we got ready for bed, Lana Rae snuggled up next to me and we quietly cried ourselves to sleep.

Non-Striving

DAY 26	COMPLETED	REMAINING
104.8 kms in 13:10:59	2703.1 kms	4455.9 kms

I awoke to the sound of pouring rain.

The plan had been to run down Hunt Club Road to skirt the southern edge of Ottawa. But as if finding our way through the metropolitan center of a national capital weren't difficult enough, let's throw in the facts that it was Dan's first day on the job and it was raining cats and dogs. His anxiety about taking over crewing and not letting me down was palpable.

It was going to be a long day.

I waved and said my last heartfelt goodbye to Lana Rae as we backed out of the parking lot.

When we arrived at the street corner where I'd left off the day before, two local runners who wanted to run with me were standing out in the rain. I felt terrible that they were already soaked, and on my schedule. We quickly embarked westward down Hunt Club Road with the two eager and very talkative twenty-somethings. The wind howled and swirled, driving the rain at me from all angles.

I stopped briefly to orienteer, but the moisture on my phone's screen made it impossible to swipe and zoom. So instead, I called Dan the Man, who came up with a brilliant idea: we'd keep our phones going all the time so he could locate me with the Life360 app we'd been using. That way, he'd know my location and could verbally guide me. I *knew* he wasn't here just for his good looks! As we zigzagged through the streets of Ottawa, completely saturated, I thanked Dan for his problem-solving skills and ability to keep things in control.

Before long, we exited the city limits, with yet another major city behind us. We both sighed in relief. Dan knew we were throwing him right into the lion's den, but like his biblical counterpart, he managed to take the upper hand. Once I reached the Pathfinder, I grabbed new bottles, some food, and of course, a dry change of clothes.

Most provinces in Canada have kilometre markers alongside the Trans-Canada Highway indicating how many kilometres remain until the next provincial border. The very first of the vertical green markers I had seen crossing into Ontario the day before showed 2180 kilometres. My shoulders shrugged and my head sank.

You've got to remember that I'd already run *two thousand seven hundred* kilometres across *four* provinces, battled through

Covid-19, fractured my foot, and bruised every bone in my southern hemisphere. Now I'm looking at a sign that tells me that if all goes perfectly, it'll take me *another* twenty days to get across this remote and rugged province, only to be rewarded with four *more* provinces after this one.

I remember having a quiet, mental temper tantrum.

At moments like this, it's natural to catastrophize, getting ahead of yourself, starting to think "How on earth is this possible? Why even bother trying?" It's normal to look for exit doors or reasons to give up or pull back. Humans don't do well with big, scary, audacious things.

Instead, it's easier to turtle; and one extremely useful concept I'd been working on with Erin over the past year had been the mindfulness principle of *non-striving*. Non-striving is the ability to let go of the constant doing and concentrate solely on just being. Ultimately, accepting that the current moment is all we ever have puts things into perspective. The past has been, and the future is yet to come. Our effort must be focused only on what we can do *now*.

Many moments made up each day, and many days each month, and just two of those months made up this run. Out here, the weight of the unvarnished truth that the best way to get there is to be *here* is tangible.

Turtling was the only way I'd get across a place as big as Ontario, and getting across Ontario was necessary to get across Canada. I didn't need to run to Victoria. I didn't need to run to the next provincial border. I didn't need to run to the next town. Heck, I didn't even need to run to the next bend in the road.

All I had to do was take *this* step, *this* breath, and be in *this* moment, *this* experience, and *this* time, this time, not striving to do anything rather just *be*.

It's a drastic paradigm shift to focus just on the present moment.

No matter what's happening around me or to me, if I ask myself

"Am I okay?" the answer is almost always a resounding yes. Right here, right now, I am okay. I can control how I feel in this moment.

Doing so eliminates the bias that creeps in from thinking about what's ahead or behind. It leaves you non-judgmental about your own experience, and it centers you.

Despite all the road signs and markers that taunted me with what was yet to be achieved, I was just content being here right now.

And that was good. With a colossal province underway, being in a good headspace was everything.

Dan was also in a great mood all day, and we both felt that after averting potential disaster, we'd found a good groove. It also helped that he'd packed along boatloads of Mom's baking, which left me ecstatic, and I managed to eat twenty raisin cookies on our first day together.

Near the end of the day, Lana Rae called to tell me that she arrived home safely, and with my foot killing me, I limped up to the daily finish at the hotel entryway, 107 kilometres from the day's start.

I already missed her.

And now, hanging out in some dumpy motel in Renfrew, Ontario, Dan and I turned on the Blue Jays game and ate to our hearts' content.

A Hard Stretch

DAY 27	COMPLETED	REMAINING
105.4 kms in 12:48:37	2808.5 kms	4350.5 kms

Walking out the front door of the hotel to start my day's run was a simple pleasure I could easily get used to, and it helped immensely that Dan was there.

Crew selection for my journey across Canada had been very intentional, and he fell into a solid groove right away. Knowing that the most challenging portion would most likely be the long stretch across Northern Ontario from Ottawa to Thunder Bay, I had asked Dan first. Dan and I had grown up in High River, Alberta, a small town thirty minutes drive south of Calgary, and we had no other siblings, so we were close.

As kids, we had played fastball together and did quite well, especially given our limited resources. One of my earliest memories was my father Randy affixing a mattress to the wall of our undeveloped basement, with a pitching mound at the other end.

Playing in my room, I would often hear a loud *thwack* followed by twenty seconds of silence and then another thwack. Dan was fixated on wearing a hole through that mattress. Annoyed and bothered that he was earning all the attention, I'd make my way downstairs to throw a few.

My dad would sit on an old, ratty sofa with a beer in one hand and a smoke in the other while we threw balls at the mattress, and he'd direct his critiques to Dan, mentioning me only by reference to my brother. "Rotate your hips like Danny. Watch Danny as he pushes off. Grip the ball like your older brother," he'd say. I'd be downstairs maybe a third of the time that Dan was, and my dad put his attention where the effort was. My older brother was the hardest working person I've ever met, and whether it was sports or school, he clawed and persevered his way to the top.

It's safe to say that if Dan had the work ethic, I had the natural skill. Athletics always came easy to me, and this bothered Dan as we got a bit older and my pitching abilities advanced past his. We had won numerous provincial and western Canadian titles, I as a pitcher and Dan as a second baseman.

As I got older, I watched Dan's work ethic get him a long way, so I started aligning my behavior with his habits and strategies. This led me to further success in fastball, track and field, and eventually, ultramarathoning. Thirty years later, Dan and I still lived less than a kilometre apart in Okotoks, Alberta.

And we're still the best of friends. I'm very close to his wife Laura and their son, and he is very close to Lana Rae, Sharon, and my three kids. Dan has a heart of gold, and we'll probably have one another's backs until the day we die.

Sixty kilometres into the day, Danny Boy called me panicking. During the last pit stop, he said, he must have run over a screw, and now the passenger side front tire had a flat. Luckily, I was only minutes up the road, so I turned around and returned to the vehicle. Looking at the tire, it was obvious to me that the giant screw sticking out was the cause of the flat. We organized a plan to call a tow truck and try to resolve this problem as soon as possible. Meanwhile, I grabbed fifty kilometres worth of food and my credit card to stop at gas stations and was on my way, watching military helicopters doing drills to the south of the road.

As the miles rolled on without the usual pit stops, though, my foot and ankle began to hurt worse and worse. As before, it felt like something had shifted, and it ached really badly. Despite being unsafe, I ran the next several hours on the other side of the road with traffic zooming past from behind on a narrow shoulder.

Fifteen kilometres after I left Dan broken down on the side of the road, he emerged ahead of me on the shoulder with a patched tire and a big shit-eating grin. He told me about the young man in the tow truck, and how after telling him about what I was doing out here, he pulled all the stops to get the flat fixed as fast as possible. He didn't even charge us for the service!

Minutes later, a tow truck drove slowly past, and the driver yelled something muffled out the window.

I gave him an enthusiastic thumbs-up.

Later, I was updating my Facebook and Instagram feeds with a personal account of my daily activity. Most days I didn't have time to check the growing number of comments, but Lana Rae enjoyed reading them to me over the phone as I ran. I was surprised just how much I enjoyed hearing encouragement, learning that there were lots of people following my live tracker and cheering me on.

One Calgary runner had shared some rather extreme views about vaccination, and mentioned another follower named James Topp who it turned out was walking across Canada in the opposite direction to oppose mandatory vaccine mandates.

Everyone was entitled to their views on the matter, but I took offense at her leveraging my posts to propagate her own agenda. I didn't mind someone mentioning they felt that way, but she had taken to dumping links to other sites, trying to ignite a debate, and generally changing the subject to something other than running.

I didn't want any part of it.

Taking matters into my own hands, I texted her while I was running, letting her know that I didn't appreciate it and asking her nicely to halt.

Her response was refreshingly accepting and polite. I was very happy that we could come to an agreement and even happier that we didn't get into a political or ethical debate.

Feeling a bit proud of myself for not getting unproductively sidetracked and out of sorts, I returned to running with a newfound self-confidence about what I could accomplish.

That lasted until the last ten kilometres of the day, which I spent with a grimace on my face as I struggled to stomach the throbbing in my right foot. By now, the ache had spread up into my knee, causing my ankle and knee to buckle unexpectedly, which was very disconcerting.

I finished the day near Deep River, ON, knowing I'd be up a bit longer that night giving myself more soft tissue release work.

When Dan and I arrived at the hotel, Vera was to join us and share our suite. For the first time since Covid-19, she and I hunkered down with Dan for some lasagna and fish and chips, sharing a beer. As I rolled, stretched, scraped, and mobilized my aching body for hours, the three of us watched the Blue Jays defeat the Tigers ten to one.

Developing Tolerance

DAY 28	COMPLETED	REMAINING
105.3 kms in 12:33:19	2913.7 kms	4245.3 kms

I awoke with less of a limp and a smile on my face.

Sunrise marked four long weeks of running just shy of three thousand kilometres. These numbers were now starting to stack up, and sometimes it was hard to believe it was me.

If someone were to tell me a year ago that they had run three thousand kilometres in a month, I'd be hard-pressed to believe them. *Show me proof*, I'd say, and if they had, I'd highly question their ability to continue, yet alone stand on their own two feet at the end of the day.

And yet, here I was, not just surviving but thriving and oozing increasing optimism.

Not that it wasn't tough. But with less foot pain that morning, I found myself falling into a healthy rhythm early on. With the sun rising behind me, I gazed ahead at an elongated shadow of a handsome cowboy accompanying me as I headed west. Together we listened to calming classical music, plugging into a Zen state, noticing the beauty in everything that is everywhere, all at once.

Finding these moments and spending as much time there as possible are among the great joys in life. I'd keep thinking that I was a very lucky boy to be granted opportunities such as this, and I would feel endlessly grateful for the experiences. Basking in this flow-state made time pass effortlessly. In what felt like seconds, the morning flickered past my eyes and the day grew older.

I fell to reminiscing about my training leading up to the run, and how hard I had worked to ready my body and mind for the demands of such an effort. Runners often talk about their weekly running mileage as a baseline of their current fitness. A lot of friends and patients in my office would talk about their one-hundred-kilometre weeks leading into a marathon. Many ultramarathoners would train up to one hundred and sixty kilometres to ready themselves for a one-hundred-mile race. Typically, their weekly mileage would increase appropriately over months to get to race levels, peaking only two to three weeks before the big event. Structural tolerance, recovery, system building, and load tolerance were achieved in this build phase.

My build leading up to the run had me running two hundred and fifty kilometres a week. That was the most I've ever trained in my seventeen-year career, but none of it was even close to the actual distance I was planning to run. In 2018, I had been gobsmacked by how hard it was to get through the first week even after what I thought was adequate training.

So I knew better than to feel fully prepared going into *this* Trans-Canadian run. The truth of the matter was that there is no amount of training that could prepare anyone for the monumental stresses of running across a continent. The only possible way to get past the second week was to push through the first; and to complete the third week, to grind out the second.

Believe it or not, I found that my fitness actually built from one week to the next to the next. Our bodies, as I mentioned before, adapt to challenges more easily than our minds do.

Four weeks into this monster run, I was now feeling like a

machine. The fatigue I'd feel rounding out each day gradually became part of the routine as the days passed. I found the familiarity of it somehow comforting and confidence-building.

It's funny how things change. It felt *good* out here now.

It felt like home.

My run data shows that gradually, over the last 28 days, my average pace had sped to 6:15 min/km, my average day had shortened to twelve to twelve-and-a-half hours, and my average moving time to eleven hours and fifteen minutes, which would have been a respectable time for a stand-alone race.

I was happy with these stats.

Toward the end of the day, I spoke with Dan and Lana Rae about potentially increasing my daily distance. In advance of the run, I had decided that if all were going well, I wouldn't increase my mileage until at least halfway in. But feeling this good, I felt like we could do it sooner.

At first, Dan and Lana Rae pushed back, as I think they were worried it would be a five to ten-kilometre jump; but when I said I was thinking more of a one to two-kilometre increase, they were relieved and significantly more accommodating.

Still, they reminded me that the decision was made previously not to increase until 3,600 kilometres, and held firmly to the position that it was best to stick to that. Knowing that I was so immersed in how I felt about it that my emotions might overrule rationality, I gave in and went with the majority.

When my GPS watch showed 105 kilometres, I stopped, marked my place with the pinwheel and hopped into the SUV with Dan, and off to the hotel we went.

I settled in to take care of my body and eat dinner, suddenly realizing that it was just nuts that I was still blister-free!

After three thousand kilometres!

Since seemingly inevitable minefields of blisters are a recurring theme in other transcontinental crossings, I figured I must have been doing something right. I dropped everything and emailed the Altra Running crew and the people at Swiftwick Socks to let them know about this incredible milestone. Faithful supporters for years, I knew they'd be thrilled to hear how well their gear was working for me out here.

Eating Contest

DAY 29	COMPLETED	REMAINING
105.1 kms in 12:39:41	3018.9 kms	4140.1 kms

Knowing that these days of feeling good were limited, I milked as much from them as I could.

Riding high on the emotions from the day before, I ate an extra-large bowl of oatmeal while Dan loaded the last items into the truck. He's struggled with falling asleep and staying asleep all his life, and last night had been rough for him. Moving from hotel to hotel would be hard on most, but for Dan, it was proving most difficult.

After dropping me off, he drove ahead to a local bakery to load up on baked goods for our aid stops. These bakery stops quickly became the cornerstone of my happiness. There was just something about proper baking and the liberal use of butter, flour, and sugar that makes my heart sing.

Calling Lana Rae for our regular me-on-the-road-her-drinking-coffee-in-bed chat, we talked non-stop as the rain came down. I listened to her voice go from groggy to crisp as she woke up. After seeing what the run could do to our frayed psyches, we had begun making this daily coffee date a priority. It gave us structure and time to connect that we both needed and enjoyed.

A couple of hours later at a scheduled pit stop, Dan opened the trunk to unveil a huge box of mouth-watering cakes, squares, tarts, muffins, and scones.

You would have thought I had just won the grand showcase prize on "The Price Is Right" as I squealed and danced in celebration! These priceless delicacies, each looking perfectly scrumptious, made my soul complete. Dreaming about how each one of them would taste as I devoured them one by one, the only conflict in my mind was which one I would devour first.

Ultramarathoning legend Ann Trason once said that "ultra marathons are just an eating and drinking competition with a little bit of running thrown in." When you need to eat 9,000 calories per day, elimination diets and salads that aren't first put in a blender are just not an option. Many ultrarunners preach the importance of low carb or transitioning to more efficient fuels such as fats. But running across a continent isn't a one-day or one-week event. It's a multi-month endeavour.

Falling behind on calories and protein is the kiss of death. Training yourself to eat almost anything is the only way to go, and the preparation to do this starts years in advance.

Prior to every run for the past fifteen years, I'd eat difficult-to-digest foods and larger portions than were comfortable. Initially, this creates significant gut distress, causing faster gastric emptying and dicey races to the next gas station, porta-potty, or ditch. But just as running uphill makes you better at running uphill, eating and running makes you better at eating and running. So that's how you train: you fill your stomach, then you run, and you get better and better at it.

The other big part of the puzzle is the prevalence of taste fatigue. Ask any runner, and they will tell you that what you think you might want in advance of your run is almost never what you want in the moment.

Even your favorite foods or fail-safe, easy-to-digest staples for your race will at some point induce the desire to vomit. And some super-long-distance runners, myself included, ironically find that when we most need food, we've lost our appetite.

The gut is a funny place. It sends you strong messages: NO, YES, DON'T YOU DARE, or *GIVE ME THAT!* An ability to eat a wide range of foods gives you more choices before your gut says "no."

Baked goods were my primary source of fuel. Since I was eating every twenty minutes and aiming for 450 calories per hour, I had to make the most of every fuel stop. I'd stuff fruit and Coke down my throat, eating as much as I could since it was difficult to run while eating or drinking.

The other challenge was getting in enough daily protein to support my muscle system. In my day-to-day life, I aim for 150 grams of protein, whereas on the road I strived for 240.

As a practical matter, my options for protein were shakes, extra meat sandwiches, and nut butters spread on anything. In the morning before the run and during the evening after the run, I always ate protein. But since anything over 15 grams per feeding stressed my digestion, timing and calculation were critical.

An all-you-can-eat buffet sounds fun at first; but the truth is that force-feeding yourself to the point of feeling a bit sick multiple times a day gets old quickly.

Therefore, food that went down easy in mass quantities was always in demand.

Digesting carbs and fats while running was a lot easier than digesting protein, and I ran from one bakery item to the next as the day wore on.

Then there were the flies and mosquitoes. I had been warned in advance about their prevalence in Northern Ontario; and in the last twenty-four hours, they seemed to have doubled in size and population. As annoyed as I was, Dan was even more annoyed. I noticed that he'd stay in the vehicle until the last second before opening the door and popping the hatch.

When standing still, we were an easy target, and the mosquitoes took full advantage. This quickened our pit stops from minutes to seconds, making us ultra-efficient.

Dan later told me that the next hour would be spent swatting bugs. Through practice, he also expertly discovered the perfect combination of open windows and slightly open sunroof to vacuum the little buggers out of the car while driving at high speeds.

I thought this was hilarious, and we both had a great laugh about it.

As the day wound to a close near Sturgeon Falls, mowing my way through half of the treats Dan had bought, I felt fat and happy. We called our parents to let them know all was good and that we had survived another day out here.

Another successful day!

At the hotel, I went through my regular evening routine with the same urgent efficiency we'd used escaping the flies. I wanted to get everything done and close my eyes before 8 p.m.

Nothing ever goes well for this long, I thought as I got ready for bed. *But as long as I'm on a roll, I'm going to do everything in my power to keep it rolling.*

Efficiently Consistent

DAY 30	COMPLETED	REMAINING
105.3 kms in 12:36:23	3124.2 kms	4034.8 kms

It's Groundhog Day again! I rolled over and looked at the alarm. 4 a.m., it read, almost mockingly, just like yesterday.

Sitting up, I stretched my arms above my head and slowly

moved my broken body to the bathroom. I brushed my teeth, got dressed, lubed up all the parts that chafed and rubbed, and made my way to the desk where I always ate my oatmeal, checked the weather, and Theragunned my legs.

There's nothing sexy about this routine, but it's what I do every day, because it works. I habitually turn my brain off while Dan runs around like a chicken with its head cut off, talking to himself about what he forgot to do

I didn't say anything because I was certain I smelled ten times worse, but he's starting to smell—Mom's extra baked treats displaced some of the clean clothes he originally had in his luggage.

In fact, it's very possible that our combined bad smells have worsened the bug situation.

Day 30 officially started with the usual press of buttons on my GPS watch and Garmin In Reach at 5 o'clock in the morning.

I was on pace to finish the run in Victoria on Day 66, breaking Al's record by a full six days. I found myself getting so excited at the thought of success that I had to consciously force myself to stay in the present moment. Getting ahead of myself and getting lazy have gotten me into a lot of trouble in racing in the past. Laziness, especially, can lead you to take your eye off the ball. That's when things get catastrophic.

Perhaps because of that, though, my morning pace was a bit spicier than usual. I found a good stride early. In the afternoon I'd be running through Sudbury, where we knew there would be some construction. Dan and I had researched the latest on that the night before while eating dinner.

Typically, the first fifty kilometres including two pit stops, take me five hours and twenty minutes, give or take five minutes. As I came upon the 50 km pit stop, the clock read 10:13 a.m., exactly as predicted. Lana Rae repeatedly labeled me the human metronome, and I couldn't disagree with her.

Ralph Waldo Emerson is famous for saying that "a foolish consistency is the hobgoblin of little minds." But my consistency was anything but foolish; efficiency and staying within myself were the name of the game.

To do that, I ran everyday, all day in Zone 1. Zone 1 is a physiological state where the exercise intensity approaches the aerobic threshold, but the intensity is so low that all lactic acid accumulated or produced in the muscles is utilized. Put more simply, it's the "go all day" zone.

In Zone 2, the exercise intensity creeps just above the aerobic threshold, so there's a slight buildup of lactic acid. Running in this zone is like setting the trigger on a time bomb. I could run for twenty-four hours in Zone 2, but certainly not for two months.

The very slight differences in how the body behaves in these two zones, including such things as breathing, muscle strain, mental fog, and ability to talk often go unnoticed until they've gotten out of hand. But the best measure of whether you're overdoing it remains heart rate.

My heart rate when I jump from Zone 1 to Zone 2 is 134 beats per minute. So as long as I stay sub-134, I should theoretically be able to go forever; so staying Zone 1 makes a lot of sense when you're banging out over 100 kilometres/day. Another benefit of staying in Zone 1 is that you use less energy in a given unit of time. That means burning less calories, utilizing more fat than carbohydrate, producing less cortisol, and causing less muscle damage.

Dropping the ego and the jazzy feeling of blowing and going is hard.

Being patient is hard.

Working on efficiency is easier.

The key to efficiency is to effectively control all or most of the variables. That means an efficient morning routine, no wasted time on lengthy pit stops, no stopping for media, and always moving forward.

And it didn't stop when I paused my GPS watch or InReach for the day. Staying on task in the evenings was key as well. Meals would be ordered and delivered within minutes of getting to the hotel. We'd park as close as possible to the ground floor hotel room. Hotels were lined up and booked weeks in advance by Lana Rae. If someone wanted to talk to me, they'd have to call me while I was running.

All these things added up allowed me to squeeze in as much running as possible within a twenty-four period, given that I still needed eight hours of sleep. Lack of discipline or failure to be efficient would directly limit my production of miles and jeopardize the entire project. After all, it *was* a speed record I was trying to break and there are only twenty-four hours in a day.

The focus on efficiency boiled over onto crew operations as well, and all of us involved discussed it thoroughly prior to the start. Lana Rae, Wayne, Myron, Dan, Shep, Joel, and Mike all agreed to run a tight ship and signed on the proverbial dotted line.

As I was out running, their wheels always turned in the background, making things happen on time, and it wasn't easy. In fact, one of the reasons that each crew member was limited to a two-week stint was the substantial workload each of them assumed. I was the only one who could ignore where we were staying, what we were having for dinner, where the grocery store was, how much gas was in the tank, or whether we were low on supplies. Like Christmas morning, poof, stuff would just magically appear.

At the time I was running across Canada, fellow crosser and super-speedy ultrarunner Michael Wardian was running across the U.S. for a cause, averaging 84 kilometres a day. Looking at his numbers, he was out on the road running for roughly the same time I was, yet I was able to travel a half marathon further each day. It wasn't a race, and his pace was effectively the same as mine. However, not being as pressed for time as I was, he spent more time at the crew vehicles, chatted with people, and devoted time to fundraising efforts.

That's the difference efficiency makes. Michael and I were roughly comparable runners, but owing to the different nature of his run, he and his team could afford to loosen the reins on efficiency.

In some ways, breaking a record was about everything *but* the running.

But back to Sudbury.

Pretty much as expected, Sudbury was full of construction and narrow, half-chewed-up shoulders. The winds swirled as we called it quits just west of Sudbury in a town called Lively.

When Dan came back with dinner, he was carrying only one dish of chicken parm, saying that he wanted to save me money by not ordering himself an entrée. We had plenty of bakery items in the car getting stale, so his plan was to eat those.

Something you need to know about Dan is that he hates wasting food. I had even seen him earlier that day eating around the moldy bits of a loaf of banana bread. Like the two rats in the movie *Ratatouille*, one of us was picky and discerning, the other would eat anything if the price was right and it was still (mostly) edible.

But I couldn't watch Dan eat around mold while I scarfed down delicious hot comfort food, especially not after he had dropped everything to help me. We got into the kind of big debate that only family can have, and after a few raised voices hugged it out and came to an agreement: I'd accept him and his thrifty ways, but only under the condition that he let me buy him dinners.

Protest

DAY 31	COMPLETED	REMAINING
105.1 kms in 12:26:33	3229.4 kms	3929.6 kms

After thirty days of running two and a half marathons every single day, I was shocked that I still didn't have a single blister on my feet. Based on stories I've heard about other transcontinental crossings, I had fully expected that by this point my feet would be covered in painful blisters.

I'm really not sure what to credit for my good luck. Some of it has been a trial and error process of finding the best gear. I've tried a lot of different shoes over the years, and landed on Altras for the extra-wide footbed. Every ultrarunner knows that blisters have ruined many a good race, which is how I ended up with a drawerful of Swiftwicks that have done a champion job of reducing friction and keeping my feet intact.

I also think simple body mechanics probably deserve some of the credit. I've run so many miles that I've been able to hone an efficient and compact stride. I've also been told that I have limited moving parts and that my stride frequency is very high.

Either way, I was ecstatic to have one less thing to worry about.

But things you don't have to worry about have a way of being replaced by things you do have to worry about. As we got rolling, I noticed that the flies and mosquitoes seemed to have doubled in size and population overnight. I fully expected to see warning signs for bugs the size of birds as we advanced into northern Ontario.

Vera had excitedly reported the previous night that today I'd cross paths with James Topp, a military warrant officer relieved of his duties after refusing the Covid-19 vaccine. A man on a mission, he had donned his uniform, gathered like-minded individuals, and was now walking east up to 50 kilometres/day to Ontario and Parliament.

Along the way, his campaign had picked up steam, aligning with hundreds of familiar faces from the anti-vaccine Freedom Convoy and picking up loads of media attention.

All summer, vaccine protests had been everywhere, and it was all that Canadians were talking about. Even I, buried in preparations for this run, had heard rumblings of this moving protest headed my way.

I understood why Vera couldn't wait to capture our encounter on film.

But I dreaded it.

While I'm pro-vaccine, I respect the right for others to have their own views. But I felt uneasy as our own quiet campaign of two approached his loud campaign of hundreds.

I just wanted to make it to Victoria as fast as I could. Anything else would distract me and get me off my game.

Nearing the forty-kilometre stop, I looked ahead to see Dan's vehicle parked beside four large motorhomes covered in banners and Canadian flags.

Oh Lord, I thought, *they're already here!*

Planning to make the stop as short as possible, I perched on the back bumper while I cracked open a can of iced tea and started stuffing watermelon into my mouth.

Within seconds, a couple of foot soldiers in James' war walked up with big smiles, extended their hands for a shake.

As I introduced myself and offered a fist bump, the taller of the two laughed and still with an outstretched hand, told me that there was no need to fear that so-called virus.

I paused, then smiled and thoroughly shook his hand, sharing with him that my preference for fist-bumps was more for his health than mine, as running alongside the highway with no bathrooms ain't pretty and I had just taken a huge dump about a mile back.

I've never seen a person so confused and repulsed at the same time.

He swiftly pulled away from our dirty embrace, and I crushed the rest of my tea and hauled my ass back out on the road.

Knowing from Vera that James was very aware of my run and the opportunity for publicity, I braced myself for what I thought would be my inevitable meeting with him.

We soon entered a construction zone with traffic backed up for about a mile. Running against traffic, I spotted giant flags and a commotion on the other side of the road. Chuckling to myself, with no means or desire to dodge traffic to get to the other shoulder, I watched them pass east as I picked my way west through the construction zone.

That was the closest I came to the notorious James Topp and the closest I'd ever come to participating in an anti-vaccine rally. We heard sirens not long after they passed, finding out later about a collision between two motorist onlookers.

As with the friendly farm dog I encountered earlier after getting lost, God had provided me with just what I needed, when I needed it. I decided to never again curse running into a construction zone.

Partly because of the anticipated commotion, my running economy had been on point for the day and the kilometres had clicked by with little effort. In fact, my heart rate had dropped from 132 to 123, despite the faster pace. If there was one indication my system was adapting, this was it.

Despite the terrible bug situation, Dan made time to clean up trash in the ditches near where he parked, and used two large rocks as dumbbells to get in some strength training while he waited for my arrival.

Yet just hours later, that lighthearted mood had inexplicably vanished, and he seemed in a horrible mood.

I asked what was wrong, and he quickly snapped back, "Nothing!"

Later that evening, he finally confessed that he had stashed his wedding ring on the RV's back bumper before his impromptu weightlifting session, driving off without first retrieving the ring.

Minutes later he realized in a sinking moment of horror what he had done, and spent the next several hours juggling crewing with returns to the pit stop to search for his precious ring, but to no avail. The ring was lost.

Given Dan's truly horrible day, I tried my best to hide my excitement about the day's great running stats, and we drowned our sorrow about his loss in burgers, deep-fried mushrooms and the Blue Jays game.

Pick Your Battles

DAY 32	COMPLETED	REMAINING
105.8 kms in 12:29:37	3335.2 kms	3823.8 kms

The next morning, while eating my breakfast and Theragunning my crusty, tight muscles and the scar tissue in my right foot, I watched Dan grunt and groan about the hotel room. When he snapped that he hadn't slept well, I chalked it up to the loss of his ring and decided to give him room and double down on appreciation for everything he was doing.

As I hit the road for the day's 100+ kilometres, the only thing worse than the pain in my foot were the swarms of starving mosquitoes and flies circling my head. The only satisfaction I found was watching the black cloud of voracious bugs zoom right past me when I'd stop without warning to stretch out my calf.

Later that day, I mentioned to Dan that the water bottles he was prepping for me seemed lighter on electrolyte powder than usual. This might sound trivial, but balancing your current sweat rate with a precisely measured intake of sodium, potassium, and magnesium is crucial for ultrarunners. He rolled his eyes with exasperation, saying he'd pay more attention.

I wasn't convinced we were entirely on the same page, and that anxiety solidified at the following pit stop, when he handed me a ham sandwich with only two slices of meat. I grabbed another eight slices from the cooler and stuffed them inside the mixture of hummus, avocado, and ham, knowing that I had to keep forcing thousands of calories down just to offset the energy I was burning with each day's run.

Telling Dan I'd need ten slices of meat at the next feeding, he gave me a skeptical look and said "Really, Dave?!" I explained the need to manage calorie and protein depletion at length, but his face told me that he wasn't convinced.

As I resumed running west, I called Lana Rae for a fresh perspective since my frustrations and explanations clearly weren't meeting the need.

While acknowledging that the food requests were non-negotiable, she also reminded me that despite our lengthy history, Dan and I were two distinctly different people. No one can get under your skin like family and the usual social filters are often absent. And family can be the last to see that their youngest snot-nosed kid is now an elite athlete determined to control his environment and performance

Lana Rae also pointed out that Dan was the only crew member who wasn't a competitive ultrarunner, and thus most likely didn't identify with any of what a run like this entails. While

Myron and Wayne probably didn't enjoy my *prima donna* tendencies either, they were ultrarunning friends who knew very well what success required.

I ended our call resolving to lead with gratitude and patience, and started by showering praise on Dan at the next pit stop for picking up a huge amount of trash from the ditch as he waited.

Maybe I overdid it, but it was sincere appreciation, deserved and necessary.

As he handed me a cinnamon bun stuffed in a reused plastic bag smeared with hummus and avocado, I reminded myself:

Pick your battles, David Randall Proctor, pick your battles.

Dan retreated into the distance and I devoured that cinnamon roll with nothing but patience and love for him.

Around sixty kilometres, I found myself in the middle of a real-life Frogger video game, surrounded by dead frogs and turtles. These little guys had sought refuge in the pond across the road, full of hopes and dreams about tastier flies or attractive potential mates with shiny shells. They risked it all for a better life, and the pungent smell reminded me of all those who didn't make it.

And yet, one persisted.

Just ahead of me slowly walked a brave soul the size of a pie plate. As he took his first step over the thin white line, I felt an overwhelming urge to help this critter out by giving him a lift across the highway.

As I approached, he retracted his head and hoisted his rear end, looking quite scared. As I bent to grab the sides of his shell, he launched himself with his front legs and thrust his head toward me a full eight inches, snapping at my fingers and only narrowly missing.

I jumped back screaming like a schoolgirl. His head now tilted quizzically toward me, I cussed him out.

"That's not how you treat someone who wants to help you!

You're gonna have to figure out how to get to the other side yourself, big guy!"

I may have thrown a few less family-friendly comments in there as well.

As the adrenaline surging through my body slowly subsided, I continued running west, laughing at myself.

Live and learn. Or *don't* learn and don't live. I felt sorry for the little guy, but not *that* sorry. Jeez.

Thus far on this adventure, I had encountered bears, wolves, moose, beavers, and coyotes: but this was my very first animal attack.

I feel like we've been conditioned to fear large carnivores, but I learnt something very important that day: the real danger is snapping turtles.

The day had been hard. My foot normally starts feeling better in about half an hour, but today a lengthy five hours had passed before it improved, testing my patience and all forms of mindfulness.

Constantly aware that I wasn't even halfway to Victoria yet, a sort of survivalist mindset had swirled in my head off and on, with complex questions about the legitimacy of continuing when so many signs point towards possible catastrophe.

Yet I also know that second-guessing past decisions and doubting outcomes before they even happen has gotten me into a lot of trouble in the past, so at times like these, my advice to myself is simple: *never make decisions running uphill.*

I finished Day 32 with just over 105 kilometres under my feet again. There hadn't been a day yet that I had missed my mileage target, and that felt good. What felt better was knowing that I was only burning through two-thirds of my energy reserves every day to achieve this. As much as the foot pain had been crippling, my confidence ultimately remained high.

That night, I could see Dan was still frustrated and out of his element. Rather than risk worsening it, I quietly worked through my evening routine and tucked in for the night.

CHAPTER 7: WESTERN ONTARIO

Superior

DAY 33	COMPLETED	REMAINING
106.2 kms in 12:42:42	3441.4 kms	3717.6 kms

We awoke to heavy rainfall in the morning of June 16, marking Day 33. It had rained all night long, at times waking us due to the loud tin roof. The anticipation of being wet and cold all day brought back flashbacks of long, hard days in the Maritimes.

It had been another tough night for Dan. He's had sleep issues his entire life, and we had known that the break from his usual routine and the constant move from hotel to hotel would be a problem.

Eating my usual oatmeal, I curled into my seat, not looking forward to the day. It rained cats and dogs as we drove to the start—but as we parked, the downpour miraculously stopped and the sun came out.

We both laughed at our auspicious good luck, a happy moment that was a welcome change from the recent tension between us.

I spent the first half of the morning chatting with my lovely lady as I ran and the other half listening to classical music and meditating, trying my best to mentally manage my foot pain.

There's a saying, "Stomp your toe to cure a headache," and at some point that morning I suddenly realized that the 10-year old vertebral injury which has hurt every single run since, hadn't hurt in weeks. In fact, I couldn't remember the last time I noticed it.

Perhaps 3500 kilometres of road camber had realigned my mid-back somehow; or perhaps the monstrous volume of miles had somehow fixed the problem.

Whatever it was, I was just so damn happy to be pain-free, at least in my back.

As the great Forrest Gump says: "Well, one less thing."

Forty kilometres into the day alongside the shoulder of the highway, Adam Khatava and his family met me with fresh bakery donuts that were so good they brought a tear to my eye. Adam's an old running buddy, and we hadn't seen one another for over six years, since he moved to Sault Ste. Marie for work and to raise his family where he had been raised. He's a speedy ultrarunner and good-hearted family man, and I was happy to see he still had the best head of hair going.

We talked nonstop, catching up as we approached the Sault.

I ran a plan past Adam that involved roadways on the east side of the Sault to avoid the major city. He agreed it was a good plan, but pointed out that the roadways were not passable via car and were more like offroad trails. Yet the thought that there might be some variety in the day got me excited as we veered onto the alternative roads skirting the city.

I quickly realized Adam was right. This route was more of a

grassed-over trail with lots of hills and expansive pools of muddy water. It rained lightly as we ran joyfully across this welcome break from the tedious, mind-numbing paved highway miles. Now past the city limits, he gave me a big hug, wishing me good luck for the journey ahead, and peeled off to run back home.

I was once again alone on the backroads until they merged again onto the familiar Trans-Canada Highway—this time, the legal part of it.

It would be my home for the next seven hundred of the most remote kilometres.

The sun's position in the sky shifted as I headed north, which would be my heading for the next three days as I skirted the third largest lake in the world, Lake Superior. Spanning over eighty-two thousand square kilometres, it was the largest of the Great Lakes dividing Canada and the United States, and together with the rest of the Great Lakes, accounted for eighteen percent of the world's fresh lake water.

At the seventy-kilometre pit stop, Dan mentioned that he was going to drive ahead and put a load of laundry in at the Inn to maximise use of time. When we got back to the inn at the end of the day's run, he'd transfer it to the dryer. I told him I didn't think that was such a great idea given that we'd be leaving it unattended for four hours, during which time someone could steal our clothes. I told him that those clothes had been integral to reducing chafing, that they had been perfect so far, and that not only would I hate to lose them, but it would be somewhat catastrophic for them to go missing.

Noticeably perturbed, Dan agreed to wait until the day was done to start the laundry.

Merging back onto the Trans-Canada Highway ninety-five kilometres into the day, I laid eyes for the first time on the ocean-sized body of water that would be my companion for the next full week. The solid wall of wind, thunderous crashing waves and the smell of marine life left a lasting, unsettling impression of the sheer power of such a massive, living thing. The fickle, drastic weather of the Great Lakes deservedly occupies a place in legends and folklore, and the stories are almost always cautionary tales to sailors and people of the north brave or foolish enough to walk their shores.

As I finished the day's running, I spoke openly with the Lake, asking for passage and promising in return reverence. It may seem odd, but as time passed on my journey, I feel more and more in touch with the world around me, and a sense of oneness, blurring the lines between where I ended and everything else began.

If that sounds trippy, let me tell you: running *is* my drug and this high is worth every penny.

Stopping my watch and InReach, we packed into the SUV and drove back south for twenty minutes to the Inn, where ribs and mashed potatoes were waiting for us.

Today we had reached one of the biggest milestones: the halfway point, and still on pace for a record, I was feeling good enough, getting fitter by the day, had established a healthy routine, already grown a grizzly beard, and had dropped only ten pounds or so (losing thirty is common among transcontinental runners). I was over the moon about how things are going.

To celebrate, Dan and I shared a beer; and despite his mood, Dan made every attempt to celebrate with me this important landmark in this journey.

Brothers' Quarrel

DAY 34	COMPLETED	REMAINING
106.2 kms in 12:54:17	3547.6 kms	3611.4 kms

I could tell Day 34 was going to be...interesting...as soon as I woke up.

For Dan, staying up late finishing laundry, being frustrated that his younger brother had made him do it, and not sleeping well combined to create a tornado of discombobulation. Dan paced the room packing and getting organized, constantly talking to himself, quite a bit of it decidedly negative. I knew best to stay quiet and let him sort it out. The last thing he needed was my suggestions; and during the twenty-minute drive north to the day's start point, I could tell he was trying to keep his cool while the disdain in his eyes told a very different story.

As I exited the vehicle, barely able to open the door, an impossibly strong headwind swirled off the lake and pushed back, almost as if in refusal. I tightened the fastener on my hat, pressed start on my devices, and got running north. As I left, I said a prayer for Dan that he could find some peace, since I could tell he was not having fun at this point. I tossed in an extra prayer to the Lake gods to dim the switch on the wind a bit, but as the day went on these prayers went unanswered. With zero cell reception I had a lot of time to ruminate.

How could I make Dan's experience better? What's the meaning of life? And if a bald man is washing his face, where does he stop washing?

Adam had warned me of the hills that were coming my way, and he was not lying. The hills bordering the lake along the Canadian Shield were no joke. The frequency and grade of the climbs were the hardest so far in Canada. I think that with the limited population in the north, the government, when building these roads, had somehow neglected to blast the apexes off these hills, leaving an eight percent grade instead of the six percent found in other provinces. Now 3600 kilometres into the run, the difference was noticeable. That plus the gale-force headwind sucked the joy right out of the day. The one silver lining was that the mosquitoes that had pestered us for the last several days had probably been blown all the way south to Mexico.

By the time noon approached, the temperature had fluctuated wildly at least four times, and I had changed in and out of jackets so many times I felt like I was at the Golden Globes.

Earlier in the day I had seen a sign that said NO SERVICES NEXT 160 km.

I decided not to tell Dan about it. He was already under a lot of stress, and the thing was what it was.

Seven hours into the day, after finally getting cell reception, I was able to call Lana Rae back home. What little time she hadn't spent working had been entirely devoted to studying maps to better plan our logistics. This is one of the many reasons I love her and feel like we make a perfect team. Her meticulous, no-stone-unturned approach, when combined with my laid-back, go-with-the-flow attitude minimizes catastrophes but leaves us wiggle room to quickly adapt to what we encounter and improvise a stellar back-up plan.

Lana Rae was quick to tell me that I had entered an area of Canada with significantly limited support in the way of stores, gas, restaurants, and hotels.

I told her I had noticed the sign earlier in the day but didn't want to mention it to Dan given his depressed mood. After careful deliberation we agreed that she was going to call Dan to share what she has learnt and to develop a plan for meals and groceries.

A half an hour later I got a phone call back from Lana Rae. She was both frustrated and worried that Dan had not planned ahead, and that there was no plan at all to acquire dinner for tonight. She said that Dan was short on the phone and showed a great deal of frustration about the situation in general and missing that detail in particular.

I told Lana Rae I'd talk to Dan at the next pit stop about what to do next.

Lana Rae reminded me that options were nonexistent and that I'd probably go without dinner tonight.

Minutes after the call ended, I ran into Dan alongside the desolate highway and jumped feet first into the discussion about dinner. Dan was adamant that we would have to go without dinner and instead just eat the running fuel that we already had in the truck. He looked half mad at himself that he had dropped the ball, and half frustrated that he already knew what my response would be.

I told him that already a month into a run with zero comforts, I looked forward to having a warm meal at the end of the day. I looked into his eyes with desperation, asking him if he could find a way to get a warm meal.

With a look of resistance on his face, he said "No." Vera caught the moment on film, and I could see a look of sadness on her face behind the camera.

I ran north away from the pit stop, trying not to be upset and trying to erase the memory of how good those ribs had tasted the night before.

I understood my brother's frustration, and I understand the complexities of logistics, but I also felt that Dan hadn't heard me when I voiced my concerns about eating protein bars and baked goods for dinner. The concept of rewarding yourself is a slippery slope, and I've been cautious in doing so; but the fact of the matter was that in a world of discomfort, bookending the day with a hot comforting meal made tough times tolerable.

For the remainder of the day, Dan and I were quiet at the pit stops. Neither one of us wanted conflict, but neither of us had felt heard.

 In the final hour, Lana Rae delivered some news that gave pep to my step: Vera had stopped filming and driven out of her way to buy spaghetti and tomato sauce from a camping store so Dan and I could have a hot dinner. When Dan picked me up at the end of the day upon a long steep climb, we were both in a better place, laughing about the situation and hugging it out.

We stayed in a tiny, leaning, rustic cabin bordering the lake in a run-down campground. To say that these accommodations were dismal would be an understatement. Nothing was clean, nothing worked, and we feared a stiff wind would topple the cabin over in the middle of the night. We decided not to complain to the owner after he told Dan at length about how he was dying of terminal cancer. A dirty shower and skittering bugs just seemed to matter less after that.

Vera arrived a little later. The three of us hugged each other, and Dan and Vera got started on boiling water for the spaghetti.

As I drifted off, I closed my eyes with a full tummy and a full heart.

Thank you, Vera. You know how to keep body and soul together.

Tension

DAY 35	COMPLETED	REMAINING
106.5 kms in 12:44:25	3654.1 kms	3504.9 kms

The rain continued throughout the night and the better part of the next day, and the hills and wind off Lake Superior were downright mean.

My foot hurt like hell and my pace was dismal. To make matters worse, I found myself needing to stop and pee every fifteen minutes. I had noticed that my electrolyte drinks tasted off, like they had been mixed with less powder than usual in the last couple days, so I brought that possibility up to Dan.

Nope. Same amount of powder. That wasn't the problem.

So what was going on?

At the next stop, I asked Dan where he had gotten the water.

He said it had been from the bathtub faucets in the hotel rooms.

That clicked for me: I had probably picked up a parasite from the well water. I asked Dan how soon we'd be able to buy a supply of bottled water, and at that point he launched into a long rant about the cost and environmental impact of bottled water and told me I should be fine drinking this water. He was digging his heels in again and I wasn't sure why.

As delicately as I could, I reminded him that I was in the middle of the longest, fastest run in the history of Canada and that I was deeply in tune with what my body needed.

"There are things that are up for debate," I said, "but this isn't one of them."

I eyeballed the number of canned Cokes and tea we still had, telling him I'd drink those until we could remedy the water situation.

I've always felt like I was the black sheep in my family. Growing up, I never felt satisfied. To this day, I hardly feel satisfied. I've always admired people like my brother, mom, and dad for being as content and happy with the normal, mundane aspects of life.

If the key to happiness was wanting less instead of desiring more, then I had been going about it wrong for the past forty-one years. I *love* exploring risk, doing the hard things, and pushing boundaries to find out whether I reach the bottom of the well before the end of my rope. There's a saying that *doing hard things makes for an easy life; doing easy things makes for a hard life.* It was a mantra of mine long before I heard the quote.

My family has always scratched their heads and politely questioned my motivation, drive, and struggle to stand still. To them, I must appear to be a tormented soul. We *all* struggle to understand why others do what they do and feel what they feel.

Nevertheless, I generally felt that they had accepted me and my ways even when it made them uncomfortable. After decades of watching me run ultras, my family, once in opposition, now just shrugs their shoulders and says, "Dave will be Dave." But even with the most accepting family, during extreme moments it's common to question the actions of loved ones. This was one of those times.

I wish I were satisfied with non-expansionary things. I wish I could be still and happy. And I'm working on that, believe me! In fact, I just installed a hammock in the backyard this summer.

But perhaps this was why Dan was so upset. Maybe witnessing me out here pushing my limits made Dan very uncomfortable, and that made him shrink, seeking safety.

I had to remind myself that he loves me, and who on God's green earth could be upset about that!

I stopped my electronics and got into the vehicle, and neither of us said much during the awkward drive to the hotel. While stretching and eating dinner I put a movie on the TV to make it a little less uncomfortable.

Amends

DAY 36	COMPLETED	REMAINING
106.2 kms in 12:27:16	3760.3 kms	3398.7 kms

We awoke the next morning at 5 a.m. with the same uneasy tension lingering in the air. During the long drive to the start point, I broke the silence by addressing the uncomfortable atmosphere between us.

Dan nodded in agreement, and I brought up "decoupling," a concept that had helped Lana Rae and me earlier in the run. Back then, it had helped us reframe our situation by seeing me more as an elite athlete and less as a whiny, controlling boyfriend.

I shared with him that changing the lens you're using to view a situation can make a big difference, and I thought it might help us.

Then I laid out a scenario for Dan.

He's a big baseball fan, so I asked him if he'd want to help if the star right fielder and designated hitter Vladimir Guerrero Jr. asked him to support him for a game, helping with water bottles and equipment.

Dan's response was a simple "of course."

I told him that I tended to downplay my achievements in the running world, and that perhaps that had affected how my family viewed what I was attempting.

"What Vladimir is in the baseball world, I am in the ultrarunning world. I understand that I don't make millions of dollars playing this sport, but I'm in the midst of something truly elite and record-setting. Can you try to see me as Vladimir, and less as a younger brother competing for our parents' attention?"

Dan fired back that it wasn't Dave the runner, but Dave his brother, that he loved, and pointed out some of my behaviors that he found off-putting.

I agreed with him, acknowledging that if I acted that way at a family barbecue, he'd be completely justified in kicking me out.

But this was a different environment, I explained, and it was a side of me that was new for him to witness. When I've got my game face on, I'm intensely focused on what I can control.

Gradually, as we continued talking, our tone settled.

Dan admitted that he felt way out of his element, and when we stopped the car at the start, I saw a hint of tears in his eyes.

We both promised to try to do better for each other, hopping out of the SUV after a long, heartfelt hug and reminders that we loved each other. I closed the door, feeling that we had worked something out, and life would be better for it.

As usual, the first ten thousand steps felt like the fiery depths of hell. It began with my feet, then my ankles, knees, hips, and finally my back. It was like cooking an all-day stew: first rapid boil, then rolling boil, rapid simmer, simmer, and finally a slow simmer that would last for the rest of the day. But the morning's familiar body pain seemed more manageable given the resolution we had reached in the car just minutes ago.

After all, I was that guy, and this was my job, to get out and run, and to set everything else aside while I was in the Vault.

The day before I had started my big run in St. Johns thirty-six days ago, Lana Rae and I had come up with a way to keep my attention focused: keep my eye on the ditch and take a picture of the most interesting pieces of junk that I found. It gave me something to do all day, and it was fun to post the "ditch find of the day" on social media.

Most people couldn't comprehend running over a hundred kilometres a day, but they could connect with seeing weird junk in the ditch; and surprisingly, this became quite popular. I received hundreds of comments and private messages from people eager to know what the ditch find of the day would be.

What was even more surprising was how much I got into it myself. I enjoyed connecting with people over something as silly as ditch finds. I made a habit of texting my mother the many ditch photos, asking her to pick the best one. It kept me connected with my circle back home in a way that let everyone feel involved. As lonely as I felt at times and as much as I missed my people, we could always connect at the end of the day about the crazy junk I saw in the ditch.

Some of the hilarious items I had found included handcuffs, a deep fryer, a bathtub, a Relationships 101 book, a full bottle of ketchup, a vacuum, a manikin, an "If I were king of the world" book, a printer/photocopier, a vehicle safety light, a toy stegosaurus, a sloth stuffy, a pregnancy test, and a hedgehog planter pot. And these were just a fraction of the items!

Around the seventy-kilometre mark of the day, I nearly stepped on a pair of sunglasses resting on the shoulder of the highway. Bending over to take a picture, I noticed they were in mint condition—Ray-Ban polarized aviators that would retail for around 250 bucks. After taking the picture, I tried them on, transforming instantly into a devastatingly handsome smooth operator. Until that point, I hadn't kept any of the ditch finds, but since these glasses considerably improved my look, I tucked them away in my vest pocket.

Thirty minutes later, I ducked into the bushes as nature called. While squatting briefly, I was swarmed by hundreds of blood-sucking pests the size of pterodactyls. Bug butt bites (say that three times fast!) are no fun, so I rushed the process and got out of there as fast as humanly possible.

Minutes later, I reached into my vest pocket for a snack and found that the sunglasses must have fallen out during my bathroom break.

I took this as a clear message from the Ditch Gods that I was not to take what I came across on the journey. The Ditch Gods had spoken, and I had no choice but to obey.

I finished off the day after running 106 kilometres, now my new normal since passing the halfway point.

As we settled into the motel, Dan and I had a really good laugh about losing the Ray Bans, ate our body's weight worth of food, and tuned into the Blue Jays game.

Two-Stepping with Terry

DAY 37	COMPLETED	REMAINING
105.4 kms in 12:32:07	3865.7 kms	3293.3 kms

The morning of Day 37 was remarkably better then days past. For one thing, Dan was upbeat and laughing as we got organized for the day.

These relentless hills of northwestern Ontario had been taking their toll on my drained body, and that was more than evident in the day's Theragun session. My GPS watch routinely read over one thousand meters of elevation gain every day at a grade distinctly greater than anywhere else in Canada. But it wasn't the climbs that were bothering me as much as the steep descents. They were crushing my hip flexors and quads.

The ritual closing of the car door before starting my electronics reminded me of the soul-sucking repetitive miles ahead of me in this hellish land.

Piled on top of my already-broken body, the remote location and unimaginable distance from the comforts of the finish line stirred up a disturbing internal discourse. In a pace like this, feelings of utter despair could ignite into a fiery inferno.

Pain loves attention.

I kept telling myself: *don't give it air. Don't give it space. Don't give it attention.*

Let's try a little game.

I want you to take a deep breath.

Now, empty all of the air from your lungs.

Do this three more times.

Now, I guarantee that for the past few minutes you've been breathing—yet you haven't noticed it once.

Why is that? It's the power of attention.

When you focus attention on something, that attention makes it *everything.*

Try now to *not* think about your breathing.

You'll find yourself thinking about *not* thinking about it. It takes a while to truly empty your mind of attention to something once it gets your focus.

Pain is such a primitive feeling that it demands more attention than anything else in the world. Distress comes when the attention you pay to a painful situation gets magnified in a feedback loop of attention. You catastrophize.

The simplest solution to this problem is to not notice it... just like your breath. Don't give it air. Don't give it space. Don't give it attention. Repeat.

Lake Superior was angry today. Its weather system often changes on a dime. One second there was no wind, just a couple white billowy clouds in the sky, and temperatures were in the low twenties. Minutes later, looking up in the sky I noticed a cloud swirl and the sky turned black, the wind kicked up to over one hundred kilometres an hour, the temperature fell to 5 °C, and giant hail fell from the heavens. My cowboy hat shielded me a bit as I changed into my rain poncho. But it seemed that as quickly as I got dressed, the clouds disappeared, and the weather returned to normal.

This was just the way it was out there.

Thirty minutes later I came upon Dan at the pit stop. He told me he hadn't noticed a thing. There were two more storms of this same nature that day, and both made me think about the lyrics of Gordon Lightfoot's *The Wreck of the Edmund Fitzgerald*:

> *Superior, they said, never gives up her dead when*
> *the gales of November come early.*

It was the kind of day given to such wandering thoughts and imaginings.

All day, I envisioned the mirage of the one-legged Canadian hero Terry Fox hobbling ahead of me, treading the very same steps forty-two years ago, not knowing he was running his last days. I'm certain he knew that the cancer that had taken his legs had returned and understood that he was dying. Sadly, his journey came to a tragic end as he was escorted via ambulance from the shoulder of the highway just east of Thunder Bay. It put me in an even more somber mood than the lake had done.

This was a place of spirits, and of unfinished business.

Growing up, I had been schooled in the lessons of inspiration that Terry had taught us all in his Marathon of Hope to raise funds for cancer research while showing every Canadian what was possible if you just tried. Forty-two years later, he is still remembered as the most inspirational Canadian hero of all time. His moonshot goal of raising twenty-four million dollars, one from each Canadian, has since ballooned to well above eight hundred and fifty million dollars and counting. But as a runner, he was also my personal hero, and the image of Terry stayed with me for a long while. I'm not ashamed to say that as lonely as these remote miles had been out here, I'd gotten used to running alongside my fallen hero as we made our way west.

Sad as it was, I knew this two-step would end soon, and it simply broke my heart. Tears poured down my face as I failed to compose myself. The importance of this moment and this man in my life was hard to describe. I wouldn't be here if not for him, but I knew we would have to part company soon. As I slogged out the miles, the slobbering mess I had become was witnessed only by wildlife and the occasional trucker.

I ended the day with mixed emotions, as we had finished right in front of the famous Coach House Motel where Terry stayed an extra night, skipping a day of running, to swim with a ten-year-old boy who had lost his leg to bone cancer.

Dan and I slept in the same room where Terry's crew had slept. Vera slept in Terry's room.

I lay down on the bed and stared at the same ceiling that Terry had probably seen four decades ago. The motel owners had not renovated a thing since the day Terry and his crew had stayed here in 1980, which I greatly appreciated.

But somehow, I knew I wouldn't get a wink of sleep.

Legends Never Die

DAY 38	COMPLETED	REMAINING
106.5 kms in 12:20:44	3972.2 kms	3186.8 kms

Stepping out from the motel that morning I knew I was stepping into a minefield of feelings. All day I ran with Terry. The trees had grown and new asphalt had been applied to the road, everything else was the same. This would be the closest I'd ever come to witnessing greatness from my hero's eyes, so I soaked up this unique opportunity looking around, knowing this is what he experienced.

Eighty kilometres into the day during a steep ascent, my left knee abruptly gave out. I felt a stabbing pain followed by numbness drifting down my lower leg and foot. I yelped and limped in pain as I crested the hill, feeling a sense of urgency. The impossibility of the lengthy descent ahead prompted me to take out my phone and call my brother.

It felt like a tracking issue with my patellar tendon. I just *knew* I needed a release in my vastus lateralis ASAP. Playing it safe, I slowed my run to a walk as I felt a burning sensation spread below my knee, signalling a tendon tear.

Dan pulled up, parked the crew vehicle in a wide spot on the side of the road.

As soon as he popped the hatch, I lunged in to grab the lacrosse ball.

Vera filmed with a giant smile on her face as I sprawled facedown on the narrow shoulder on the hard rubber ball and buried it in my upper outer quad. I grimaced as I rocked back and forth over the new nodule in my leg. Vehicles sped past just feet from my head as the trigger point slowly softened. Minutes later, when enough release was achieved, I slowly rose to my feet hoping I'd find resolve.

Walking felt good and running felt okay. But given my panic thirty minutes ago, okay was good enough. I could make it. I could keep going.

What didn't escape me was the strangeness of this sudden leg pain along this particular stretch of the highway. The leg that hurt was not the one with constant foot and ankle problems. It was on the other side—the same leg that remained intact for Terry Fox. Like the blood of Christ, his ghost delivered a timely reminder of the lessons he had taught us while still here.

If that doesn't drive home the point that legends never die, nothing will.

We finished the day at 107 kilometres, now my *new* new normal. I spent more time than ever that night doing muscular release and joint mobility work.

To say I was scared of a recurrence of the sudden leg pain would have been an understatement. The chance of injury was always out there, and with four untouched provinces remained the single most deadly dagger that could be shoved into my journey.

Today had been the rudest of wake-up calls.

I fell asleep that night a little less comfortable, knowing that one false step might not only spell disaster but possibly break my heart.

Highway of Courage

DAY 39	COMPLETED	REMAINING
107.2 kms in 12:09:04	4079.4 kms	3079.6 kms

Despite last night's anxiety, I slept deeply.

I clapped my hands, barking, "It's Groundhog Day!" as I swung my legs out of bed. Ever since Dan and I made amends a couple of days ago, we'd been getting along famously, and seemed in a great mood as we organized ourselves. This would be Dan's final day out here with me as Lana Rae had scheduled his flight home for tomorrow morning. I couldn't tell if Dan was happy because today was his last day with me or if he was actually starting to have fun. Either way, I was beyond relieved to have my "real" brother back with me again.

The stretch of road I'd be running today was called the Terry Fox Highway of Courage. It extends between Nipigon and Thunder Bay, marking the final miles of Fox's historic Marathon of Hope in 1980, and I was still feeling emotional from the weight of the last couple of days.

Men look to male role models for inspiration. The men in my life have played a pivotal role, but men like Terry, whom I'd never met, were just as vital. His lessons of persistence, courage, and vulnerability were evident in every step of this run.

Today, I paid homage to a hero.

I was pleased that my knee and leg felt much improved from yesterday. The lacrosse ball had dramatically eased the burning in my knee, leaving me with a deep bruised ache that was more than acceptable.

As I ran up a hill, my phone rang. It was Terry's brother, Fred Fox.

Almost immediately, I felt at ease. The excitement in Fred's voice calmed my nerves, which I did my best to hide. He jumped right in, asking me numerous thoughtful questions, telling me that he had been following my run and was very impressed.

Hearing this made me blush, as I wasn't expecting the conversation to go this way. I thought I'd be the one asking all the questions. Instead, our mutual interest in each other's stories became evident as we rambled on like childhood friends.

The conversation grew familiar when I asked him about Terry's temperament during the Marathon of Hope. He said that his younger brother would become very controlling and bossy throughout the day and even into the evenings.

When Terry felt that his needs weren't being met, he'd get agitated and frustrated. Fred and his team couldn't reconcile the transformation of this normally subdued, gentle younger man into the control freak he became on the highway.

While others seemed to tolerate this shift, Fred, their other brother, and one of Terry's childhood friends really struggled with it.

Despite trying to ignore and overlook it, he found it impossible not to not exchange harsh words on occasion.

"Well, ain't that interesting," I exclaimed. "My brother Dan and I are going through that exact same issue and have probably used the exact same words said between you and Terry forty-one years ago on this exact stretch of the highway."

"I guess it's better late than never," I said to Fred, "but I'd like to help you understand maybe where Terry was coming from, if that's okay."

"Yes, please," he said.

"Two things," I replied, "If Terry is anything like me, in an environment where you have very little control, we runners seize complete control in the places we can. It's a survival thing, plain and simple."

I explained that I had run thousands of marathons in my life and was always scared as hell out here that something might go wrong.

Terry, on the other hand, had run one and only one marathon—and upon completion, decided that he could do it every day, hundreds of times across the country.

"If I'm scared, Fred," I continued, "then Terry must have been downright paralyzed with fear. I've been putting my fear square on Dan's shoulders because he's 'safe.' I'm guessing that you were *his* safe place, Fred."

There was a long pause on the other end of the line.

I broke the silence with a simple question: *Could he offer me any advice from a guy who's been on the opposite side of the relationship?*

Fred responded immediately.

"Be patient. Understand that this is a very confusing time for your brother, and always know that he loves you with all of his heart."

I could tell from Fred's tone and delivery that his mind was transported back to a place where he could see, smell, taste, and feel Terry's memory as if it were yesterday.

It felt as if Fred were talking not to me, but to his brother, saying something that until now, had been left unsaid.

The uniquely beautiful exchange ended with the usual formalities; but I knew that we both were changed forever.

At the next pit stop, I spotted a familiar sight: Dan swatting mosquitoes behind the SUV. I proceeded to run directly into my big brother's arms, giving him a lengthy embrace. Laughing, mid-hug, Dan asked, "What's this all about?"

"I love you, man, always have and I always will," I said, and I meant it.

"I love you too, David," he said.

We finished the day about ten kilometres short of the Terry Fox monument just east of Thunder Bay, with another 107-kilometre day in the books. I was stoked to see my good buddy Shep when we pulled into the airport hotel, as he'd be taking over crewing responsibilities from Dan.

Dan spent the last couple of hours running errands and chasing from one bakery to another, frustrated to find that they were all closing for the day or out of anything to sell us. To make matters worse, we got lost and drove past the hotel twice.

It was official: Dan was seriously done with being out here. Everything about him screamed, "Get me back home!"

On the third try, we finally pulled up in front of the hotel to Shep's glowing, shit-eating grin as he stood there waiting. Every ounce of his soul screamed excitement, and for that, I was endlessly grateful. After a huge hug and introductions, Dan busied himself showing Shep the ropes while I tended to body care and ate a giant burrito.

As Dan headed to the hotel pub, Shep lay down on his side on the opposite hotel bed from mine, his head resting in his hand, and said, "Okay, now tell me everything!"

We stayed up for the next hour or so geeking out about the details of the run, and something told me that Dan was feeling no pain when he returned to the room later that night.

Unconscious

DAY 40	COMPLETED	REMAINING
105.4 kms in 13:48:21	4184.8 kms	2974.2 kms

The next day marked forty days on the road, and my scruffy, unkempt beard showed it.

I hugged Dan, thanking him for everything he had done, as he helped us out to the car and headed out to catch his noon flight. Like a strong drink, Dan was one part loving me and two parts done with this shit.

Shep, on the other hand, was literally vibrating the entire fifteen-minute drive out to the day's 5 a.m. start. His plan was to drop me off, head west ten kilometres to the Terry Fox monument, then run *back* to meet me so we could run a bit together.

Less than an hour later, I'd pass the landmark marking Terry's last step. From that point there'd be no holographic vision of Terry coaxing me on like my own personal Obi-Wan; I'd be on my own.

Shep met me on foot just as I exited the highway and headed up a wet, grassy hill to the memorial. He remained quiet as we climbed the hill, giving me space to gather my thoughts. It was not my first time setting foot here, but by far the most memorable.

I stood looking up at the west-facing warrior, my fallen hero, and paid my quiet respects. The words I had been rehearsing for days will stay between me, Terry, and God; but I can tell you that I made a promise to him that I'd see him soon in Victoria. Then I tipped my hat and ran down the hill back onto the highway continuing west.

I try to avoid major cities as much as possible, and Thunder Bay was easy enough to skirt. One right turn and I was able to avoid the city all together.

The wildflowers were abundant that day, possibly due to the heat. It was in fact the warmest day we'd encountered so far. I had wanted to avoid the crippling heat; in fact, avoiding the hot, humid summers of eastern Canada was the principal reason I had started in mid-May. Now forty days in and dealing with my first day over 30 °C, the weather overall had been a blessing.

Shep continued his practice of driving ahead and running back all morning. Knowing the responsibilities and exhaustion that previous crew members had encountered, I wondered just how long this high-energy back and forth would last.

Shep drove up to the fifty-kilometre stop, parked the SUV, then ran back to me again shouting, "Woot woot!"

It wasn't long until we reached an overpass bending to the left with a strangely elevated, narrow sidewalk and a very narrow shoulder covered with rumble strips bordering the white line.

I remember commenting on how strange it was, and deciding to jump up on the sidewalk. The last thing I remember hearing was Shep's "Man, look at that view."

Bang. Lights out.

The next thing I remember, Shep had his arm under my armpit, his other hand holding his phone up to his face, and he was walking me off the overpass.

My surroundings were muffled, blurred, and made no sense. Filled with confusion, I wanted to ask what had happened, but it was as if I had forgotten how to talk.

I listened to the distant, muffled voice of my friend on the phone with what sounded like a 911 dispatcher.

It took me a while to realize he was talking about me.

The cloud lifted enough that I could now murmur, "What happened?"

"You fell and hit your head," said Shep as he continued trying to carry on a conversation with 911. "You were unconscious for 20 or 30 seconds and now you're bleeding a lot from your head."

"Can I sit down?" I asked.

"Of course!"

I sat down on a guard rail, hanging my head to collect my still-swampy thoughts. I could tell that Shep was getting more and more frustrated as he talked to the 911 operator.

"Shep, I'll be fine," I said, trying to sound convincing. "You should hang up."

There was a lengthy pause, then Shep looked at me and replied, "Are you sure?"

"I'm pretty sure," I said. "You can always call them back."

Shep had served in the US military as a paramedic years ago, so I was in capable hands. He started asking me questions. *Who is the Prime Minister? What is my birthday? What province are we in?*

I was able to answer all of his questions except for the day of the week, to which I simply replied, "I have no fucking idea. Every day is Groundhog Day!"

Shep laughed.

Our car was about two kilometers ahead, and we decided to run to it slowly, and he could call Lana Rae on the way to fill her in.

I remembered that I had promised Vera that I would let her know if something important happened so she could film it, so I texted her: *Fell and hit my head. Lots of blood.*

She quickly responded with *OMG. On my way.*

Those two kilometres seemed like an eternity. My head felt like it weighed a hundred pounds, and I was almost screaming in pain.

My body was defiant, not wanting to cooperate, almost like it was on strike. Emilio, my salamander, now wielded a megaphone, barking every excuse in the book for why I should turtle. His voice was loud and convincing.

To make matters worse I looked behind me to witness my coyote's teeth gripping my leg, whipping its head from side to side and trying to rip tissue from my bones. They were ganging up on me. I looked up to the sky for my dragon but it was still too cloudy to see him.

My eagle emerged from the clouds and for a moment we locked

eyes. In that moment I heard Erin say, "This is this. It doesn't need to be good; it doesn't need to be bad; it just has to be." My eagle turned westward, as did I.

Shep and I arrived at the vehicle, and I sat on the back bumper called Lana Rae, listening carefully to her instructions about what to do next. Having her act as my frontal lobe at a time when I couldn't think straight was so helpful.

On speaker, Lana Rae talked us through managing the current situation and its thus-far unknown consequences.

Chiming in, I proposed making the most of this stop, then proceeding forward in five-kilometre increments to see how things played out.

At that point Vera arrived, slammed on the brakes, and hopped out of her car, camera in hand.

Before leaving, I looked at myself in the mirror. Blood dripped down my face and stained my clothes. I looked like a badass character from *Yellowstone*, but not in a good way.

The plan now was to see Shep every five kilometres for the remainder of the day to mitigate risk. I spent the next half an hour focusing on mindfulness to forestall catastrophizing.

In my experience, moments like these are ripe for making a mountain out of a molehill. Your mind wants so badly to admit defeat, identify or even create problems, and find reasons to be a victim. Stress overrides our system, and we decide to put our reward aside in order to survive. We judge our situation and our prospects pessimistically. From there, it's easy to see everything as a hopeless catastrophe.

Step by step, I made the conscious decision to starve these worries of oxygen.

Shep continued his habit of parking ahead of me, then running back. He was super-diligent in quizzing me about the head injury, and I knew he was relaying info back to the team at large.

Vera shadowed us the remainder of the day; and five kilometres at a time we achieved eighty, ninety, one hundred, and finally one hundred and five kilometres.

When I reached the day's planned stopping point, Shep and Lana Rae sighed in relief.

At the tiny cabin that evening, Shep and Vera cooked us breakfast for dinner. My head was pounding, my body was covered in blood, and I felt like I had been run over by a semi. It had been a long day, taking an hour longer than any of our days so far.

It was a shit storm, but I felt a deep sense of pride for just getting through it.

Like a Dog

DAY 41	COMPLETED	REMAINING
107.5 kms in 13:08:38	4292.3 kms	2866.2 kms

With no time for body care the previous night, I awoke on Day 41 feeling like hot garbage. Everything hurt. My legs, ankles, feet, and hips throbbed. My left arm, shoulder, jaw, upper back, ribs, and head felt destroyed. I sent Shep's videos from the previous day to my physiotherapist Tyson and strength coach Carla, hoping they'd being able to suggest remedies for some of the body pains.

The first steps on the highway were the very definition of suffering. It seemed like every bone, muscle, bursa, ligament, and tendon in my body hurt twice as much as it had on previous days. Giving myself a stern talking-to, I slogged forward, grunting and groaning every step.

The one ray of sunshine was my buddy and fellow ultrarunner Shep. We had met via Facebook four years ago, when he followed me during a six-day race. He wanted to do similar things, and asked point-blank what he needed to do to achieve them. He was perpetually realistic, confident, and most of all, positive. In fact, I'd never met anyone as positive as him, ever.

We'd been super-tight ever since our first run together in Calgary, and in a very short time, he had become one of Canada's strongest multi-day runners, winning Outrun Backyard and competing twice at Big's Backyard Ultra in Tennessee in the United States. He was capable of outworking and outlasting any runner out there.

My 36-year-old friend had grown up in Alaska and didn't have the prototypical runner's body. He looked more like a bodybuilder, and carrying around extra muscle could be a detriment for a sport like ultrarunning. Nevertheless, Shep refused to give up his day job—carrying around a chainsaw all day in the woods as he maintained trails for Sinister Sports.

Shep's superpower lay not in his physical strength but his attitude. He was literally a human version of a dog: tenacious, friendly, and faithful. I have never once heard him say anything negative about a person, place, group, idea, or thing.

In a world full of assholes, this absence of negativity was refreshing. You know how when you get home, your dog thinks you are wonderful and looks past your flaws, greeting you excitedly? Shep had that same look in his eyes. He saw nothing but awesomeness in people.

Shep also had his eye on running across Canada in the future, so he paid very close attention to the details of my run, details that other crew members were either unaware of or wouldn't dig into.

All day he had a hard time hiding his worry. He was a terrible actor and his eyes told the story. I think he eventually grew tired of asking how I felt, because my answer never deviated from "I feel like a bag of smashed assholes."

As I ran further away from Lake Superior and into the land of a thousand lakes, Northern Ontario, I was surprised at just how well my cardiovascular system was functioning despite the mountain of pain I felt everywhere else. One day short of seven weeks into the run and its daily 100+ kilometre grind, my fitness was building to a point where I was feeling less and less fatigued.

These 740-kilometre training weeks are really paying off, I thought as I finished the day close to the motel.

That night's motel bordered a small lake with a dock, and after settling into the room, Shep played on the dock, doing tricks and backflips into the water as Vera filmed.

That evening, as I ate loads of food, I noticed something had changed. During the past seven weeks, Vera's camera had been pointed in my direction. Now, with shirtless, handsome Shep around, Vera's attention was squarely on him!

Like It's 1991

DAY 42	COMPLETED	REMAINING
107.3 kms in 12:46:16	4399.6 kms	2759.4 kms

Shep bounced out of bed promptly at 4 a.m., fully awake and ready to roll. He made his way happily around the room getting organized for the day.

My head still felt like I'd been hit with a baseball bat, but after the previous evening's extended body care, my ankles, feet, and legs felt slightly improved.

Checking my phone, I noticed that Carla and Tyson had replied with recommended exercises to activate my lateral hip stabilizers—the same exercises I had been considering—and I got right to work.

On the highway, I got to thinking about Al Howie and what he had gone through to set his record thirty-one years ago. Al was well known for his love of beer, so much so that one of his sponsors had been Labatt Brewing Company. I would often enjoy a half a can of beer at night with dinner and just marvel at stories that he would polish off an entire six-pack each night during his run. I couldn't imagine running the next day with a hangover.

Up until Thunder Bay a few days ago I had the privilege of running alongside the memory of Terry Fox.

From here on out it'd be just me and Al.

Al's record stood at 72 days, 10 hours, and 23 minutes. I was on pace for 66 days, shaving 6 full days off the record, and that was an important milestone for me.

The way I saw it, even if all hell broke loose and I needed to take a full day off running, I could do that every eleven days and still break the record. Now, with only twenty-four days remaining and not having taken even one day off, I had earned a very generous buffer against calamity.

That math lifted an incredible amount of stress.

If I could run through Covid-19, a foot fracture and a concussion without a day off, I could believe that I might never need a rest day.

Shep continued his habit of driving ahead and running back to me like clockwork. Since starting with me three days ago, he had consistently run sixty-to-seventy-kilometre days while not missing a beat with crewing responsibilities. His form hadn't suffered, his smile hadn't faded, and his attitude remained rock-solid.

The guy was truly a beast.

We wrapped things up at yet another run-down northern motel, and the smell of lingering cigarette smoke from decades ago was all too familiar by now. The decor, as always, remained stuck in the seventies. That suited me just fine. I figured Al had viewed the same tired wallpaper and the same execrable paintings as he laid his head down on the same stained bedspread.

Limbic Overdrive

DAY 43	COMPLETED	REMAINING
105.3 kms in 13:30:31	4504.9 kms	2654.1 kms

Rain banging on the metal roof woke me up before the alarm did.

"Let's get *swimming*!" Shep exclaimed.

But rolling slowly out of bed, I noticed again that something didn't feel quite right, and I couldn't put my finger on it. Nevertheless, I worked through my usual morning routine of getting oats, lube, getting dressed, Theragunning and the like.

We were planning on driving east only twenty kilometres to the day's start, so it afforded Shep time to drive back to the motel after dropping me off to pack things up. Mornings like these made things a lot easier.

Getting out of the SUV, I immediately felt wet and cold. In addition to the torrential downpour the wind was gusting at an unreal clip. As vehicles passed, I felt extremely irritated and bothered at the noise that the tires created as they cut across wet tarmac.

My phone rang. It was Lana Rae for our usual morning coffee chat. "Hello," I answered with a bite in my voice.

Later, Lana Rae told me that I had sounded pissed off from the start of the conversation. Our conversation continued as she carried most of the chatter forward, noticing my poor mood.

A semi truck drove by. The noise, the wall of water slamming into me, and the fact that he was quite a bit closer to the white line than I preferred all pissed me off. At that point I stopped running, I turned my body to face the truck to flip him the bird and yelled obscenities at the top of my lungs.

Shocked, Lana Rae paused mid-sentence, asking, "Hey Dave, are you okay?"

I told her what had just happened.

She mentioned that I'd been off this morning and asked me if I slept well last night.

I barked back at her that I slept just fine, but I just couldn't handle these *asshole drivers* out here.

She tried her best to calm the situation, but I kept coming at her with reasons I was still bothered.

At her best, Lana Rae is not exceptionally tolerant of negativity; and hearing all of this nonsense, she had pretty much had enough. She responded to my outburst with a tone that was part dismissive, part irritated, and *all* get-right-under-your-skin.

I erupted in a fit of rage. I won't go into details, but there are two important things for you to know. First, I was wrong; and second, I was wrong.

The battle ended shortly after names were called and ugly comments were made. It was not one of my proudest moments.

When Shep caught up with me later, I was in tears, still yelling at passing vehicles like a madman. To his credit, he tried his best to calm me, but couldn't come anywhere close. Nothing was breaking me out of my mood.

The rain stopped five hours into the day, and I had hoped my mood would improve. Instead, when Lana Rae tried calling numerous times, I refused to pick up the call. My crying continued so much that at one point in the day, I increased my fluid intake to avoid dehydration.

Six hours into my run, my phone rang. It was Erin Zelinsky.

Crap!

I had forgotten about our 11 a.m. therapy appointment. She asked about my day, and I told her about everything that happened. The anger, the sadness, the hopelessness, the frustration, and worst of all, the knowing that I was being completely unreasonable, yet unable to stop it.

"It's not your fault, Dave," she said.

That wasn't what I'd expected to hear. "Huh?" I replied, confused.

"It's not your fault. This is normal. You need to know that this is *normal.*"

Erin explained that this type of behavior was not unheard of after a concussion. She told me about brain injuries and their effects on the prefrontal cortex and the limbic system. Essentially, she explained, the blow to my head three days ago had scrambled up my thinking so badly that my feelings were taking over and I was acting like a three-year-old child after not getting ice cream exactly when he wanted it.

The good news was that this was controllable with some clever planning.

I perked up in attention.

Erin asked me what I would do if I were driving and my brakes started failing.

What would you do, she asked, *to mitigate a crash if you saw vehicles stopped on a hill up ahead?*

I mentioned that I could gear down to slow my vehicle.

"Good idea," she said.

I could also locate exits or pull-offs from the road to take prior to reaching the stopped vehicles, I realized, so that's what I told her.

Erin's applause was audible. "Now we're talking, Dave," she said. She went on to explain that the rest of my brain was working just fine, but that I needed to acknowledge that my brakes weren't in great shape and plan accordingly.

This made total sense to me at a time that nothing made sense. I told Erin that walking me through it had lifted a huge weight off my back, and I'd forever be grateful. "But what should I do to make things right?" I asked.

"Sorry goes a long way, Dave," she said. "Lana Rae and Shep are good people and they love you. Just be your authentic self and I'm sure it'll all be good."

I hung up and called Lana Rae immediately. Erin was right. It didn't take long for Lana Rae to forgive me and to help plan a path forward knowing this wouldn't be the last time things went sideways. The next time I came across Shep, we hugged it out.

Mr. Positivity smiled and gave me the old Jerry McGuire line, "You had me at hello."

Day 43 had been the hardest day out here so far, and to put a nice red bow on it, I was rewarded with my very first blister. Even so, it was another 105-kilometre day in the books; and looking back on it, I'll stand by this one simple truth: give me physical pain over emotional pain any day!

Lake of the Woods

DAY 44	COMPLETED	REMAINING
107.2 kms in 13:05:16	4612 kms	2547 kms

Shep's spirit made it near impossible to be in a bad mood. Nevertheless, waking on Day 44 wasn't easy. A whopping headache accompanied an array of extreme body aches that encapsulated areas of my body I never knew I had, and my monkey-brain clung to its sour state.

Today's run would encroach on Ontario's Lake of the Woods district, a part of Canada known for its extreme beauty and small chunks of land tucked between countless crystal-clear lakes. The wildflowers and bird life that populated this Rainy River district were so abundant that it made you feel like you were standing in a painting. Yet despite the angelic birdsong and early morning sunrise illuminating the still waters, I struggled to break free of the anger nestled in the recesses of my head.

Lana Rae and I resumed our usual coffee date at 5:10 a.m., just ten minutes after taking my first step. She answered my call in her usual welcoming voice, almost hugging me through the phone. We chatted about the usual things, what we had dreamt about, what the day ahead looked like, and various other thoughts on our minds. Then she mentioned something about cleanliness.

I don't know why, but just like that, I was full-on angry. I remained silent, trying to envision Erin's analogy of my brakes not working well.

Lana Rae picked up on my silence and inner spinning and changed the topic, craftily steering around points of conflict to avoid flooding my emotions.

After a while, I admitted that I was struggling to keep my emotions in check.

I actually found myself capable of laughing at the craziness of it all; and together, we decided to shut down the conversation before I ruined it.

Shep's hippie-like 'nothing bothers me' attitude was contagious, and it couldn't but rub off on me as he continued his badassery of driving ahead and running back to me. It was just the tonic I needed. Every time I'd see him approaching, he'd let out this war cry that would instantly make things fun and relaxed.

Whether he knew it or not, he was a modern-day running Buddha.

Around seventy kilometres into the day, I ran through Kenora, a beautiful community nestled in the heart of the Lake of the Woods. A number of locals came out to see me as I passed through, and I even stopped briefly to take a selfie in front of the forty-foot-tall sculpture Husky the Muskie. We'd be circling back to Kenora at the end of day to stay the night.

The remaining four hours of the day, I was immersed in natural beauty, and it had an amazingly calming effect. Looking out at the majestic lakes, I pondered the last twenty days I'd spent running across the biggest province in Canada. I thought about the first sign I'd seen entering Ontario, the one that read 2185 kilometres.

Twenty-five kilometres into tomorrow's run, I'd cross into Manitoba, leaving Ontario in the rearview. That feeling of achievement nourished my soul, and from it grew a newfound sense of belief in my team and our plan; and a belief that despite all the setbacks, injuries, frayed relationships, and my own imperfections, I was worth it.

CHAPTER 8: GROWING PAINS

Following my failed attempt to run across Canada in 2018, I had wanted to dig a 20-foot hole, climb inside, and pull the lid in after me. Such a public endeavour brought lots of attention, but the humiliation was too much to bear. I had no problem risking big; that came easy. The problem was that I had never learnt how to emotionally suffer defeat or embarrassment.

Returning home to answer all the laboured questions was not fun. It was like a funeral: people were sad and sympathetic but didn't know quite how to act or what questions were appropriate. I had put my entire soul into the effort. After all the time, sacrifice, anguish, and effort, they knew I'd come home empty-handed and crushed, and they were right.

Adding to the emotional pain was the immense amount of physical pain I had endured. I had beaten up my body...and for *what*?

MRI results showed a significant L5 S1 disc herniation, creating a pain I've never felt before. Even breathing hurt. Moreover, the nerve pain in my back, hip, and leg were out of this world. I now had a new sympathy for anyone who had ever suffered from neurological pain. The only position where I could find any sort of comfort was lying prone on the floor or bed.

Not just that, but I had young children to look after, a 40-hour-a-week job to return to, and bills to pay. I know this is what a lot of people do, but returning to it in pain after such an undertaking shocked my system like jumping into a lake in winter.

Working as a massage therapist, standing or slightly bending over people all day was profoundly uncomfortable, but I forced myself to look past the discomfort. The good and bad news was that after setting things aside in my practice to run across the country, business was extremely slow. Since money was getting tight from the loss of income, this created tension at home.

Eighteen years into an extremely busy massage practice that was typically booked solid for weeks, for the first time I saw gaps in my schedule. I used this time to lie prone on the massage table, traction my spine, or do my own rehab exercises.

I also suspected that many of my existing patients were reluctant to book appointments because they feared awkward conversations about my failed run.

I was seeing Shari MacDonald and Tyson for physiotherapy support. They are both masters in intramuscular stimulation (IMS), which is a dry needling technique that addresses soft tissue release in hard-to-release muscles. Working with them, I discovered a unique position standing up, slightly bent, with my leg rotated and pelvis tilted anteriorly, that "flossed" the affected nerve and gapped the related joint in a way that provided immediate relief. I'd imagine when doing this that my little disc was wiggling and worming its way back into place bit by bit.

Since I was more than happy to run for extended periods, and had zero problem with commitment, I devoted a minimum of 6 hours every day to moving my body in and out of that unique position, believing all the while that it was repairing itself. This became my life.

A few weeks after the end of my run, talks with the Rare Disease Foundation (RDF) started back up again. Despite the run's premature end, the Outrun Rare campaign was an enormous success. Our little independent campaign turned out to be the largest single fundraiser for rare disease in Canada ever. We raised well over $300,000, raised loads of awareness, and caught the attention of policy makers in Ottawa.

Third-party fundraisers are charities' dreams come true. There is little or no liability on their end, no effort, and all the reward. Charities depend on these numerous, usually small, events to fill their pockets as they go forth and do their good work.

The problem with Outrun Rare was that we very quickly became not so small. With our recent success and potential for further gains, the Outrun team and I thought it would be a good idea to join forces with RDF. Our two charities started discussions right away, dreaming up the campaign for the next Outrun Rare run across Canada.

I knew for sure that given the status of my health, I wouldn't be ready to attempt the run again until the summer of 2020. RDF was more than accommodating given the circumstances and very grateful that I'd even consider it again.

After many meetings with my own Outrun volunteers, we all agreed that if we were to go big next time, we needed more support. Outrun Rare was made up of thirty volunteers who met on Sunday nights after their kids went to bed. We all had full time jobs, many had young families, and surprisingly no one except for Sharon and me had direct experience with rare disease. The volunteers that made up our force were mostly a bunch of ultrarunners, family, and close friends who cared.

The ultrarunning community is a force of nature: many of its people are relentless to a fault and strive further than any other group. These wonderful humans routinely turn their insides out in order to achieve what most would deem impossible. This was my *army*, but the problem was that we had no idea what we were doing. We had no experience running a charity—just *running*.

RDF, on the other hand, knew exactly how to run a charity. They had employees specifically trained to execute campaigns of this nature. Their Board was made up of brilliant and diverse people with a structured aim to support the community I belonged to.

With humility, they admitted that the passion and drive developed with the Outrun Rare campaign was impressive. The executive director at the time even described me as "the guy on the Trans-Canada Highway lighting himself on fire for his son." Every part of RDF wanted to join forces with Outrun Rare and maintain the passion-fueled brand we had created together. For that reason, I sold the intellectual property of Outrun Rare to RDF for one dollar and was now assured that this next campaign would be a huge success.

Besides, I needed their support. I now knew firsthand that it was impossible to both run across Canada in record time, knowing the extreme and all-encompassing effort it would take, *and* stoke the fire beneath a significant charitable cause that demanded attention to millions of little details. I felt foolish for even trying.

The contract came through, and with my signature, the deal was done.

The beginnings of the relationship were a lot of fun. The board was optimistic, and we spent large portions of the day exchanging emails and phone calls, exchanging dreams, and talking ideas. As time went on, the board saw firsthand what our group of dedicated volunteers were made of. Motivating staff at a charity had always been a challenge, but propelling this group was as easy as cake. They backed my vision and matched my drive.

With the failed run behind me, and still recovering from a herniated disc, I now also had a lot of time to devote to the early planning stages of Outrun Rare 2020.

Eight months after ending my first attempt, I started running again after witnessing progress in my recovery. Eight months was a long time to be without my main outlet for stress, and some of the habits I had picked up during the run were a bit hard to stop. I was still eating like an ultramarathoner and had gained fifteen pounds while losing considerable muscle mass.

Running can be an exceptional endocrine regulator, and without my daily 100-kilometre run, my mood was unbecoming and I was difficult to live with. Sharon and I were sparring more often, and an already stressful, busy life raising three kids became more challenging.

She and I were polar opposites, and what we had once seen as strengths we now started to see as our greatest weakness as we navigated family, financial, marital, and lifestyle challenges.

Outrun Rare acted as an outlet, a wonderful distraction from the plethora of challenges that lay just under the surface of my fumblesome attempt to re-inject myself into a normal life. Sharon and I would work in parallel but never too closely on this project that mattered to us both, and at the end of the day we could both say that even if we had nothing else in tandem, at least we had that.

Carrying extra weight and losing loads of fitness was humbling. Running is hard, and it's easy to take for granted how easy it is when all your cylinders are firing.

Now, as I returned to running, I needed patience and a detailed plan laid out for me. That was much harder than you might think because I had neither patience nor a detailed plan.

I'd never been coached in my life. Now, I employed a running coach and started working with a strength and conditioning coach to get back what I had lost. My strength coach Carla Robbins "built me up from the basement up", explaining to me that you "simply can't fire a cannon from a canoe." Starting slow and focusing more on consistency rather than brute volume was something new for me. It didn't take long to see the results from the changed approach as both the run coaching and the strength coaching produced results I couldn't argue with.

Up to this point in planning Outrun Rare 2020, I had just relied on the assumption that I would get there, hoping that the thousand things I was doing in my training would culminate in readiness. With the progress I was seeing in my recovery and training, my lengthy career in ultrarunning, and my tenacious attention to where I needed to be and how to get there, I began to nurture a sense of hope again. As my fitness built and the training volume increased, my mood improved, my back pain was almost gone, and a belief started to creep through the cracks again that I might be able to return to running—even across Canada—without significant pain and in record time.

Time is a bitch, though; it's the ultimate score keeper. As my ability to run further increased and my mileage crept above 120 miles a week, running again started again to put a strain on other parts of my life. At this point I was working 40 hours a week, co-parenting three kids, directing Outrun Rare activities another 35 hours a week, and now running and strength training around 20 hours a week. If you're counting, that's 95 hours a week, and I was burning out big time.

The stress fell especially heavily on Sharon.

When I asked RDF for more support resources, they simply couldn't provide them. That meant less sleep, less me time, and less family time, all while prioritizing commitments that I'd made to others while trying to convince myself that it was sustainable.

The obvious answer was that it wasn't.

I spent the next year in and out of mental and physical burnout, showing up big-time and executing in a masterful way, only to drift away weeks later, vanishing from the world and hoping that nobody noticed I was missing. While in hiding, I would send just enough texts, respond to just enough emails, and attend just enough meetings to give the impression that I was in a good state.

In reality, I was miserable, broken, tired, and just didn't know how to stop the machine I had constructed and fired back up again.

In writing this book, I wanted to let it all out, to be honest about my deep, dark, ugly gremlins. One of those gremlins was my sense of self-worth. I remember returning from Italy in 2015 after setting the Canadian record at the IAU world 24-hour championships. I was sitting on the back deck with Sharon, drinking a glass of Gewurztraminer, when the idea of a Trans Canada run came up.

My initial thought was that I would love to give it a go. After exceeding my expectations in Italy, I believed for the first time that maybe I could do something like that. The feeling and the idea got me extremely excited; and we talked about it openly for about ten minutes until I started feeling strangely uncomfortable.

The awkward, unpleasant feeling gave way when I started dreaming about how we could turn the run into a rare disease campaign to benefit kids like Sam. Maybe it was because it was something bigger than me, and deep down I found it easier to believe in the cause than in myself. Maybe it made it safer to dream big if I weren't sticking my neck out alone and just for myself.

The bottle soon emptied, and the next day, aligning myself with other big dreamers, the project took on a life of its own.

I loved every second of it. I was no longer just existing, I was creating. This huge canvas had been laid before me and the sky was the limit. The campaign was all about rare disease. We'd create national attention for access, support, awareness, and above all, research dollars. I was high as a kite on the idea, and it drove me to do more.

A brave soul free of limits is a force of nature, one that could transform the world if everything went right. The scary thing was what could happen if it went wrong.

While soaring high, making plans and executing them, I'd remember what had made me feel ugly and uncomfortable when Sharon and I had talked about the run over glasses of wine, dreaming up the whole thing. My first feeling was that I wanted to do it for myself; then I would feel a pang of guilt and selfishness and immediately hate myself.

I had loathed myself for putting my wants and desires first. Never in my life had the negative self-talk been as brutal and ruthless as it had in those moments. My salamander's voice would climb and fill my every cavity with punishing comments. Worst of all, I would believe them, leaving myself feeling stupid, selfish, judged, sad, diminished, and scorned.

The feeling of loathing penetrated my every cell, and I'd overcompensate to prove to myself that I *was* a good person and that I cared more for others than myself. I would simply turn around, straighten up in my chair, and make the rare disease component bigger.

See Dave, this IS about rare disease.

Get uncomfortable. Go get another sponsor.

Get uncomfortable. Raise the fundraising goal.

Get uncomfortable. Develop a new awareness strategy.

Get uncomfortable. Employ a music artist for a theme song.

Still uncomfortable? Good, aim even higher.

Unfortunately, this never-ending treadmill led to an eventual cliff. The problem was me, but I didn't know it; and worse, I was driving myself to that cliff. The other problem was that people love following visionary leaders.

Visionaries are hard to find in this mass-market, consumer-driven world. We love producers—people who dream and do big things. Most of the time, those producers, if they're self-aware enough, find themselves acting increasingly independently of their own lived experience. They've got a head of steam on the engine, and they're riding it at full speed.

And now, it was far more difficult to stop the speeding train full of passengers than it was to stop a single conductor.

By the time we flipped the calendars from 2019 to 2020, Outrun Rare was ready to roll for a May 15, 2020, start in St. John's. Sponsors and finance were nailed down, my training was solid and thanks to some good counsel from my coaching, my fitness was epic. Logistics looked good and the entire Outrun Rare volunteer group was efficient.

The only problem was that my cyclical burnouts were still occurring despite my repeated calls for further support from RDF. The board and the Executive Director explained that the resources simply weren't there; and while I understood, I was still frustrated and exhausted by doing so much of the work myself.

As the months leading up to the run ticked by, temperatures rose. The mounting stress and anxiety matched with our moonshot goals put everyone on edge. At the same time my personal demands increased, so did the requests from the Rare Disease Foundation and during one fateful board meeting, the hornets' nest cracked open to catastrophic effect.

Both the foundation and I made decisions to protect ourselves, and it became increasingly clear they wouldn't be working with me in the future, nor I with them.

My heart broke again.

I had started my whole effort because of the love that I have for my son and truly felt that this was my best way to support him. I had believed in it so much that I'd signed away the rights to my own organization's name for a dollar.

And now, in those moments, I felt like the people on the other side of the table had ripped all of that away from me. I was befuddled and quite simply lost my faith in humanity. How could anyone, much less a foundation who said they supported families like mine, take such actions? I felt lost, without hope, and decided to never trust anyone with my best interests again.

Later, I spoke with a friend about what had gone down and was able to make some sense of things. Leaving that conversation, I better understood RDF's side of the argument and how they found themselves in a tricky spot. I took time over many days trying my best to walk in their shoes.

Gradually, it started to make more sense. Our mutual optimism had shadowed obvious issues associated with running a fundraising project like this. It had just taken this long for them to come to light.

I don't blame myself for not seeing it at the time, and in all fairness, I can't blame them either. I'm sure we both could have conducted ourselves better in the process, but we're all imperfect.

With a lot of the work we had done just flushed down the toilet, I worked hard to rediscover my motivation, and realized that we still had something money can never buy: momentum and drive. Upon hearing the news about RDF, our team was now more driven than ever. It more than made up for the sadness and loss of the project we had worked to build with RDF.

With my training on point, many relationships already in place, a motivated team, and an extreme personal desire to make this dream happen, we didn't skip a beat. We met often, discussed great ideas, and had consistent follow-through.

Yet in the background, dreadful whispers of a global Covid-19 pandemic got louder.

More team members started sharing concerns about logistics, health, and government policies forbidding the kinds of activities that featured someone traveling from town to town, possibly coming into physical contact with infected people, spreading the disease as he went.

We faced a paradoxical challenge: our campaign was intended to be a very public awareness campaign. Make it public enough and loud enough and it would backfire as irresponsible and disrespectful to immunocompromised people or those living with disabilities, precisely the group we were looking to support with our campaign!

Yet reducing our campaign's visibility guaranteed that we would reach neither our awareness nor fundraising goals.

By late March 2020, the pandemic had quickly escalated. Within a week, cross-border travel was banned, workplaces shut down, professional sports leagues canceled games, and we quickly found ourselves in the full-stop Covid-19 lockdown.

While the world reeled in shock at the gathering storm clouds of a 100-year pandemic, we at Outrun Rare called a meeting to discuss our future.

I started the meeting with a neutral tone, trying not to shift the energy one way of the other. I truly wished to hear my team's thoughts. I told them that I trusted them and loved them more than they knew; and that I would be content with whatever we decided as a team over the next hour.

Over the Zoom feed, one by one each of our twenty-two volunteers took turns delivering their thoughts on the pros and cons of progressing with Outrun. Screen after screen showed sad eyes as each person explained why they thought the run should not happen.

Not one person on that call thought we should move forward. It was hard to take. Halfway into the call, I poured a tall glass of bourbon out of sight of my screen. I didn't want them to see my sadness, but I'm sure the wet eyes and sunken features displayed obvious despair.

By the end of the call, we made the decision. Outrun Rare 2020 would need to wait a year.

The next week was a personal struggle. Aside from the anxiety everyone across the planet felt at the emerging health crisis, I was also mourning yet another loss. And I had to consider the very real possibility that I might never finish the run.

In all our planning, none of us had ever considered the possibility that the outbreak reported months before in China would turn into a global health catastrophe, obliterating our venture as if it had never existed.

I found myself awkwardly bored, not knowing what to do with myself. My training runs quickly shortened, mostly as the result of a "what's the point?" mentality, and I looked for something to fill the sudden availability of energy and time.

One of my Outrun volunteers called me one day with a big idea: to take the energy we had stored in the now-deferred Outrun project and create an online backyard-style running race. Invented by Lazarus Lake, backyard ultras require competitors to run 6.7 kilometres every hour until they can't or simply won't. The last remaining runner wins.

I thought this was a great idea, and we talked for hours about ideas and concepts that seemed half pie-in-the-sky and half-doable. I told him we'd need a small nimble group to pull it off, and it would need to be concept-to-completion in about two weeks.

We exchanged a virtual high-five and got busy working on it. That evening, I convinced a team of three others to get on board, and we left the next meeting with a to-do list.

Since we weren't working and no one had anything better to do, we moved quickly. My task was to contact the top 30 ultrarunners in the western world and get them on board. I emailed everyone, openly cc'ing the rest of the list so each recipient could see who else was on it, hoping to perhaps spark FOMO within some of them.

My message was simple: I told them that all of their races had just been cancelled, and only one race had been started: the

Quarantine Backyard Ultra.

Due to regional restrictions, our event would allow runners to run on their treadmills, outside in their neighbourhoods, around their living rooms, or even their own backyards. This would all be recorded on a live Zoom feed and be available on You Tube. There was no cost, no profit, just a group of people within the tightly knit global running community wanting to have fun.

At first everything looked perfect. We were all doing our tasks and we all did them very well. Registration opened and numbers were huge.

Then two team members took control of the project in a way that to this day still baffles me. The remaining four of us started panicking. Our names were all over this. Most people had called this Dave Proctor's race; and yet, we were excluded from any decision-making.

In an effort to restore equilibrium, I privately extended an olive branch and thought we came to an understanding. I shared the news with the others, and we all thought our team effort was back on track, only to see it fall apart again over the next few weeks.

As my position diminished and I stood back watching yet another dream crumble in front of my eyes, my inner voice spoke up.

Dave, you had this coming to you, you fucking idiot.

You let people in and handed them trust.

You looked past the obvious possibility that they had alternative motives for being your friend and helping.

It was true: I had seen goodness in them and trusted that they had only good intentions toward me. Yet I now suspected that their motivation had been to promote their coaching business while leveraging my success in the sport.

My heart broke a little more, and I felt stupid. I tried distancing myself from the event; but as I said, my name was all over it. I stayed close enough to see it, and far enough away that I didn't have to touch it.

Following the event, I was mad; and I couldn't tell if it was at myself or at others. Sharon and I struggled to connect. The disintegration of my relationship with RDF continued, which further shook my trust in others and lessened my faith in humanity.

I felt like there was only one person to blame: me.

The common denominator in the equation was me.

I hated my life, and I hated me. Why did everything I touched fail?

I couldn't make sense of things.

Then one day, my 15-year-old daughter Julia emerged from her girl-cave and asked, "Dad, do you want to make a TikTok video with me?"

I jumped to attention, declaring that I would love to. I love dancing and being silly with the kids and making short, choreographed dance videos with my teen was a dream come true, especially during the early days of the pandemic when we all had time on our hands.

Every day we made a new video. We'd practice the choreography for hours at a time, then do endless recordings until we both got it right. To this day, I've never felt this close to her, and deep down I think she loved doing it with me.

As the summer passed and I struggled with self-doubt and self-hatred, Sharon and I split. We had both tried our hardest, given it everything we had, and I will always love her. The looks on the kids' innocent little faces as they heard the news was, and always will be, the most sorrowful moment in my life.

So at the age of thirty-nine, I packed up my bags and moved into my brother's basement. I tried to hide, stay busy with friends, and not drink too much while evading others in Dan's basement.

It's impossible for most people not to pick sides when a couple separates. People assign their own fears, ideals, and virtues at a time like this, when judgement is tempting and easy.

The guilt of leaving weighed heavily on me, made worse by the piles of shame delivered to my front step by the many who felt they had an opinion that needed to be heard. I lost a number of friends, many of whom never returned texts, signaling loud and clear that they were not on Team Dave.

I knew I'd miss them, but if that was all it took to break it off, maybe it was better. Those friends who did stick around more than made up for the loss of the others.

I will always remember one dear friend's response. After giving me a hug following the separation, he looked me square in the face and said, "Life is complicated." That level of love and acceptance was true friendship.

As May 2021 and the rescheduled Run Across Canada approached, my running was ramping up again. I was more determined than ever to accomplish the task that had evaded me for so long; and despite feeling broken, I remained hungry.

I wanted to finish this feat so badly I could taste it. Swimming in a pit of sorrow, all I wanted was to crawl out and achieve something great, something I knew was in my wheelhouse, and perhaps something that would make me whole again.

My friend Stephanie, co-founder of Outrun Rare, decided to approach the Canadian Organization for Rare Disorders. CORD was the one foundation other than RDF that served the Canadian rare disease community at large.

Since the bridge was already burnt with RDF and I still believed we had a unique, large-scale opportunity to create awareness and advocacy for rare disease with this run, I thought they might want to join forces.

Our initial meeting went well, and they were very impressed with the 2018 movement we had created. We discussed and debated ideas, but sadly, following that discussion, our emails never received a response and after a while we stopped trying.

Instead, Stephanie and I settled on a small-scale awareness campaign that would spread the message about the need for further access, support, and treatment for rare diseases in Canada, still the only developed country in the world without a federal rare disease strategy or an orphan drug plan.

As my training mileage ramped up, however, Covid-19 had different plans. With the second and third waves now rippling across the country, the federal governments unleashed further lockdowns. Provincial governments doubled down, deploying inter-provincial travel bans limiting movement of non-essential travelers, including transcontinental runs.

Even if they had intended to let us through, our campaign's intent had been to be as loud as possible. Given the heightened state of frustration, the court of public opinion would have tried and hanged us before sundown. I could just imagine people saying, "I can't go visit my mother, yet this guy is allowed to do *this*? How *insensitive!*" For that reason, 2021 was a wash and we needed to put the run off yet again.

Looking back, it was a good thing it never happened in 2021. I was a mess. I was struggling to find equilibrium with Sharon, the kids were struggling big-time, and when your kids are unhappy, Dad's not doing so well either.

The good news was that a gift from God appeared in my life when I least expected it. Still raw from the separation and convinced that I was not ready and probably not worthy of dating, my friendship with Lana Rae evolved, and we started dating in early 2021. Our romance ignited in a way I thought only happened in fairy tales, and we couldn't get enough of one another. I'd never felt like that before, and it was scary.

I wanted nothing but to hear her voice. We spoke endlessly about all manner of things, and I had never met anyone as intelligent and interested in learning as she was. She listened attentively, and when she spoke, her message landed in a way that changed me.

One common discussion we had circled around self-worth. She knew that this topic was one I struggled with after I had shared the bulk of my deepest fears, including my recent split with RDF and the Run Across Canada saga.

She spoke sweet, angelic words that I only now started to believe. "It's okay to want greatness. It's okay to make your dream your only purpose. Pursuing your own dreams for yourself is enough." For once, somebody had given me permission to believe it was okay to take this on for myself, by myself, if only because I was worth it.

I felt alive. For the first time in a long time, I felt excited and driven about my project, which now had no title, no beneficiary, and no start date. And for once, that was more than okay. This was my run, for me and as much as that made me feel a bit weird, it felt great to finally own those feelings, and I loved it.

But would others? Would they still be on board with the stripped-down, super-efficient "Project Dave"?

With a much smaller friend group, it was easier to run this idea past people whose opinions I valued. It was unanimous. One by one, they all told me that they loved it. They said "It's about bloody time," and "Dave, this will be great for you!" They all lined up to come out and crew me for portions of the trek, committing their time well in advance, knowing that if we pulled this off, I'd call on them in due time to come suffer with me.

And I loved them for it.

The next thing I was worried about was my existing sponsors. How would they receive the news of our stripped-down, subdued, and hopefully final attempt to break Al's record?

To my relief, they were eager to help. One sponsor said, "Dave, we have always been on your team. We supported what you supported. You've done enough and it's about time you did this for yourself." Hearing this made me glow. I've always cared way too much about what others think of me. I had thought all along that they were here for the charitable component first and me second, but now I realized it was the other way around.

Not long after the sponsor calls, I was talking to a friend about my struggles with self-worth and financing the run. We dove into a very deep conversation and shared stories about greatness, professional desire, risk, and belief in oneself. My friend is a very successful businessman who's taken this road many times before—and it hasn't always been a cakewalk for him either.

His advice was to go for it. It was obvious that he believed in me, and we shared an affinity for doing hard things. Nearing the end of the conversation, he asked what the budget for a run like this would look like.

When I told him, he didn't hesitate. "My company will sponsor you for that dollar amount, go make this happen."

Everything was lining up, and I felt called to finish the run once and for all.

The feelings of guilt, shame and loss were now being replaced with courage, belief, and strength. While the outside world saw me as a broken bird, those close to me saw a spark they hadn't seen before. My training ramped up again, my fitness grew steadily and I was running stronger than I ever had. As I started working with sports psychologist Erin Zelinsky, my 80% complete game climbed to 99%.

I awoke in the morning thirsty and went to bed at night satisfied. I owed nobody anything and had the freedom to do what I wanted. I was on fire.

As the calendar closed in on my start date of May 15, 2022, I felt confident as fuck.

CHAPTER 9: MANITOBA

The Hundredth Meridian

DAY 45	COMPLETED	REMAINING
107.7 kms in 12:53:38	4719.7 kms	2439.3 kms

In 2018, my record attempt ended here. Today, we would break new ground.

Waking in Kenora on day 45 was like any other day. Alarm sounds, get dressed, eat breakfast, and break up crud in my legs with the Theragun.

We were loading up into the SUV when I noticed a homeless guy sleeping outside of the Super 8.

A week earlier, I had found a five dollar bill in a ditch and had resolved to pass it along when I met someone who needed it more than I did. This was exactly such a person and moment, so without waking him, I tucked it under his arm to protect it from the wind.

Thirty-five kilometres later, we arrived at the starting point west of Kenora. The morning was picture-perfect, and the hills were already noticeably smaller and the trees less dense. Within the next twenty-five kilometres I'd run into the province of Manitoba, welcoming the Prairies and saying farewell to Ontario and the Canadian Shield.

Shep was buzzing around. He, too, picked up on the importance of the geographical transition. In fact, it was on days like this that I remembered why Shep was here. Shep lived for the journey, and if the significance of running clear through the Shield and into farm country didn't ignite him, then nothing would.

Ten kilometres into the day, a woman pulled up in her vehicle, hopped out, and excitedly asked if she could run with me for a bit. Sandi and I had met in 2018, as I passed through Kenora after stopping my run. Her own family had been deeply affected by rare disease, so the wrapped RV with rare disease messages all over it had instantly caught her eye. Then, I was broken and in enormous pain. Now, we comfortably chatted and caught up for the next half hour.

Before leaving, she announced that had left me a ditch-find ahead, marked by a large Canadian flag. Shep and I kept our eyes peeled, and not long afterwards, found a cooler full of local craft beers!

WELCOME TO MANITOBA, the sign said as I looked up; and just like that, the big ol' province of Ontario was done and dusted. After stopping to take some pics, we proceeded into my sixth province. Only a few steps later I looked to my right and saw the familiar kilometre marker signs. For the previous twenty days I had watched as the numbers slowly decreased from 2,185 to 1. Now standing before me stood a new sign telling an entirely different story. This one read 490, and the first thing that popped into my mind was that it was totally runnable.

Over the next twenty kilometres, as if the world were giving me a break, the hills flattened, the trees thinned out, and suddenly I was standing on a flat road. I looked to my right and saw a potato field. Looking left, I saw a corn field. When I turned around and looked back, I saw a wall of trees. I'd skipped from one tectonic plate to another and crossed the hundredth meridian, made popular by a song from the band *Tragically Hip*. It's the line of longitude that separates the humid eastern provinces of Canada from the arid western plains, and it's commonly observed to occur just east of Brandon.

This location, however, described it to a tee.

Shep and I blasted the *Tragically Hip* song and sang at the top of our lungs. Playing both lead singer and selfie filmmaker, Shep captured our singing on camera. To our delight, we found out later that the band had shared our video on Instagram!

The greatest gift that the prairie provinces gave me was a tremendously wide shoulder to run on. With so much real estate, I finally found safety in running with my back to traffic. My ankle and foot were very appreciative of the change in camber as the road now sloped away in the opposite direction.

We concluded the day bagging another 107 kilometres. My fitness continued to build and the 107s were starting to feel easier as time went on. Shirtless Shep and I cozied up to a huge pizza and got on the phone with my buddy Jeremy, who would be my running buddy and guide through the confusing roadways of Winnipeg the next day. Jeremy was stoked, Shep was full of energy, and I was on cloud nine. In a pizza-induced coma I fell asleep in my Normatech recovery pants and dreamt of wide, flat, prairie highways as far as the eye could see.

Flashbacks

DAY 46	COMPLETED	REMAINING
107 kms in 13:09:33	4826.7 kms	2332.3 kms

Seconds after the alarm sounded on Day 46, both Shep and I shouted in unrehearsed union, "It's Groundhog Day!" We erupted in childlike laughter as we sprang out of bed.

Yes, you read that right. I *sprang* out of bed.

There was just something about Shep that put me in a good mood. We had something great going out here, and I wasn't sure if it was our methods, attitude, or even our combined good looks; but whatever it was, we were having a blast, and that made me happy.

We had been having car troubles with Lana Rae's Pathfinder, and he took it to be worked on in Winnipeg later in the day. That meant I'd be without his support for a four-to-five-hour chunk of the day, but luckily my buddy Jeremy would be running with me during that time.

Shep had his own reasons for wanting to be at the dealership. Yesterday I had picked up a ransacked wallet in the ditch, and when Shep called the number on the wallet's ID, he connected with a young woman whose car had been broken into months ago. They planned to meet up at the dealership, where she was overjoyed to retrieve what was remaining. Well, there was our good deed for the day!

Taking the first steps of the day, I was overjoyed that I had been bestowed a hefty tailwind, unusual in the prairies. And the big sky sunrises were worth waking up for. The auburn glow of the moist earth reaching up to welcome the sun's embrace had a very auspicious energy about it. The quiet roads, interrupted only by the early morning Canadian Pacific Railway trains chugging by, create a stillness that was hard to duplicate.

Around thirty kilometres into the day, I crossed the unmarked-yet-solidified-in-memory spot where I had taken the final steps of my aborted 2018 Trans Canadian Run. Memories of the misery I felt at that time made my eyes well up. I felt bad for my past self, for what it had to go through, yet equally grateful that in the present, I was doing well. I telephoned Wayne, who had crewed me to this very spot in 2018 and reminisced about those final days. The active therapy was a lot more cleansing than I would've expected.

With Mother Nature's hand on my back, the running was effortless. Looking ahead at the 45-kilometre point, I saw a giant and very familiar billboard on the north side of the highway marking the geographical center of Canada.

Jeremy and I caught up on the run into Winnipeg, a city that strangely avoided linear east-west and north-south roads in favor of roadways that darted in all directions like cockroaches scattering in a freshly lit room. This awkward city planning made navigation extremely stressful, and I was doubly grateful to have the settling influence of Jeremy in tow.

Running on a pathway, I noticed a woman and her three children ahead. As soon as I could make out her face, it dawned on me that it was someone I knew. "Lisa!" I shouted, and Jeremy and I stopped as I landed a big hug. We had first met almost twenty in my downtown Calgary massage practice, and now her kids were drawing pictures of me with my cowboy hat. Pretty cool!

I knew that I had to get a roll on, but basked in the joy of seeing her happy with her own young family. And like a true friend, she had also left fresh banana bread up ahead with Shep.

On my way through Winnipeg last time, I had only one regret: that I didn't stop at the Bridge Drive-In ice cream shop, lovingly known locally as the BDI. This time, making sure I wouldn't die with that regret, we stopped and ordered "The Sleeping

Beauty," a masterpiece consisting of a half-pineapple filled with strawberry and cherry sundaes, topped with sliced bananas, diced pineapple, whipped cream, cherries and peanuts. We hardly came up for air as we hucked it down our throats before continuing the run.

As we passed through the city, it was great meeting local runners who came out to join me, seeing their smiling faces and hearing their encouragement. They celebrated my luck with the weather, since just a few days ago Winnipeg had reached a roasting-hot 37 °C. Today it was *twenty*-seven degrees, and with the humidity that felt plenty warm enough.

We finished off the day west of Winnipeg, back on our old friend, the Trans-Canada Highway.

And again, Shep didn't skip a beat, putting in another sixty-kilometre running day.

107 kilometres done, body care checked off, and having eaten my weight in dinner, I hit the hay. By now, I had the routine down to a tee.

Letting Go in the Prairies

DAY 47	COMPLETED	REMAINING
107.2 kms in 13:13:48	4933.9 kms	2225.1 kms

Shep told me upon waking that we'd be joined by a couple running legends at the start of the day's run at 5 a.m. Yin and Janel, along with numerous friends, had run across Manitoba in 2021 in 7 days. I was eager to share some miles with these fellas and hear their stories about the adventure.

Arriving at the start location as the sun crept across the farm fields, I saw two people approach our vehicle, seemingly appearing out of nowhere. I was a bit confused but resisted asking them where they had parked. Instead, we just started running.

Immediately into the run they both launched into a thousand questions about the run: how, what, where, when, and of course why. After a healthy exchange of storytelling, the conversation morphed into a debate on ideas of self-actualization and believing in yourself. I love these types of people, the ones who *don't* feel they have all the answers, who are instead intensely curious and have more questions than answers. Everything was fair game. Whether we talked about belief patterns, ideologies, or mental constructs, one thing was consistent: they were eager to grow.

Yin told me about his seven-day run the previous year. He said that the aching in his legs a few days in had been the biggest hurdle to overcome. He said that without the urging of his friends to get moving in the morning, he had felt hopelessness and a deep desire for the ache to just go away. He asked me how, after 47 days, I was able to reconcile these feelings. I assured him that I felt the same ache that he had.

I found myself launching into a story about how hunters capture monkeys in the wild. It was common practice to take a hollowed coconut and drill two small holes in the back, feeding a cable through both holes and fixing that around a large tree. Next, the hunter would drill a third hole in the front of the coconut just big enough to feed a half of a banana through, and along would come a monkey, smelling the banana inside. It would squeeze its hand inside the coconut to grab the banana, but now with a closed fist around the banana, it couldn't pull its hand free. The monkey would pull for minutes, hours, at times even days, but remains stuck. At any time, it could look above at the trees and see hundreds of bananas, but having this one in its grasp, would not let it go. All the monkey needed to do was let it go.

"We are eerily similar," I said. "For us to be free of torment, we need to let go."

I told Yin that I let go of any desire from comfort six weeks ago; otherwise, I would surely have drowned in my own misery. The first week had been the hardest because I could still remember vividly what comfort felt like. Letting go of the things that don't serve you to achieve a desired outcome is vital in both work and play. I looked him square in the eyes and said, "Comfort has no place setting at *this* table."

The boys peeled off after saying their farewells and it was again just Shep and me. As the tailwind turned into a deafeningly strong headwind, I sent a quick email to reschedule our weekly *Chasing Tomorrow* podcast recording for later in the evening, so we could record indoors.

As soon as we hit 107 kilometres, we called it a wrap!

That night's lodging was a super-dumpy motel; but I had to admit that I was starting to enjoy a certain sort of charm shared by these critter-infested dives.

Shep got to chatting with another traveler outside, so I had the place to myself; and with a half-chewed mouthful of spaghetti and meatballs, I fell asleep.

Cyborg Status

DAY 48	COMPLETED	REMAINING
107.4 kms in 13:08:11	5041.3 kms	2117.7 kms

Day 48 was Shep's last day with me on the run, and that made me sad. Not only had he run 60-70 kilometres per day with me, but on top of that he hadn't skipped a beat with his crewing duties.

The guy was *unreal*, and I could see he had a real shot at breaking the Trans Canada running record in a few years. Despite his late night, there he was, at it again at 4 a.m., full of piss and vinegar.

Shep was killing it out here, and what had made it even better was the chance to deepen our friendship.

My buddies Joel Campbell and Mike Huber were supposed to fly into Regina and drive a rental car to meet us at the end of the day near Brandon. It would be the fourth crew swap so far, leaving just one swap remaining.

I loved having fresh "meat." New crew brought an excited energy and shifted the dynamic for me. I learnt after 2018 that it was easy to get annoyed, exhausted, and bored crewing. Plus, crew members had lives, jobs, and families they couldn't just abandon all summer.

These 6-to-15-day rotations were a perfect balance, and Joel and Mike were sure to bring the energy I craved.

The morning was cool and crisp with not much wind: a perfect day for a 100-kilometre jog.

Nearly seven 740-plus-kilometre weeks of running had done something to my body which to this day I struggle to understand. Aside from my foot, which remained terrible but not worsening, and my general leg stiffness, which was constant, I was feeling better week by week. Having the patience to stay below my aerobic threshold had set the stage for adaptation and avoided lactic buildup.

I've always thought there was fit, then super fit, then ungodly fit, and somewhere above that was cyborg territory. There was no doubt that I was well into cyborg status at this point. Slogging out ungodly miles didn't seem hard anymore, and the fatigue you'd think I'd feel later in the day never came. The daily mileage wasn't the limiting factor; it was the non-negotiable 24 hours in the day, and the need to find time to eat, treat, and hit the sheet.

Since my speed had only improved marginally and I had no interest in taking unneeded risks, I had been stuck maxing out between 105 and 108 kilometres each day.

All things considered, I felt scarily invincible. The delicate line between hyper-confidence and foolish cockiness was one I crossed multiple times by accident. When that happened, I would find myself coming back down to earth by either calling my parents, my kids, Lana Rae, Dan, or my friends.

The flat prairie roads felt like a celebration and a well-deserved reward for getting this far this quickly. Even so, I knew from experience that I shouldn't celebrate yet. Despite already completing 5000 kilometres, I still had over 2000 to go, and that included the Canadian Rockies. As I had found out all too well in 2018, anything could happen out here on this unforgiving highway.

A couple local runners came out to share some miles, and I even shared a beer with one of them as he stopped at his truck—a real treat mid-run.

Shep continued his amazing 60-to-70-kilometre drive-and-run routine; but despite his exhaustion, I knew he'd immediately miss being out here once he left.

As we ran, I noticed a Jeep driving eastward towards us down the highway. As it passed, we heard screaming like teens on spring break, and followed the sound of screeching tires on asphalt as the Jeep executed a sharp U-turn to pull up just ahead of us.

Joel and Mike had arrived! They spilled out of the Jeep, running back to us to give big bear hugs all around. Right away I noticed Mike's silky smooth "porn" moustache. "Damn, that looks dirty!" I said to him jokingly.

Mike's only response was to give me a slow wink.

The boys went straight east to the hotel in Brandon while Shep and I rounded out the 108 kilometres for the day. We got back to the hotel and met Joel and Mike in the parking lot.

These crew transitions were always interesting because everyone was eager to learn what they needed to do and how to get it right. The boys asked twice as many questions as the last rotation had, with triple the amount of interest.

They had brought me a Terry Fox shirt for motivation, and we immediately cracked some of the craft beers we'd been carrying since Kenora. With this much energy in the room, I knew I'd be just fine for the next week.

We all tucked into our respective beds and the lights went out.

Seven Weeks

DAY 49	COMPLETED	REMAINING
107.7 kms in 13:12:02	5149 kms	2010 kms

By morning, I'd logged seven long weeks of running.

Right away, I noticed that four grown men in a hotel room made things a bit cozy but sped up preparation for the day. The plan was that Shep would drive the rental car back to Regina and fly out from there. Mike wanted to run the first forty kilometres with me, then he and Joel would trade positions and Joel would run the next forty.

Having quality company all day was something I was definitely looking forward to.

After saying our goodbyes to Shep, we were on our way. Getting rolling and watching the boys watching me was interesting. It was fun knowing they had both been paying close attention to the run and were now here in the flesh. Both Joel and Mike were huge Terry Fox fans and knew every minute detail of his 1980 run. They were both uniquely inquisitive, and that, paired with their love for ultrarunning, left them on the edge of their seats.

The first four hours of the day were spent in non-stop chatter with Mike. We ran on golden-wheat-bordered highway in the morning glow, catching up on the happenings thus far. He asked very insightful and deep questions, seemingly trying to stir up a debate about ideas instead of the usual play-by-play about how the run had gone so far.

Mike is an unassuming man. Standing 5'9" and 48 years old, he's even skinnier than I am. In a short span of time, though, he had evolved as an accomplished runner, working hard but quietly. He and his wife were raising three teens, and he beamed in pride when he spoke of them.

Mike was also a high achiever. In addition to raising a wonderful family, he was also an extremely successful realtor in Maple Ridge. This guy never rests. Whether it's on the pitch as a soccer coach, exceeding sales targets, coming home with random flowers for his wife, or pushing physical limits as a runner, Mike rarely loses.

One thing I could do all day with Mike was philosophize about life, love, parenting, business, and belief. He was that rare person who could eloquently convey his thoughts but remained both humble and intelligent enough to allow them to be changed.

Before the 2018 Outrun Rare campaign we had put out a press release to rally attention, had lofty fundraising and awareness goals, and an enormous PR campaign prepared and ready to achieve our targets. I'd do four to five interviews a day, and even after the run started I continued daily interviews. As great as it was to get the word out, those interviews were also a distraction and source of stress.

Knowing that the media tempo had to change this time, we had gone in the other direction, perhaps a bit too far. On this run, there had been zero media outreach, but also much less stress.

Despite our intentionally low profile, I was still surprised that so far, the most prominent running publication in Canada hadn't reached out at all, not even to get some quotes to add to boilerplate they'd gathered from elsewhere. Not one article had been written. Nothing. Even without a massive media campaign, I would have expected at least a *little* interest. After all, I was on track to break the record for the fastest run across Canada!

The media vacuum bruised my ego a bit. I'd done a good job thus far controlling it rather than letting it control me. In the past, my ego had often hijacked my values, personality, and ethics, leaving me compromised. Nonetheless, in a moment of weakness, I texted one of their writers offering an interview—and quickly forgot about it.

Thirty kilometres into the day, I got on the phone with CBC Radio to do a live interview. It went well and lasted only about ten minutes. This was only the second interview I had done so far in this run; and in comparison to four years ago, it was like night and day. It wasn't high-profile. It wasn't stressful. The reporter asked questions, and I answered them. They signed off and that was that.

I was just grateful to see that the run still mattered to someone.

Mike wouldn't shut up about how beautiful the farm fields were. I sometimes forgot that people from coastal cities rarely frequented the prairies. Canada is the world's largest exporter of peas, lentils, durum wheat, mustard seed, canola, flaxseed, and oats, and our crops are known internationally for their quality. The brilliance of the bright canola and the glow of the wheat were outshone only by the good people who lived here. I was honored to call myself a son of these prairies and wore my cowboy hat proudly.

Yes, Mike, it's beautiful, I thought. *Glad you noticed.*

At the forty-kilometre stop stood a man with a boyish grin plastered on his face. He was lathered in sunscreen and raring to go for a jog. It was Joel's turn!

A quick bathroom break and we were on our way. The importance of the SUV and their tall doors in these prairie provinces was crucial. In previous provinces I could simply duck into the trees to relieve myself, but out here there were no trees. The land was so flat that if our dog ran away, you could watch him for days before losing sight of him. For restroom breaks, a physical barrier was sorely needed. We'd typically open both doors on the passenger side to create a box. There in the door, I'd have all the necessities for wiping and lubing. I'd then secure waste in a baggy in order to not litter. The efficiency of this routine was much like that of a Formula 1 pit crew, minus the power tools.

As Joel and I got running, much like Mike, he got right into it with a million well-thought-out questions. Joel and Mike had been university roommates and were very similar.

Working in the energy sector in downtown Calgary, Joel had a special talent for honing in on details. Joel was also the kind of guy who went for long runs continually stopping at every dog he passes not only to pet them but to make friends with the owners. He was also a passionate sports fan and willing to debate in detail any number of social issues affecting culture and society. There were no limits to the depth of his character. He was just a well-rounded guy who was interested in everything.

One thing that Joel and I had in common was that we were both easily bothered by others, but in very different ways. We'd often get into debates about some social issue or another; but I always respected that he never took any of it personally and was always willing to change his mind. His wife Caelly was a very lucky woman, as she was married to the most thoughtful man I'd ever met.

Nearing the end of the day, the three of us posed shirtless, myself tanned, sinewy, and sporting an unkempt and lengthy beard, and the two of them pasty-white and fresh-looking, at the "Welcome to Saskatchewan" sign.

A fellow traveler started chatting with us; but when he learnt what we were doing he launched right into comparing me with a well-known runner that I frankly didn't respect much. It triggered me, and I started responding in ways that immediately made me feel terrible about myself. Panicked, I tried to soften what I had said, and made an excuse to get the hell out of there.

I spent the rest of the day's run hating myself for how I came across to a complete stranger. It seemed I wasn't quite out of the post-concussion woods yet.

Following the 108-kilometre day we drove ahead to a complete dive of a motel whose exterior made the dank, stained, cigarette-smelling rat traps we'd stayed in before look like the Waldorf-Astoria.

When we pulled up, a group of cheap-beer-drinking prairie hillbillies were barbecuing in the parking lot and eating steak with their bare hands. Half shit-faced, they came over with smokes dangling from their mouths and said they needed to find out what we were doing there, as though we needed permission to stay at a place like this. We definitely didn't fit in, even given my verging-on-ZZ-Top facial hair, but after I filled them in about the run, they wanted selfies with me and offered us beers.

As we got to know them, I came to appreciate these small-town, blue-collar workers, as they reminded me of my extended family: simple people who say what they mean and mean what they say.

Surprisingly, the inside of the motel was newly renovated and very spacious, yet another reminder to never judge a book by its cover.

Joel stayed up a bit later having a beer with the group outside.

Not long after, we turned out the lights, knowing I'd just run clear across six provinces, with three still to go. 5149 kilometres in 49 days and six days ahead of Al Howie's speed record, I looked forward to entering the land of the Rough Riders.

But for now: *sleep.*

CHAPTER 10: SASKATCHEWAN

Blinders

DAY 50	COMPLETED	REMAINING
108.2 kms in 13:22:56	5257.2 kms	1901.8 kms

Waking up on Day 50, I felt recharged. The day before, I had passed into Mountain Standard Time and was rewarded with an extra hour of sleep. This was now the fourth time passing into a new time zone, and the extra hour of sleep felt *so* damn good. The next and final timezone crossing would be in the Rocky Mountains.

While getting ready for the day, Joel told me that there had been a fatal shooting years ago from the rooftop of this very motel.

My foot felt especially terrible all morning long, but...well, I'd learnt that some days are like that. When I stopped to check on it, the inflammation and mobility hadn't worsened noticeably, so I kept on going.

The boys swapped back and forth running with me all day, picking up the conversation right where they'd left off the day before.

On our morning call, I spoke with Lana Rae about her jumping back into crewing in Medicine Hat instead of three days later in Calgary. We planned logistics, and I could tell that she wanted to be out here just as much as I wanted her to be.

I called my mother for my daily check-in. Her big-hearted nurturing tendencies had a way of wandering off into worry if she didn't hear from me. At home she'd have my live tracker up on her computer all day, watching it tirelessly. She has a hard time wrapping her head around things she doesn't understand, and my running had always been a cause of stress for her. I'd call her every day and paint an edited version of the day, carefully omitting the scary stuff and playing up the fun stuff.

Often she would comment that I wasn't as out-of-breath as she imagined I'd be. I'd remind her that *this is my craft, Mom, and I've been training all of my life to excel in these conditions; so yes, I'm more comfortable than most would believe.*

I'd also try to call my parents when traffic or the wind wasn't terrible as the background noise was too much for them, especially my father. My dad played the role of the cheerleader and would always follow up with a comment about how he didn't know how I could do it. When my mom wasn't around, he would remind me to call more often as Mom needed more reassurance that I was okay.

The carefully controlled structure of my day eliminated most tasks not directly relating to running. My crew did everything aside from running, so I could clear my mind and dedicate every second of every day to putting one foot in front of the other. Fifty days in, I began to worry if I'd remember how to do everyday tasks such as shopping, mowing the lawn, or emptying the dishwasher. Life had become so simplified that even the most basic things seem to elude me. Once, I had completely forgotten the pin number for my credit card and the password for my email. To test myself, I would walk through in my head where the dishes go in my kitchen, and the steps to change the oil in my car. The way I saw it was that the brain took up so much energy as a vital organ that the run challenged the limits of energy expenditure, then I should be responsible for as little as possible.

Lana Rae and my crew were providing me with everything I needed to focus on running. I had to trust that they were doing a much better job than I could.

About three hours before the end of the day, I was tending to nature in a ditch pit-stop when I felt a couple of pinches on the bottom of my foot. After whipping my shoe and sock off, I saw a large maroon tick scamper away. After checking both feet and my legs, we all agreed upon a no-ditch policy going forward. I wasn't about to argue the point. Ticks have always given me the heebie-jeebies.

We closed the book on another 108-kilometre effort by sinking our teeth into a delicious deep-dish pizza later that night.

Now officially off the clock from the day's running, my foot reminded me that we had unfinished business. It throbbed agonizingly all night, and I repeated in my mind:

Don't offer it space, don't give it attention, don't allow it room to grow.

Piercing Pain

DAY 51	COMPLETED	REMAINING
106.7 kms in 12:29:01	5363.9 kms	1795.1 kms

I awoke the next day to see Mike on his phone.

He mentioned that he had been having a couple issues back

home; that one of his kids was acting up and the other was managing his business and its employees from afar. He reassured me that everything was under control, but I could tell that shit was going down and that he didn't want me to worry about it. On one hand. Mike desperately desired to be out here; on the other, he wanted to manage those conflicts as best as he could at a distance.

That duality I knew too well.

By far, the largest struggle I'd yet to overcome had been abandoning my kids to be out here. I hadn't seen them in just under two months, and for a dad who was very present, that was like torture.

I'd tell myself that I was doing the best thing for them by being out here, showing them firsthand lessons on goal setting, mindset mastery, expanding boundaries, leadership, strategic vision, preparation, and shattering limits. Those bullet points look compelling in a PowerPoint presentation but do very little to lessen the guilt, knowing I had been absent for daily homework, soccer games in the backyard, important conversations, and making lunches.

All the things that I had signed up for when deciding to be a parent I was now neglecting. And though I tried to call them daily, sometimes I felt as if they were screening my calls in order to avoid another valuable life lesson from their old man.

Around fifty kilometres into the day, with a forecast that called for rain but so far had only produced threatening clouds and a nice, strong tailwind, I was running alongside Mike on a wide shoulder with our backs to traffic. I'd keep listening for the sound of tires crossing the rumble strip so we could jump out of the way.

Suddenly, mid-conversation, I felt a very strong wind from behind, and turned to see a large pickup truck driving on the wrong side of the rumble strip. It must have crossed the rumble strip way back, because I hadn't heard it coming. Seeing, hearing, and *feeling* this idiot blowing past us at 100 km/hour only inches from my arm made us both jump six feet in the air.

Mike, who is typically a pretty laid-back dude, started yelling F-bombs at the top of his lungs, running faster as if to catch up with the asshole and kick his ass.

Speaking for myself, this wasn't the first time and probably wouldn't be the last that I'd had a close call with a shitty driver. In the past, I'd been working with Erin on releasing stress, fear, and anger so that I didn't carry it forward. If I allowed the fear of traffic to permeate my mind and stagnate, the energy it'd take to manage it would be enormous. By itself, stress was exhausting, but out here it could be crippling.

There was no better release than tilting my head back, arms stretched, and yelling it out.

I stopped dead in my tracks, took a deep breath, and having regained my composure, screamed at the top of my lungs, "FFFFUUUUCCCCKKKK!" Then I looked at Mike and said, "Now that's done, let's keep going."

The clouds cried on us for the remainder of the day. At least this time, the rain waited for the truck to pass, sparing us the demoralizing wall of water.

I had seen a lot of wet days by now and had gotten used to the sloshing of my feet. As we got closer to Regina, the capital of Saskatchewan, the traffic picked up approaching rush hour. The increased traffic and soaking wet roads gave me a brand-new problem: a pounding headache. I'd never suffered headaches in my life, and this new sensation was certainly not welcome.

Mike had swapped out with Joel by now, and I ran alongside Joel and the traffic picked up, so did the pounding in my head. Noise-cancelling earbuds seemed to help, but not enough. Joel mentioned that maybe the headache had been a result of my concussion ten days ago, and that seemed very plausible. As we entered the city, I glanced constantly at my watch, praying that the countdown to the end of the day would come faster.

My head felt like a ticking time bomb with a very short fuse. At one point after a small overpass, the pain became too much, and I knelt down and started crying like a baby.

Joel softly put his hand on my back and gently urged me to get going. He said we only had five kilometres to go before reaching the hotel. I pleaded with him to call Mike and get him to drive back to pick us up. This was the first time in fifty-one days I had ever wanted to stop early. I felt I just couldn't handle it anymore.

I could see the sympathy in Joel's eyes as he struggled with urging me to continue. He didn't want to push me anywhere I wasn't capable of going, but we had so little left to go, and he knew how I'd feel once we'd reached the hotel and I unpacked all my mental baggage about stopping the day early.

After an uplifting and truly motivational speech, Joel convinced me to slow our pace. "Let's see how the next kilometre goes," he said. "Baby steps. We'll get there."

Slouching my head and nearly dragging myself forward, we proceeded silently, cursing at all the vehicles generating the piercing noise that penetrated my skull.

Stopping my GPS watch in the hotel lobby, I retreated to the quiet hotel room in extreme pain. This feeling in my head was both inescapable and unusually unpleasant. The rest of the night was a disaster. Flooded with immediate despair, I felt angry and sad. Maxing out on zopiclone, Advil, and Tylenol, I closed my eyes hoping that this pain would be gone when I woke.

Survival Over Reward

DAY 52	COMPLETED	REMAINING
107.5 kms in 12:45:08	5471.3 kms	1687.7 kms

Finishing right at the hotel allowed for a bit of a sleep in, and I noticed when the alarm went off that the headache had vanished.

This made me extremely happy.

We got rolling, and due to Regina's ring road, I only needed one left turn to skirt the city. The sound of tires on wet asphalt from the handful of cars passing by still caused an incredible piercing sound that promptly rekindled the previous day's headache. Thinking about how I had suffered during the final hour of that run and projecting that forward for the remainder of today filled my soul with dread.

Lost for words, Joel would divide the long silences with the occasional, "You've got this", "One step at a time", or "Hang in there."

At moments like this, it was easy to locate the proverbial exit doors. Those exit doors lined the road with large neon signs that glowed with all the reasons that quitting made sense.

Slow down, buddy. Sit down, take a nice long break. You don't have to put up with this. You can take a long lunch, then stop for the day. Go take a nap. Hell, you can rest for a whole day. Nothing bad will happen. Come on, you know you want it....

All day, every day, for the last fifty-two days, the exits had been there. Some would be hiding in the trees, and some would be so close to the shoulder I'd need to twist my body to squeeze by. The difference between today and most other days was that I was intentionally looking for them. I'd pretend that I wasn't, but I spent a lot of time locating them and contemplating the what-ifs.

Just open that door, maybe walk inside. Might be a comfy quiet couch in there.

Moments like this reminded me that we choose our pain, and my choice was either the pain of the doing or the pain of the regret.

Given my headache, I strongly considered forgoing my weekly therapy appointment with Erin, but the boys convinced me otherwise, so I connected with her at 10 a.m. Right away, she reminded me that humans will always choose survival over reward, that the survival instinct hijacks our decision-making process. We're built to favour living to fight another day over the risk of failure or death. In Canada, in 2022, death is not a realistic outcome, but thousands of years of mental programming had hardwired our deepest instincts to plead with us for safety when we were in trouble.

Those instincts are wrong 99.999% of the time—yet we perceive them as fact and give up without even trying.

In other words, it was normal to feel this way, but that didn't mean I had to succumb to it. I had a choice. I could take the feelings of the moment at face value, or I could take a closer look at the situation. A closer look would tell me that this was a transient feeling and that I'd be just fine. I had plenty of food, water, warm clothes, shelter, and comfort. I was healthy. The worst thing I had going was a very uncomfortable headache, but I'd manage.

Hearing this flipped a switch somewhere in my head. Taking control of how I viewed this problem changed everything. When I ended our call, the headache was still there, but I had a different point of view. The boys noticed the difference immediately and couldn't praise Erin enough.

Minutes later I got a call from a writer at the Canadian running publication I'd texted earlier with no reply. Shortly after answering, though, I could tell something was off. We'd spoken many times in the past, but this time she seemed inexplicably cold and quickly launched into a barrage of questions challenging the legitimacy of this run.

She quizzed me on very specific details of my Strava profile, the live GPS tracker on the Performance Tea website, a two-kilometre section missing from an area in Ontario, and much more.

The tone, delivery, and questions felt like a deliberate attack on my ethics and character. For example, she questioned why the live tracker only showed the previous four days. I suggested that she click the large button labeled "Show All", and after clicking she curtly replied, "Okay, that resolves *that.*"

It didn't take a rocket scientist to figure out that she was suggesting that I was cheating. As we talked, I was getting increasingly agitated and found myself taking walking breaks.

I felt as if a crazed vigilante were trying to take me down, dead or alive.

And it seemed to me that her questions and lack of research reflected both incompetence and gross professional negligence. At the same time she pressed me on Strava details, she told me that she actually hadn't visited my account. In hindsight, I should have asked how she came up with these questions if she hadn't even acquainted herself with my public Strava data.

I did my best to remain calm while we talked, but ended the call furious, and called Lana Rae to share what had just happened.

Post-concussion, today's headache, and now this!

Aside from being pissed-off and sympathetic, she did drop an "I told you so." She had warned me in recent days to be careful, that if a writer wanted an interview then they'd reach out to me. This time, my ego had gotten the best of me, thinking that they should be interested in a story like mine, and it had come back to bite me on the ass.

I remained pissed the rest of the day.

The boys and Lana Rae did their best to calm me. The noise from traffic was still bothering me big time, so the boys thought it was a good idea to get me off the highway and onto a side gravel road where it was calmer and I could collect myself. This was a great idea, and it was nice to have a noise reprieve even if it lengthened the run slightly.

With about thirty minutes left to run, I heard from the boys that her article had been published.

I took a walk break to read it. Instead of celebrating the monumental effort, the insubstantial article did its best to cast doubt on the run. Despite my corrections of the reporter's misinformation, they had still elected to publish it, perhaps hoping to discredit me, perhaps simply hoping to attract attention.

At the end of the day, we retreated to the hotel, where I sent a lengthy email proclaiming my disappointment in the article. Unsurprisingly, I received no reply.

A month later, a friend of the late Al Howie published a post on my personal Facebook page, saying that he could not congratulate me on the speed record as he had questions about the run's legitimacy.

I now wondered if someone had fed this reporter false information in hopes of protecting his late friend's record. The data he cited on Facebook was the same data that she had walked me through on the phone. It looked to me as if someone had contrived a plan to use this publication to spread doubt about my record attempt, rather than approaching me directly with questions.

Surely the running publication had better things to do than pick on a trivial glitch in satellite data or engage in conspiracy theories about how I had completed 99.999 percent of the run but inexplicably fudged or omitted .001 percent of the data. Strange people do strange things, but the sad thing was that this once-reputable publication had doubled down on its terrible judgement, perhaps at the request of someone with vested interests and a highly visible agenda.

I went to sleep angry in hopes that I'd sleep it off and feel better in the morning.

Shaky Ground

	DAY 53	COMPLETED	REMAINING
	106.6 kms in 13:17:40	5577.9 kms	1581.1 kms

I woke on Day 53 still angry.

The boys intentionally kept it light, telling jokes and picking on one another, and this effort of theirs did help some.

When we got out to the gravel road where I had finished the day before and spotted the marker, I walked east one hundred meters and started running.

The morning's sunrise had Mike oohing and aahing all morning long. He'd run ahead to snap pictures of it, grinning ear to ear.

A few minutes into the day the hard packed gravel shifted to a deep loose gravel, and my right foot soon screamed in agony. It was obvious that my fractured foot did not enjoy the unstable surface. I asked Mike how long we had to go until we emptied back onto the Trans-Canada Highway.

Mike looked at his phone and guessed about ten kilometres.

After thinking about it for a bit, I told him I could stick it out but was looking forward to the familiar asphalt again. What I hadn't seen coming was how paying attention to the loose gravel to find foot placements upset my head. The post-concussion headache had returned, and it truly was the pits. Running in silence, I tried my best to remember everything Erin and I had discussed before and repeated to myself, *we always choose survival over reward. But I'm not dying out here. I'll be fine.*

Twenty kilometres into the day, Mike and I reached the point where Joel awaited with the car at the Trans Canada highway. I told the boys that I needed a ten-minute nap in the front seat before I got going again, and they both agreed that was a good idea. I sat there with my head in my hands and even the slight wind was an irritant. I could tell that the boys felt that their decision to take me on gravel late in the previous day was now causing trouble. I told them to not sweat it, and that I would have made the same choice.

The next several hours I struggled to mitigate the foot and head pain, but as time went on things got better.

As my thoughts drifted, my mind kept circling back to the debacle with this running publication. Aside from letting my ego get the best of me, I had been frustrated by a couple things. First, it really bothered me that media these days gravitated to bad news instead of good news. Second, you don't need to look far to find catastrophe, so this tendency turns judging others into entertainment. Ordinary people watch hours of reality television every week with one goal in mind: to make fun of others and to feel better about themselves.

The damage this does to the hopes, dreams, and lives of real people is unconscionable.

During the 2022 Badwater 135, Ashley Paulson had crushed the field; but due to technical failure—really, just a battery that ran down—the media circus tried to discredit her before she even had time to produce her data. When her data and reports established that her performance had been legitimately documented and confirmed, the media were nowhere to be found.

Starting a dumpster fire, walking away, and denying responsibility should be considered a crime.

What I find even more appalling is that the media only gives us what we want. The judgement of others isn't a new phenomenon, but it has ramped up in the past couple decades. Real news is overshadowed by allegations of cheating and false narratives designed to intentionally cut down the tall trees and make those who dare nothing feel better about their mediocrity.

Come on, people, we're better than this!

My pace for the remainder of the day was sluggish at best. The one silver lining was that I got to run with Kevin, a proper cowboy from Swift Current. We had run together during my first Trans Canada attempt in 2018, and his attitude was contagious.

Nearing the end of the day we noticed an open bag peeking through the tall grass in the ditch. Now, if you've been reading this far, you know that sometimes the Ditch Gods giveth (cold beer from friends) and sometimes they taketh away.

Well, upon closer examination, the bag turned out to be a drug kit with syringes, rubber bands, and a crack pipe—literally not my bag.

But definitely the Ditch Find of the Day!

Due to the slowest average pace that day, I didn't have much time for body care, so I missed out on very necessary minutes massaging, stretching, rolling, pain relief, and otherwise coaxing my body into getting ready for another day.

Instead, I went to bed with my foot in pain, and there wasn't anything I could really do about it.

Tough Cowboy

DAY 54	COMPLETED	REMAINING
107 kms in 12:46:52	5684.9 kms	1474.1 kms

The tiny motel room had us three grown men packed like sardines.

I felt bad because the farts I had during this run were legendary due to the volume of junk food I had been consuming to get calories, salt, carbs, fat, and protein on board. My gas had been so bad last night that the smell even woke me up. So it was perhaps not surprising that, as we went through our usual morning routine, we were all anxious to hit the road.

In typical fashion, I connected with Lana Rae on the phone at 5 a.m. Our morning "coffee in bed" regime has been unshakable since we first started dating. She loved the mornings just as much as I did, and it was truly a treat to enjoy something special together. We chatted about a lot of things, but mostly about how much we are looking forward to seeing one another in less than forty-eight hours.

Despite injuries and considerable discomfort, my fitness had really developed into something special. Seven and a half weeks of continuous 100-plus kilometre days had me feeling more comfortable running than sitting, walking, or lying down.

As the day grew older, the land that opened in front of me looked more and more like home, with familiar farms blanketed in abundant crops tended by hardworking people. I could almost smell Alberta, and it smelled good.

About fourteen years ago, I signed up for a race with a deathly hot forecast. Shortly before the race, I bought a case of beer that came with a cowboy hat. It gave better coverage than any other hat I owned, so I wore it for the race. I ran well, stayed cool, and won. Ever since, it's been my hat of choice.

Prior to the 2018 Outrun Rare run, I had partnered with Smithbilt Hats to create the very first running-specific cowboy hat, the "Outrunner," and a portion of sales had gone to the Rare Disease Foundation. My trusty Outrunner was keeping me company for every step of this run too. It was comfortable as all get-out, provided shade, protected me from hail, kept me dry in the rain, but most importantly, looked sharp.

What was even more amazing was how it made me feel: like a superhero. The hat was my power suit. Wearing it, I felt like the real thing: smart, capable, and confident.

Every morning, when I stepped onto the road, the first thing I did was put my hat on. Just like that, I transformed into an unshakable stone-cold killer who got the job done. *Dave Proctor, Toughest Son-of-a-Bitch in the West. And Man of Few Words...So Pay Attention.*

It was the hat I wore to the Gunfight with the Open Road. Maybe that should even be the title of a Clint Eastwood movie, the one where he plays the grittiest, roughest, toughest old bastard around, the Man Who Will Not Die. There ain't no quit in this cowboy, and the only justifiable reason for failure was being hauled off the highway on a stretcher.

At midday I had the pleasure of doing my weekly podcast interview with *Chasing Tomorrow*. This week was special, because it wasn't just Performance Tea's Joe Gagnon and me on the line—we were hosting my modern-day running hero, Pete Kostelnick.

In 2016 Pete broke the 36-year-old record for the fastest run across the United States by running 4,938 kilometres from San Francisco to New York in 42 days, 6 hours and 30 minutes, averaging 115 kilometres per day. We had become good friends over the years, and his record stands as one of the greatest athletic achievements of all time.

As I ran, Pete and I exchanged stories that only two guys like us could. I told him that I felt very lonely out here but was worried about being even lonelier after I was done, as there was almost no one that had an experience comparable to mine. Pete said that he felt the same, and still did to this day. We rambled on, at times giggling like schoolkids about our very personal shared experiences. We took turns saying, "I know, right?" and shared experiences we knew only a handful of people in the world would understand.

I left that conversation feeling like a million bucks and I couldn't wait to tell the boys all about it.

As I finished the day with my watch reading 107 kilometres, we drove back to a ratty motel. The rooms were so tiny we opted to get two of them; but I speculated the real reason was the horrid smell of my farts.

I stayed quiet. I could use a bed of my own anyway.

We ate our weight in noodles as Vera filmed away.

Alberta-Bound

DAY 55	COMPLETED	REMAINING
106.6 kms in 12:12:30	5791.5 kms	1367.5 kms

Day 55 would be my last day running in Saskatchewan, as my maps showed I was due to pop into Alberta about 90 kilometres into the day.

While I got ready in my room, I heard a commotion next door. Joel announced with concern that Mike had quite the evening and this morning things had been worse. The situation with his teen had escalated, Mike had chipped his front tooth opening a pop bottle, and to top it off, he had just locked both of them out of their motel room. The good news was that everything needed to get me running was already in the car. The plan was for Mike to drive the two of us out to start the run, and he would circle back to sort out the room thing.

When I got out to the SUV, Mike was already sitting in the driver's seat, completely still. If he had been a cartoon character, it would have been one of those with a red face, clenched fists and steam coming out of his ears.

I tried to lighten the mood. "Teeth aren't tools, Mike."

The joke fell flat. Mike's gaze didn't shift an inch, and he remained both silent and expressionless.

218

After some time, Mike got around to mentioning that his right knee was now starting to bother him, so he'd need to shorten his 50-kilometre run days with me to something more manageable. That was fine, I said, but Mike appeared disappointed in himself. He had been a very generous friend with so much going on in his life; and yet, he still remained out here with me. That meant a lot.

On the drive out I gently reassured him that if he needed to get back to patching some holes in his professional and personal life, I totally understood.

Mike forced a toothless grin and said, "It's all good. Things will sort themselves out."

From the get-go that morning, my pace was rocket-speed. My legs and spirit felt good.

One reason for the bump in my pace was my excitement about crossing into Alberta. I was raised in Alberta and will always call Alberta home. I felt a special pull at my heart as we approached the place I associated with restful times, even though until I reached the finish, zero rest would be granted.

Another reason I was excited was that I knew that at the end of the day, I'd be in the arms of the one I love. As we'd discussed, Lana Rae was driving out from Okotoks to Medicine Hat and would meet me at the hotel that evening. With this constant pain and discomfort I had been feeling, I ached for the comforts of her embrace more ever. The longing for her brought me to tears many times in the past several days, and that morning was no different.

The third reason, and a very understandable one, was that I would be breaking in a new pair of Altra Riveras today. The relieving cushion of a new pair of kicks is better than sex out here. I had brought twelve pairs of Riveras on this trip, and I'd worn through nine of them so far. The plan was to cycle three pairs at a time, marking them with a Sharpie as one, two, and three. In a three-day period, I'd wear one pair all day and then cycle them out for the next pair, then the next. Then another three the day after that, and back around to pair one. I would go through this cycle six times, and on day eighteen I'd toss them and start a new cycle with new shoes. After 630 kilometres, a pair of shoes would be properly worn through. Today I'd be breaking in a shiny new pair, and felt like I was dancing the foxtrot on the moon.

I thought many times throughout the day how incredible it was that I'd only developed two blisters so far. I'd seen pictures and heard stories of other crossers whose feet were carpeted with blisters. Just the sight of it was hard to stomach. I prepared myself mentally for this kind of suffering, but God knows why I hadn't encountered it. Maybe it was the socks, maybe it was the shoes, maybe it was luck—or maybe it was all of the above.

I'd glance occasionally at my watch, expecting to see the usual 6 min/km pace. Instead when I looked down, I saw 5:30 min/km. "Boy, I love that girl," I exclaimed. The Saskatchewan hills flattened as the valleys opened up in front of me. This was the last breather before the fields broke back into foothills and abruptly launched us into the Rocky Mountains.

The boys got out and ran with me throughout the day. As Mike pulled back his mileage, Joel was picking his up, running his first 50-kilometre day with me. He and I had been running in tandem for a while when I looked up, and for the first time in 5780 kilometres, saw a sign that said:

WELCOME TO ALBERTA

I broke into tears as we approached, trying to keep my composure as I noticed Vera standing ahead with her camera facing me.

Oh my heavens, this feels good.

I stopped for a quick food break. I didn't stay long. The boys shoveled in some watermelon and I drank a Coke. As I took my first steps into my home province, I played one of my favorite songs on repeat the rest of the day, Paul Brandt's *Alberta Bound*.

    I'm Alberta bound.

This piece of heaven that I've found.
Rocky Mountains and black fertile ground.
Everything I need beneath that big blue sky.
It doesn't matter where I go;
This place will always be my home.
Yeah, I've been Alberta–bound for all my life.
And I'll be Alberta–bound until I die.

The remaining fifteen kilometres were my fastest across the country as I floated across the earth towed by my heart. Upon completing the usual 108 kilometres, we still had to drive another 40 kilometres to arrive at the hotel in Medicine Hat.

And there she was, standing at the loading dock of the hotel with a smile so big that it mirrored mine. I sprang from my seat and swept her into my arms.

The boys told us that they were going down to the restaurant to eat dinner and not to expect them back anytime soon as a few beers might be involved.

And Lana Rae and I fell asleep that night entangled in one another's arms, holding tight and never wanting to let go.

CHAPTER 11: THE CAPTAIN'S CHAIR

—Lana Rae Ledene

It was early in our relationship when Dave started to talk about making another attempt to run across Canada in 2022. I didn't yet know Dave when he made his 2018 attempt; I had just followed a bit of his journey online and heard tales from our mutual physiotherapist about his journey.

When Dave started talking about the run, he was planning to use it as a platform for an awareness campaign, heading across the country with a caravan of RVs. He wanted me involved, but I was hesitant. I couldn't live out of an RV for weeks, nor did I want to live in a media circus. I'm a relatively private person, and I don't like being followed around by a camera or being in the spotlight in any way.

I told Dave I'd do it, but in order for me to stay sane, it had to look very different from his first attempt. I agreed to get onboard if he made three changes.

First, it had to be scaled back and simplified.

Second, I asked him to do this for himself, for his dream, and for his future. I knew that if he wasn't doing this for himself and if he didn't think he was worthy of this goal, he would never be successful. I felt strongly that Dave had to do it for Dave

Oh, and I also felt strongly about hotels: we had to stay in hotels every night. Other trans con attempts I'd read about often involved sleeping in tents, cars, trailers and even ditches. I travel a lot for work and l was no stranger to living out of a suitcase— but I needed a proper bed with clean sheets and blankets, and a shower every day that didn't run out of hot water.

Dave agreed, appointed me as his crew chief, and we went into planning mode. My one goal throughout planning and execution was to set the run up so that all Dave had to think about was putting one foot in front of the other every day, and nothing else.

I had his route, which was fairly straightforward. He planned to run 105 kilometres a day, so we marked out 105-kilometre segments on the map and I went to work. I booked the hotels for the first two weeks of the run and always had them booked out by only two weeks. If we had a major setback, I didn't want to go through the hassle of cancelling and rebooking forty-plus hotel rooms. It was tricky to say the least, especially in remote parts of Ontario that offered only hunting and fishing lodges many miles away from the Trans-Canada Highway.

I also had to figure out where and when the rest of his crew would fly in and out of major cities and coordinate our schedule and theirs without causing havoc for Dave's timeline. When I was out there with Dave for the first two weeks it was fairly easy to assume the crew chief role. I was there. I could control everything. I was also on vacation from work, so I didn't have other obligations competing for my time.

My two weeks on the road with Dave came to an end and I left him in New Brunswick. After returning home, leading the crew from Okotoks took on a life of its own. I was no longer on vacation and was juggling Dave's needs with a fast-paced sales job at Canada's largest financial institution. I'd be up at 4 a.m. most mornings, looking at where Dave stopped the night before, and poring over maps, making sure the next few hotels were as close to our 105-kilometre endpoints as possible. Dave and I talked for hours on the phone every day, sharing stories from the road and updates from home. Other days were spent trying to calm him, navigate his mood swings, and provide solutions for problems that were happening many, many miles away, often in other time zones.

When Dave's brother Dan started crewing him in Ottawa, it became evident very quickly that the crew duties were a lot for one person to manage, especially for someone who didn't have prior experience with competitive ultrarunning and didn't have an instinct for what Dave needed out there. To help out, I started taking on dinner obligations. I'd find out what local restaurants were close to the hotel and place an order for pick-up or delivery so dinner would be available for Dave within 15 minutes of his arrival at the hotel.

That was the thing I liked doing the least. Dave's dinner was one of the few true luxuries he looked forward to every day, and I always wanted to get it right. He loved anything that resembled comfort food, and he didn't make ordering dinner easy on me. I'd call him and announce, "Dave, I found you ribs and mashed potatoes for dinner, your favorite!"

He would reply by asking, "Are they side ribs or back ribs?"

I'd think to myself, *Good grief, does it matter?!*

At the beginning and end of every day, Dave's crew took on the role of sherpa. I think we had about 5 bags we had to lug into the hotel room every night and back out to the SUV in the morning. The bags were full of breakfast supplies, recovery tools, toiletries, a change of clothes for Dave, two coolers, water jugs and dirty laundry if it was laundry day. It was a great day when we arrived at a hotel and they had a luggage cart!

Finally, July 8 arrived: the day I was going to join Dave on the

224

road again. I had hardly slept a wink the night before and it seemed like forever since I had last seen his chiseled face.

Dave and I spent our first hour of every day on the phone together; but this time, we had been unable to connect all day. A Canada-wide Rogers Network outage meant I could not see where he was on the tracker, I could not speak to him on the phone, or even text him or any of his crew. Given that the entire country was disconnected and it was impossible to connect with colleagues and clients anyway, so I left work early that day and headed to Medicine Hat.

I arrived in Medicine Hat just as cell service resumed, and I could see Dave was finished running and headed back to the hotel with his crew, Joel and Mike. As I waited for them to arrive, I thought of the man I left behind in Ottawa. His spirits had been high and so he had moved quickly, with a spring in every step. He had looked lean and strong and his face had been flecked with grey stubble. As the SUV pulled up and I saw his cowboy hat on the front dash, I was so excited!

Dave would tell you that he threw open the SUV door, leapt from the vehicle and swept me off my feet in a big embrace.

Let me tell you what really happened.

The front passenger door opened, and as his long, tanned leg appeared, he gingerly put his foot on the ground. The other leg came out slowly and it took him a full 30 seconds to stand up on both feet. The man standing in front of me looked nothing like the one I left in Ottawa. This rail-thin man looked 20 years older, had a full ratty beard, and skin so tanned it looked like brown couch leather.

Dave started to shuffle towards me, grinning from ear to ear; that much is true, but he could barely pick up his feet and when he embraced me, I am quite sure I was holding up his full weight, which was actually very easy. It was like hugging a bundle of trekking poles. I didn't care. I was back where I needed to be.

That night, Joel and Mike wanted to give Dave a bit of space, so they took my SUV to a local car wash. They completely emptied it of all the gear bins, garbage and dirty running shoes. They cleaned and detailed my SUV and set it all back up again so that everything was fresh and clean. What a treat! I'm someone who struggles to live in a messy environment with clutter and chaos, and those two guys just spoke to my heart. Not only were they looking after Dave, but they were looking after me, too.

I quickly fell back into the crew groove with a few new responsibilities. The media were now starting to request interviews. They always wanted to know where Dave was going to stop during the day so they could be there to interview him; or they wanted to come to the hotel at night to interview him. They didn't seem to understand that Dave needed every bit of sunlight and quite a bit of darkness just to pound out the miles, nor did they seem to understand his need for food, rest, and sleep.

I gave all the media outlets the same two options: they could talk to him on the phone while he was running, or they could come and run with him on the highway. Not surprisingly, no one ever chose to run with him on the highway.

Now that we were at fifty-plus days of continuous running and it was mid-July, there were two other things I had to stay on top of that I hadn't had to worry about in the first few weeks of the run. One was making sure we always had ice on hand, and the second was calling ahead to hotels to ensure that the rooms I booked were on the ground floor or had an elevator. If I could back up to a motel room door, that was even better. Dave was in no condition to climb stairs.

At the end of each day's run, I had to help him take off his shoes and socks as he could no longer bend over. Even lifting his arms over his head to take off his shirt was a challenge. After he showered, I'd get him set up on the bed in his recovery pants and put his dinner in his lap, where he would eat until exhaustion took over.

As the days ticked by, I was increasingly worried. Every night dread and confusion filled my thoughts. I dreaded the possibility that he was too broken to be physically capable of finishing this run.

Yet I struggled to reconcile the man I saw at night with the man I saw during the day. His foot was a mess, swollen so badly that we had to ice it morning and night. If he got up from bed to go to the bathroom, he'd hold on to every wall and every piece of furniture to support his frail body and take weight off his legs and foot.

Even distracted and carrying on a conversation, it would have taken me about 10 seconds to walk to the bathroom. For Dave, it was a two-minute journey played out in slow motion.

I recall one night in particular, close to the sixtieth day, watching him shuffle around and wince in pain. I thought, *he is not going to be able to run tomorrow; how am I going to manage this? He is going to be devastated that he can't finish this run. What are we going to do?*

But I never said any of this out loud, and I doubt that Dave would have taken it well if I had.

One night, when Vera was in the room filming, she whispered to me "How is this happening? How can he run like this?"

I honestly didn't know.

The mornings weren't much better. I'd have to help put on his socks and shoes and help him out to the SUV, all the while thinking, *he isn't going to be able to run today, he can barely walk. Maybe he'll decide to take a day off or maybe he'll call me after a few hours and say that he has to cut the day short.*

Once I even thought that maybe he'd walk the entire day and we'd finish close to midnight.

But none of that ever happened.

Though Dave was clearly broken, beyond exhausted and a ghost of his former self, every morning we'd pull up to the pinwheel marker we had placed the night before, he'd slide gingerly out of the SUV, put on his cowboy hat, and start running.

Every day, he would crank out another 105 kilometres like clockwork, like it wasn't even hard.

Something happened in those moments that I still struggle to fully put into words. It was as if there were two Daves out there. Or perhaps he changed into another person when he started to run. It was as if he put all the things that didn't serve him out on the highway in the SUV, closed the door, and left them behind.

Sure, the first few steps were always shaky but he was running.

I would wait for the phone call from him telling me he couldn't continue and to please come and get him, but that call never came.

And when Dave started running every morning, there was no struggle to get in 100+ kilometres for the day. I never had to coax him out of bed and I never had to shoo him away from the crew SUV. Every day he finished at the same time, give or take 20-30 minutes.

It was as if he didn't struggle at all to get it done.

Unswayed by Covid-19, a hard hit to the head, a broken foot, and scorching temperatures, Dave's miraculous consistency was something I don't think I'll ever fully understand.

CHAPTER 12: ALBERTA

Time with the Lady

DAY 56	COMPLETED	REMAINING
107.5 kms in 12:49:18	5899 kms	1260 kms

God knows how late the boys had stayed up the previous night, as we certainly didn't hear them come in. Those 4 a.m. wakeup calls get old pretty quickly, so we decided to let them sleep in and figured they could just jump back on the crazy train at the 40-kilometre mark.

As we headed out to the start point east of Medicine Hat, sitting next to Lana Rae wasn't close enough and I kept reaching out, touching and hugging. It's easy to get annoyed with that sort of thing when you're driving, but I had caught her at the right moment, and we were surrounded by silliness and love and pure happiness at being together in this moment.

She dropped me off, and 20 kilometres later, parked the SUV and ran back to meet me so we could run together.

By the time she got back, the glow of the morning was nearly perfect as a Canadian-Pacific locomotive thundered past, giving us a big ol' blast of its horn. Lana Rae loved every bit of it— except the traffic. I'd become numb to it, but she's cautious and probably will never get over the fact that out here, vehicles zoom by at unreal speeds all day long. Nevertheless, we both really enjoyed the morning together running into Medicine Hat.

This town brought back memories of 2018, when a tornado touched down here during my run. I remembered vividly the exhaustion and chaos, the feeling that I had no control over anything that mattered.

The contrast could not have been starker. Now, I felt like I had *complete* control. I felt like four years later, I had *become* the tornado, ripping through Medicine Hat and replacing bad memories with good ones. Now, with two crew vehicles, we were better organized and more relaxed, and better able to shop for supplies and hit up the ever-important local bakeries.

The morning's momentum eventually dwindled, and around the fifty-kilometre mark, I started feeling unusually tired.

But today, my legs felt heavy and my heart rate spiked. I increased my fluids, electrolytes, and fuel, but the fatigue didn't lessen. Was this the price of yesterday's surge of speed?

Not knowing what was really going on underneath it all, I tried to be kind to my bruised body and practiced patience with my pace.

Prepared to grind out the rest of the day, my energy levels suddenly recovered at the 70-kilometre pit stop when I looked up to see a beautiful woman and a handsome man out here in the middle of nowhere, exiting an unexpectedly familiar truck. Natasha and Johnny Hubbard!

My best friends had driven out from Calgary to finish off Day 56 with me, their skinny friend, hauling out a banquet of baked goods including a donut the size of my head. It was an absolute treat to run the final four hours alongside John, who's one of the few people that truly "get" me.

We've known each other since our kids were tiny. We'd routinely get together on Friday nights after our kids were in bed to fit a long run into our hectic schedules. Suffering together through those miles after a long work week, when all we really wanted to do was sit down with a six-pack and watch the game, had forged an unshakable bond.

So today, we ran, shared stories, exchanged advice, caught up, and most importantly, added another shared experience to our long friendship as we rolled into Alberta.

As we hugged goodbye and they headed back home, Lana Rae and I rushed back to Brooks to meet my colleague and physiotherapist buddy, Tyson.

Tyson and I had met eighteen years ago as new therapists at a sports physio clinic in downtown Calgary. We became instant friends, sending each other patient referrals and treating each other's athletic injuries, forming deep insight into each other's body patterns and biomechanics.

Since then, he had established himself as Calgary's top physiotherapist for elite athletes, treating the city's top athletes, and knowing that he'd be here to work miracles on my broken body had kept me going during the last few days.

Grabbing a quick shower so I wouldn't gross him out too much, I heard his knock, opened the door to that familiar smile, and gave him a big hug.

He wasted no time getting to work. He's a master of dry needling and intramuscular stimulation, so I happily played the role of human pincushion as he expertly released tissues and mobilized joints that I'd thought were hopelessly locked up. My shameless oohs and ahhs were audible to both the boys and Lana Rae.

When I asked Tyson what he thought was causing the severe pain in my right foot, he simply said, "Well, it's hard to say." But I could tell from his expression that he thought it was bad news. And months later, back in Calgary, I discovered that he knew right away my foot was fractured—but seeing no point in telling me what he suspected I already knew, had simply packed up his stuff with a smile and wished me good luck.

Trust is everything when working with a physiotherapist. When I went to bed that evening, I knew with certainty that my trust had been well-placed and that I'd feel like a new man tomorrow.

Julia, Sam, and Adele

DAY 57	COMPLETED	REMAINING
108.7 kms in 12:30:34	6007.7 kms	1151.3 kms

I awoke at 3:30 a.m. to the familiar bruised feeling of tenderized tissue—but as always, after moving around some and using the Theragun, noticed significant improvement.

Day 57 was bittersweet—a day closer to our goal, but the final day with Joel and Mike. The boys had been spectacular, and I had enjoyed every moment out here with them. They brought a colour and a spirit that was unique and special and would be greatly missed.

On the other hand, my parents would be arriving with Julia, Sam, and Adele. I couldn't wait! I hadn't seen my kids for over two months, the longest stretch of time I'd ever been away from them, and we had big plans: a pizza party and family time.

Missing my little people felt heavy and crippling. I struggled daily with shame and regret that I was not there for them while I was out here pursuing this very selfish endeavour. As much as they reassured me that it was okay, I knew they'd rather have me at home making sandwiches, telling dad jokes, holding movie nights, and doing everyday family things.

We had started our day thirty minutes early to give me more time with the kids and my parents, and my family was at the front of my mind from the first step. I anticipated their warm embrace all day long, and it fueled me more than they'd ever know.

My three monkeys are the most wonderful people I know. My sixteen-year-old, Julia, is the bedrock of the family. I could count on one hand the number of times I'd ever worried about her. She has it all going for her: a straight-A student, always on time, disciplined, and a strong north star when it comes to values and ethics.

My middle child, Sam, now thirteen, was a tender, kind, and super-smart little man with heaps of potential yet to be realized. He was by far the most organized of the three, largely due to the demands of his lifelong rare disease, and his problem-solving and resilience always amazed and inspired me.

Eleven-year-old Adele, the youngest, was my mini-me. She and I shared ninety percent of our best qualities. She was tenacious and busy with an overactive EQ. She felt all the feelings when she wanted to, and ignored things when the moment called for it. Our similarities sometimes made me an overly-involved parent because I knew from experience what the consequences of some of her choices would be. She leaned into life with an open heart, and I hoped the world would never convince her that it was a bad thing.

I also knew that this drive to Bassano was a big deal for my parents. We've always shown up for each other and I knew we always would, no matter what—yet I also recognized that since the pandemic, their world had shrunk, and outings like this filled them with a mixture of happiness and anxiety, excitement and worry.

From the thirty-kilometre mark onward, the day dragged. It felt like the effort didn't match the outcome. But I tried to put it out of my head, knowing that one way or the other, it would soon be behind me and I'd see my family for the first time in weeks.

Mike, Joel and I kept slogging through hotter and hotter temperatures towards Bassano, and I could tell they'd miss this crazy train the moment they left. We ended the warmest day of the run so far after a very hot 109 kilometres, closing the book on Day 57.

As the boys headed home, Lana Rae and I floored it, speeding back to the motel in Bassano to finally see the kids. Before she could even park, I spotted a familiar van with familiar people getting out and yelled, "My babies! Stop the car!"

I was nearly out of my seat before the car came to a stop.

I'll never forget the looks on their faces and the harmony in their voices as they yelled "Dad!"

We collided in an emotional embrace, all of us at the same time. We cried and held on like we'd never let go, ever. Through my tears, I exclaimed at how much they'd grown, and in typical fashion, Julia responded, "Dad, you are *way* skinnier!" We were all laughing when I saw my mom and dad standing, waiting, with tears in their eyes. "Well, let's get that boy fed," my dad said, and while pulling away from the kids was hard, it made it easier that I was making my way toward Mom and Dad and one of the biggest hugs ever.

"You look good, my baby boy," said Mom.

I told her she was a good liar.

"I'm beyond proud of you," said Dad. And I knew he meant it.

The mood was sparkling as we made our way to the motel room. Full of excitement, I cuddled all the kids close at the same time; and my son Sam clung to me like a magnet and never left my side. It hit me at that moment that the lack of physical connection and affection caused by distance had most strongly affected Sam, and we started making up for lost time. Cuddles shifted to a tickle contest; and eventually, a pillow fight broke out. Pure joy and laughter filled the air, with love seeping from everyone to everyone, and somehow we managed to forget that we all still needed to eat.

Fortunately, Dad and Lana Rae came to their senses before the rest of us, and decided to make the short drive to the local pizzeria to feed the gang.

In those next couple of hours I noticed something very different and a bit surprising with the kids—the way they looked at me, their tone, and the questions they asked.

They believed.

We can talk to our kids until the cows come home, try to tell them what to do and how to act, but until the moment they witness their parent living those truths, it's all theoretical.

So although they had seen their father run all their lives, listened to my lectures about delayed gratification, self-confidence, hard work, and determination, only in this moment had they put it all together.

Seeing me, out here, doing this thing: this was proof that all those speeches, put into action with determination and effort, could make any dream possible.

As a father, moments like these come around once in a lifetime and make it all worth it.

Sensing that this was a turning point, I reminded them about everything that had gone into the run, and that I still had a long way to go. I looked all three of them squarely in the eyes, reminding them that with enough hard work, proper planning, skillful execution, patience, and dedication, they could accomplish anything.

And for the first time as a father, I felt that the message landed.

Later that evening, my brother Dan, my sister-in-law Laura, and nephew Aidan pulled in for a visit. Our pizza party was well underway, just the send-off we needed for the remainder of the run.

Saying goodbye was hard as hell, but the sleep gods were getting the best of me. After whispering individual goodnights to each of the kids, I welled up as I watched their van drive away. Lana Rae and I spooned that night, feeling on top of the world.

Now it was time for Julia, Sam, and Adele's dad to finish what he had started.

Familiar Territory

DAY 58	COMPLETED	REMAINING
107.4 kms in 12:41:30	6115.1 kms	1043.3 kms

As I awoke on Day 58, my heart was full, but my body felt like a deflated inner tube. The aches and pains had amplified, as had my resting heart rate and overall fatigue. I rolled out of bed like a sloth, noticeably moaning and groaning. Lana Rae busied herself getting organized for the day while glancing my way with silent concern.

Yet I was full of excitement, knowing that we'd finish the day dangerously close to my home city of Calgary and its familiar places, faces, and names.

Home. The simple thought of it motivated me. The quicker I finished, the sooner I'd be there.

And I knew that no matter how tough the day's run was, at day's end I'd meet my buddy and massage therapist Joe Bentley at the hotel for a much-needed massage.

Today's highway would take me through towns I've known all my life. I knew many runners had said they wanted to come run with me; but I had no idea who would show up, and when. The weatherman was promising another hot day, and it looked like we were in for 30 °C days from here to Victoria.

I could feel overwhelming tiredness creeping into crevices I didn't know I had, made tolerable only by the joy of running this flat, open stretch of highway in the morning sun with Lana Rae.

I skipped my usual nature break at the twenty-kilometre pit stop, believing optimistically that I could hold off until the next one at forty.

Then a sense of toiletary urgency (yes, I did just make that word up) struck at the thirty-kilometre mark. Hoping that Lana Rae and the SUV were nearby and I could duck behind the SUV doors for quick privacy, I called her only to find that she was at least ten minutes away.

By my reckoning, that was eight minutes too long.

I spotted a small group of trees just ahead and started sprinting towards them.

At that moment, John and Natasha sped past in their truck and pulled over onto the side of the road.

My saviours!

They jumped out, heard me yelling for toilet paper, and like the expert mom she is, Natasha took two steps, reached into the back seat, and lofted a fresh roll to me.

Like an Olympic 4x100 relay runner passing a baton, I swiped it and disappeared behind the few trees that dotted the prairie landscape.

Crisis averted!

Later, John and I laughed about their impeccable timing and watched planes crop-dusting fields for the next twenty-three kilometres. What made me even happier was knowing that Lana Rae and Natasha were getting in a good visit. They got along famously, and I knew the company would be uplifting and restorative for Lana Rae.

John struggled in the heat, no doubt picking up cues from my own mounting exhaustion. We elected to walk some of the easier hills, and happily blamed one another for doing so. Stuffing ice in my arm coolers and dramatically increasing my hydration made it bearable, although I craved fruit and salt more than ever before.

Finally, passing through Strathmore, I looked into the hazy distance and saw the grey silhouette of downtown Calgary, its office towers jutting out of nowhere like the fabled Land of Oz. Beyond that I could make out the faint outline of the Canadian Rocky Mountains, part desired destination and part cautionary tale.

Hooting and hollering, I joyously called Lana Rae, who knew exactly what I was seeing and greeted me with "Doesn't it look beautiful, David? Welcome home, handsome!"

I finished the day just east of the "Welcome to Calgary" sign, jumped into the SUV and rushed northeast to the hotel. I felt in good company when we arrived, as the legendary Calgary Stampede, known as the "Greatest Outdoor Show in the World," was already underway. During the ten days of the Stampede, everyone in Calgary dresses up as cowboys and cowgirls.

For the first time in two months, with the Outrunner perched on my head, I fit in.

When we got to the hotel, Joel Campbell appeared with his wife Caelly's home-cooked pot roast and loads of bakery treats. I couldn't tell which was better, the pot roast, the desperately needed massage, or Joe's delightfully soulful conversation.

Either way, I went to bed that night in my hometown, with a full tummy and happy muscles.

Home Stretch

DAY 59	COMPLETED	REMAINING
108.4 kms in 13:06:44	6223.5 kms	935.5 kms

The next morning I awoke to Lana Rae already on her cell, managing the logistics of running right through Calgary's main artery while fielding queries from the many runners who wanted to run with me.

Our original plan was that anyone who wanted to run with me should just check my GPS tracker online and jump in where they pleased; but due to the day's importance, Lana Rae elected to hand-hold a bit more than usual. She said that it was only for one day, and she was right.

When we got out to the start point at our usual 5 a.m. time, a handful of runners wearing headlamps already awaited us, and I recognized my buddy and strength and conditioning coach Carla Robbins swatting mosquitoes as we got ready to hit the road.

It was a treat running with Carla and the others as we approached the glowing lights of the big city, and the day's excitement muffled my declining fitness and the aches and fatigue that increasingly took center stage.

After so many lonely miles, I felt lifted up by the opportunity to talk with so many people who wanted to know about my journey. After several surprisingly detailed questions from the group, I realized that they had been following my every step since the Terry Fox Memorial via our social media posts, reminding me that at no point had I ever been truly alone out here.

I saw good friends like Brian and Cecil, alongside dozens more as we ran past cheering sections holding signs. The atmosphere was truly electric, and it seemed more than appropriate when

I spotted a sign for my main sponsor, Aspenleaf Energy. As some runners departed, others jumped in, rejuvenating the entertaining, good-vibe atmosphere that powered us down the road.

Having worked in downtown Calgary for the past twenty-three years, I saw familiar buildings at every turn, all holding countless memories. As I ran down Sixteenth Avenue just north of downtown, I passed stores I've visited and restaurants I've enjoyed, time and time again.

Gradually, as I approached Canada Olympic Park and headed out of Calgary, the group thinned to one. The construction zone that had been terrible for two years had now graduated to a full-blown disaster, and I quickly returned to reality.

This is hard, I thought, *I've got a long way to go, and boy do I ever feel tired.*

The ominous Rocky Mountains loomed before me. Their snow-covered peaks, climbing up toward the heavens, would be the last test for this withered body.

I smiled faintly, tucked my chin in, and continued.

Time to get back to work.

Calgary traffic and construction forced Lana Rae to make our second pit stop for the day at forty-seven kilometres rather than our planned forty-kilometre mark.

Naturally, nature called at the most inconvenient moment.

Hoping she could swing back with the SUV so I could use its doors to afford some privacy, I checked in with her only to discover that the exit situation basically made it impossible.

Intellectually, I understood, but I may have petulantly exclaimed that I'd just clench my cheeks until I saw her at the Petro Canada where she was waiting.

Naturally, nature's call grew louder, and I suddenly started sweating with anxiety.

Lana Rae had told me that her mother would be driving by in a white Ford Focus and would give me three honks in support right around this time. I was still trying to impress her family, and I couldn't imagine anything more disappointing than seeing your daughter's new boyfriend shitting in the ditch.

In desperation, I clenched even harder and continued on.

Out of nowhere, I heard three honks and saw Mrs. Ledene wave as she passed by. I waved back, and as soon as she was out of sight, I found a deep depression in the ditch just barely low enough to hide me from passing cars.

Ducking my head, I took care of business. Since this was such a desperate moment, and without toilet tissue at hand, I looked around for a leaf, for literally anything that could do the job—but found nothing.

With no other options, I stripped off my running shorts, used them for a wipe, dug a hole, buried them, and ran the remaining five kilometres to the Petro Canada pit stop in my underwear.

As I ran up to Lana Rae, she cocked her head sideways.

"Dave, where did your shorts go?" she asked.

I told her that it was a long story that I'll tell her one day when I was less embarrassed.

Meanwhile, standing beside the SUV was Bernadette Benson, an old friend and a Canadian 24-hour record holder, visiting from Australia to visit her mother and planning to run the next four hours with me.

Bernadette and I have never struggled to find things to talk about, and today was no different. Paying no attention to the fact that I had just run up to the SUV in my underwear, she waited while I got a fresh pair of shorts and slipped easily into conversation, as if no time at all had passed since our last meetup. We chatted the next several hours as we ran, and the honking of passers-by gave me steady encouragement for the rest of the day as the steep mountains sprawled ahead.

Towering rocks dwarfed me as I inched closer to the mountains. Each time I looked up from the thin white line painted on the asphalt, Mount Yamnuska loomed larger. I found it harder and harder to stand tall and feel confident with these giants present. It had been a long while since I had a 1000-meter-elevation day, and I was reminded that climbing is *hard*.

Approaching Dead Man's Flats, with the spectacular Mount Allan to my right and the Three Sisters peaks just ahead, I called it quits for the day at 108 kilometres. We piled into the SUV and made our way to family friends in Canmore. Myron and Catherine Tetrault were hosting us for the night, and I could almost taste Catherine's legendary lasagna thanks to Myron's mouthwatering description.

Dinner was spectacular and the company even better. Catherine poured Lana Rae a glass of rosé and I took a sip, which turned into a full glass.

I'm not sure if it was the wine or the sheer intimidation I felt about what lay ahead, but I didn't sleep much, and when I did, Lana Rae told me later than I talked in my sleep, warming her with loving words and asking her to marry me someday, filling us both with happiness.

Enter the Rockies

DAY 60	COMPLETED	REMAINING
105.2 kms in 12:45:55	6328.7 kms	830.3 kms

I awoke feeling thoroughly *un*rested.

But with things to do and places to be, I had no choice but to roll out of bed and get on with the boring, regular routine that was the beginning of every morning.

Both Catherine and Myron were already up, and extremely conscious of my need to get ready, graciously let me do my thing. Myron and a bunch of guys had decided to run the first 20-30 kilometres of the day with me to get me rolling, and I was even more grateful that Catherine, an incredible baker, had packed loads of goodies for the journey ahead.

Arriving at the start point at Dead Man's Flats, I noticed quite a few headlamps bobbing in the ditch as we pulled up. It was a strange feeling knowing that all these people had gone out of their way to meet me and join the run. I understood that by now, on Day 60, I had already done something incredible; but knowing that others had been paying attention left me mysteriously unsettled.

They were wonderful people, and I really enjoyed their company and conversation as we ran westward. My friend Mike Cameron, who had recently moved to Canmore, was a part of the group, and it was great to catch up.

The early morning jaunt past Canmore with Grotto Mountain and Mount Lady MacDonald to my right and Ha Ling Peak and the east end of Mount Rundle to my left was precious. Highlighted by the sun rising behind the mountains, the glow of the peaks was breathtaking.

The bro time with a bunch of great fellas was also exactly what I needed to distract me. The boys took me off the highway and onto the Legacy Trail, a bike path that paralleled the road connecting Canmore and Banff. This was a welcome reprieve from the usual busy-ness of the Trans-Canada Highway.

Eventually, most of the fellas peeled off, leaving just me and Jesse Kitteridge, an interesting young dude wearing his girlfriend's cowboy hat, two sizes too small, as a show of support. Jesse was a lawyer-turned-entrepreneur, and one of the wisest younger people I've ever met. His curiosity, well-thought-out questions and insightful responses had us talking non-stop for hours.

The views of Mount Rundle from the Banff side were a positive distraction from the hardship I felt inside. Every day since the Alberta border had seemed harder than the last. Fatigue settled in earlier and earlier into the day with a heavy, sinking feeling.

I knew I was reaching the end of my rope.

With eight more days remaining, could I hold on?

As Jesse jumped out, another young man jumped in, joining me for the stretch between Banff and Lake Louise. The heat of the day was at its peak, and there was no place to hide. The occasional wildlife overpass offered mere seconds of momentary shade as we quickly passed under.

I spotted Lana Rae and the SUV up ahead and slowed down to meet her. As I approached, she was picking wild strawberries alongside the ditch, which instantly put me in a far better mood than the day before, especially given the stress of the city.

When I was alone with Lana Rae and no one was looking, I sometimes cried, telling her how much I hurt, how far beyond exhaustion I felt. She'd gently remind me about all I had accomplished, that I hadn't come this far to only come this far.

It was just enough to get me away from the pit stop and back moving west on the highway.

Marveling at Castle Mountain's unsurpassed beauty on my right, I realized that I saw my majestic dragon circling the mountain, occasionally perching atop it only to let out a war cry.

Hearing it, I'd look over its way, tilting my head to peer out from under my hat brim, and give it a coy wink.

This day's effort would surpass everything I had already pushed through on this run. The time was now to do whatever was needed to get through the day.

I envisioned a long rope extending from my chest and flowing down the road that lay in front of me. It extended into the distant sky, and without looking up, I knew that the dragon had seized it to aid my progress.

Now safely tethered to this powerful winged creature, my effort eased. His support was like a tow to safety.

The long ascent up Kicking Horse Pass, an elevation of 1643 meters, was a bitch. A better name would have been Kicking Your Ass. Atop the pass was the entry into the province of British Columbia.

I'd be alone running this portion, possibly because no fool would have wanted to do it voluntarily. And thank God, because I cried the entire way. The pain was unreal. My fatigue was now next-level, and worst of all, my fractured foot hated the pitch of the highway for what seemed like the better part of two hours.

Eventually summiting the climb and crossing into my ninth and final province, I thanked the dragon for the lift.

I was officially cooked. I was so tired that I hardly blinked when I ran right past a grizzly bear eating berries just a few meters away. I'm sure he wasn't interested in a skinny cowboy anyway, unless he was looking for a toothpick.

This led me into a long construction zone that extended down into Yoho National Park and into the town of Field. My right big toe had started hurting something fierce, and as we approached numerous signs that read *NO STOPPING FOR NEXT 8 KM*, Lana Rae and I agreed to call it quits for the day at 105 kilometres.

Arriving at the insanely busy hotel in Field, our fears about finding dinner came true when the restaurant downstairs told us they were swamped and couldn't do room service. While Lana Rae went downstairs to do her magic, I looked at my toe.

Only the second blister in the past sixty days, but this one was a doozy, a pocket blister that sat just below my big toenail and required drilling a tiny hole through the nail to drain it. After minutes of drilling, I finally found immediate relief when a geyser of fluid shot across the room. I squeezed the hell out of it and tried to seal it, just in time for Lana Rae to walk back through the door with a burger and fries.

I don't know how she did it—but that woman gets shit done!

CHAPTER 13: BRITISH COLUMBIA

God is Great

DAY 61	COMPLETED	REMAINING
108 kms in 13:26:37	6436.7 kms	722.3 kms

My final province.

Dave, you've nailed eight, what's one more? I thought to myself as I rolled out of bed.

And Lana Rae matched my chipper mood as she busied herself getting ready for the day.

I was feeling much better. Since last night's blister geyser extravaganza, the pressure in my big toe had decreased dramatically.

We got out to the start point in time to witness the most miraculous sunrise so far on the trip. The first light striking the giant rock faces encompassing Yoho National Park was truly something to see. Both Lana Rae and I marveled at the beauty of the moment.

She kissed me and told me that this was going to be a wonderful day.

I got started with a long, steep seven-kilometre descent through the far side of the pass to shake out my legs. This section of the run will always stand out in my mind as one of the sections where I felt the closest to God. The still, crisp air, the silence of the soon-to-be-busy road, or just the magnificent beauty of it all left me feeling whole and complete.

If only all the miles could feel like these, I thought.

Now up in the mountains it was easier to see my progress. I'd spot a unique rock face ahead, and within minutes I'd be running past it. Then before I knew it, that same rock face would shift, showing the backside, and recede into my rear-view. These seemingly enormous structures would float by as clouds do while I ticked off one mountain at a time.

Lana Rae ran back from the SUV and joined me all morning long. Her shit-eating grin clearly showed she was having a blast. Despite what we'd gone through together, we were getting along *so* well. It felt like my wish for true partnership was coming true, and it felt like we were a team. I couldn't have organized any of the run as well as she had, and her execution on the details that mattered inspired me every day.

Neither was she shy to comment about how well she thought I was doing.

Coming from a woman I truly respected, I took great pride in that.

I climbed the final ascent before the plunge down ten-mile hill into Golden. I knew that there was a huge construction zone halfway down the descent and there might be a delay, but I knew I'd figure that out when I got there. And it was a *big* construction project. The estimated $600-million cost included demolishing part of the mountain, and I was excited to witness this modern-day engineering masterpiece up close and personal.

The long downhill was interesting. I ran by two trucks that had overheated, unable to crest the climb. Perhaps that's what I'd looked like yesterday.

As I approaching the construction zone, two young women in hardhats held up their hands, signaling me to halt.

One told me that no pedestrian traffic was allowed in the six-kilometre zone and offered a ride across. Surprised, I explained that I had run all the way from St. John's in 61 days and was on pace to break the Trans Canadian speed record. If I got into a vehicle and accepted a ride, I'd forfeit the speed record.

They seemed half-perplexed and half-expecting that I'd say that, and radioed their boss while I started worrying about the very real possibility that I might need to find an alternative route—of which there were none.

As I started checking out other routes on my phone, they returned.

"Okay, Mister, how about this?" asked one of them. "We'll drive right behind you and hold up traffic while you run. There's a pull-off every one kilometre or so where you'll need to pause for a couple minutes to let the backed-up traffic through. We'll stop there a couple minutes and repeat that until you're clear of the construction zone. How does that sound?"

It sounded perfect. They deserved a big hug but I settled on a wholehearted thank-you.

We got rolling and the ladies with lights flashing trailed in behind me. My typical 6 minutes per kilometre pace seemed disrespectful to all the vehicles I was holding up so I cranked up the pace. Not that travelling 12 instead of 10 km/hr mattered to them, but it did to me. They honked to indicate where I needed to merge into the pull-offs, and I complied.

While I stood waiting in one of the pull-offs, I saw a gentleman approach the women, aggressively mansplaining that there was to be no pedestrian traffic.

They politely explained that they had gotten the go-ahead from the boss, and that it was all good. Disappointed, he huffed and marched away, shaking his head as he went. I asked if they thought he'd speak to them like that if they were men. They rolled their eyes and said they get that all the time.

We continued this start/stop numerous times until we exited the construction zone. This definitely elongated our day; but I was, and still am, very grateful for their grace and mercy.

I ran the remainder of the hill into Golden, where I saw Lana Rae parked on the right. She wrapped her arms around me, happy that I was safe.

Grabbing a snack and filling my arm coolers with ice, I was quickly on my way. The valley was cooking and the ice in my sleeves was melting fast. Stuffing ice in arm coolers is the ultimate way to cool off. The blood vessels on the inside of your arm are very near the surface, so applying ice in that location cools your blood on its way back through the system. On days like this I'd take any cooling I could get.

The run through the valley along its windy undivided road was treacherous. It seemed as if everyone were speeding this section, trying to get somewhere fast. Vehicles hugged turns, certain that no one would be using the shoulder. When they'd see me, they'd jerk their steering wheels—and some drivers would simply remain on the shoulder. I'd take two steps into the ditch to assure my safety, but it got old fast. Nine times out of ten, the worst offending vehicles were sports cars or pickup trucks driven by white middle-aged men who looked like me. I refused to get angry about it, but I thought the consistency of it was interesting.

During a pit stop later in the day, I noticed Lana Rae was angry.

When Lana Rae is angry, the whole world knows it. She had been trying all day to call the Heather Mountain Lodge where we were staying that night. Hours later, they finally picked up only to tell her that the restaurant in the lodge was fully booked, and no room service or take-out was available. Lana Rae explained what we were doing, that there were no restaurants closer than Golden, and asked if they could they *please* find a way to accommodate us.

No, they could not.

Lana Rae was pissed! Now she'd have to backtrack into Golden to pick up a pizza for dinner.

So she circled back, as I started my long early ascent up the legendary Rogers Pass.

Along the slow climb, a couple familiar faces popped up from behind, on bikes. Jacob and Phil, two young dudes from Quebec who were cycling across Canada, had leapfrogged me several times already. These nice young men had adventure on their minds and exploration in their hearts.

I really liked them. They were about the same age as my oldest daughter, Julia. We would routinely meet up by the SUV, and Lana Rae and I would offer anything we had that the boys might need. We'd top off their fluids, ice, and sunscreen, and we'd feed them. I felt a responsibility as a father to look after them the best I could, and they were always grateful and polite.

Eventually, we split up, and after climbing the last couple hours of the day, I called it quits at 108 kilometres. As she drove west another fifteen minutes to get to the lodge, Lana Rae was still heated about paying 400 bucks to stay the night while being turned away from the restaurant.

I tried my best to calm her and snuggled up with her as big spoon and me as little spoon, and we closed our eyes, putting our stamp on yet another successful day.

Liquid Courage

DAY 62	COMPLETED	REMAINING
107.8 kms in 13:14:15	6544.4 kms	614.6 kms

Day 62 was the day I'd summit Rogers Pass. It was a big deal and I'd need to exercise considerable patience if I were to be successful. I worked through the all-too-familiar morning routine, and Lana Rae drove me out to the start point.

Exiting the car, I immediately noticed how cold it was in the wee hours of the morning. With limited traffic, and in prime bear country, Lana Rae planned on staying close and I planned on making lots of noise if I got into trouble. The day started off with a thirty-kilometre section of flat plateau followed by the twenty-kilometre uphill stretch of Rogers Pass. Following that was an incredible fifty kilometre downhill section before arriving in Revelstoke.

About three hours into the day, I got a call from Lana Rae while I was running. She sounded like she was tiptoeing on eggshells. After a bit of back-and-forth, she carefully asked if I would be upset if I finished on Day 68 instead of day 67.

I told her that I didn't care much as long as I got to Victoria on or before day 72. 108 kilometres per day had been the most I could possibly squeeze out of my legs at this point, and that would just have to do.

She sighed in relief, as she had expected me to be disappointed. Then, she launched into a whole bunch of questions regarding my mapping.

She explained that the Google Maps I had created showing 105-kilometre sections across Canada were near-perfect in Atlantic Canada, less perfect in Quebec and Ontario, and took a radical turn in Western Canada, becoming incredibly erratic, with some days totaling 85 kilometres and other days 135 kilometres.

Yet all had been labeled as 105-kilometre days!

I laughed, which made her laugh, and this is what I told her.

"Lana Rae, mapping out a run of this kind is scary as hell and takes next-level bravery. A few years ago when sitting down at my computer to do this the first time, I needed to crack a beer. I ripped through the Newfoundland part, finishing all nine days of mapping in about thirty minutes. Then, finishing the province, I looked at the island realizing the magnitude of what I had just done. If I were to just run this island, I thought, that would be huge, but the sheer size of the giant land mass of Canada made me close my laptop instantly. Minutes later, I mustered up the courage to open the laptop, cracking another beer. I got on a roll. Every province I entered, another beer got poured. As I completed Quebec, I then tackled the first day of the largest province in Canada. Needing further liquid encouragement as the route approached Ottawa, I got down to business pouring a neat glass of bourbon. All of a sudden I was cooking with gas. Twenty days on mapping across Ontario seemed easy. I lost the glass and started taking pulls from the bottle. I woke up the next morning to see my laptop still open. It showed that I arrived in Victoria on the 67th day finishing in 66 days and some odd hours. To be honest, Lana Rae, I don't remember mapping Western Canada at all, but I do remember the hangover. So yes, the erratic mapping and wild inconsistencies make sense."

Lana Rae and I had a good laugh about it as I started the big push up Rogers Pass.

Management of effort on these climbs had been my middle name this entire journey. My younger self would have grunted through these climbs and paid dearly for it later. My younger ego would not have let me play it cool ten years ago. And even though my twenty-something body could win the battle, my forty-something brain would win the war.

The one area in my body that *was* losing the war during this long climb was my right ankle. The grade of the pass is steep, reaching up to 11.1%, and at that angle the talar dome of my fractured foot locked down, feeling like bone crushing on bone. My limp worsened, driving me to tears, much like Kicking Horse Pass two days earlier.

So I did as did then. I tethered myself to the dragon, and accepted his help up the mountain.

As I reached the summit, the beauty of the surrounding views nearly erased the pain. Record snowpack still nestled atop the Selkirk Mountains made for the most beautiful view I'd seen anywhere along the Trans Canada Highway. Pain gave way to joy as I took in the glorious canvas.

I had only stopped a moment when I noticed Lana Rae parked at the top beside a rest stop. We paused and held one another, taking in the moment. Not wanting to spoil it, I pulled away just enough to tell her that my foot was in trouble. She spent the next ten minutes yanking, tractioning, and Theragunning my ankle in hopes of gaining any movement, but sadly none came. Frustrated, I got my hands down there as well, finding no relief either. I knew that a fifty-kilometre downhill on a locked talar dome would result in a serious injury.

After no luck with my foot, though, I decided I couldn't waste anymore time and had no choice but to get going.

Forty steps in, there was an audible pop. "*YES!*" I screamed with joy at the top of my lungs.

I spent the five hours gradually descending into the heat as I wound my way down past some of Canada's greatest viewpoints heading toward Revelstoke.

Closing out day 62, we retired back to the hotel. Tonight, we ate our body weight in sushi, and after cranking the AC, snuggled together and called it a night.

Hit and Run

DAY 63	COMPLETED	REMAINING
108.1 kms in 13:13:56	6652.5 kms	506.5 kms

The Weather Network called for a scorcher as we made our way through lake country. The interior of British Columbia could cook you, and today the burners were on high.

We got out to the start point just before 5 a.m. to get the day underway before it got too hot. During the first few kilometres, I checked my phone for texts and emails from the previous day.

Our Trans Canada Facebook Messenger group was full of my crew members as well as friends who had a hand in planning the big run. It was a place for passing info, debate, chat and everything Trans Canada-run related. It was typically very positive and mostly consisted of useful data valuable to the team.

This morning, though, the thread was a bit different. Lana Rae had posted, *"We need a Messenger group for the crew so we can talk smack about DP."*

The comments that followed were lighthearted ribbings calling me a diva in a cowboy hat, Diva Dave, and Princess Proctor. Now I knew that the group was just having a bit of fun with me, that it was a bit of silliness, but for some strange reason it actually bothered me, and I called Lana Rae right away to tell her that.

Her response was not what I was looking for. She told me that she was just trying to have fun and to relax. We had it out on the phone, and she told me I was being too sensitive, and that she wouldn't budge on the issue.

I hung up and typed a response to the Trans Canada group. I was about to send it, then thought about it and deleted it. I typed another response, and again deleted it. I got to thinking about the boundless support my wonderful friends in the group had given me. Then I thought of Lana Rae and her humour. I decided to just chalk it up to my hypersensitivity and let it go.

As I approached Sicamous I noticed a large group of people standing alongside the road ahead. They were making a commotion, waving Canadian flags. As I got closer I noticed the men in the group were shirtless, with painted letters on their torsos spelling G-O-D-A-V-E! Hilarious!

These fine families were camping in the area and came out to cheer me on. Across the busy road, I stopped just for a second to flex my muscles, and all fifteen of them, including children, copied my pose in celebration. How cool was that?! It made my day!

I arrived in Sicamous thirty minutes later to see Lana Rae, her best friend Stacey, and Stacey's husband Dean in front of a gas station. These are incredible, hardworking people who have always been there for Lana Rae. We chatted for a bit as I gobbled down some fruit and drank an iced tea. Dean was full of perceptive questions, as he too is a "go big or go home" type of guy.

The roadway between Sicamous and Salmon Arm was sketchy to say the least. The narrow undivided road with concrete barriers designed to save vehicles from driving off a cliff now entrapped me. Most cars sped dangerously around the bends, utilizing the shoulder as a portion of their lane. The problem was that the narrow shoulder was all I had, and with the tall barrier trapping me, I had to be ready to dive over it at any time. That required constant vigilance if I were to have any hope whatsoever of saving my life when some idiot came careening around a bend in the road.

The stress made my hair stand on end; and if *I* felt nervous, I knew how Lana Rae was feeling. For safety and security reasons, she wanted to always stay on the phone with me. She told me that after driving the stretch of highway and feeling the natural pull to use the shoulder of the road, she had a new perspective on how risky being a pedestrian on these highways was. With a couple close calls, I did my best to project calm. The truth was that I was scared senseless.

As the temperature rose throughout the day to mid-thirties, the heat was getting to me. My general system was struggling, I felt my "engine" stalling, and my foot was throbbing. Meanwhile, Lana Rae discovered that our hotel reservation in Salmon Arm had no AC. With my internal furnace revving *and* overnight hot temperatures, we decided she needed to look for another vacancy.

As I entered the city of Salmon Arm just past the 100-kilometre point, I found myself in a newly paved construction zone. The fresh black tarmac was so intensely hot it could have cooked an egg. This was nuts!

Running with my back to traffic, no lines yet painted on the freshly laid road, I knew I really should be on the other side of the road, running against traffic.

Suddenly, I felt a gust of wind on my left side followed by a punch on the back of my left elbow. I jumped into the air like a scared cat, only to see a car speed by with a newly collapsed side mirror!

Holy shit, I just got hit!

I immediately stopped, only to witness the car veering back into his unpainted lane as the driver sped up to get away. Sympathetic drivers honked furiously at the hit and run driver, but they offered small comfort.

I walked into the ditch, caught my breath, screamed "FUUUCCCKKK" as I always did when I'd gotten the shit scared out of me, and continued on, this time choosing to face traffic.

I finished the day's 108 kilometres right in town, only a 3-minute drive from an overpriced hotel with AC.

As we ate dinner in our room, we decompressed and did our best to release the fear that had almost overwhelmed us all day. Fear and anxiety had a way of cutting my legs out from under me, and I couldn't let that happen.

I was so damn close now.

I took a sleeping pill and had a beer to try to secure restful sleep.

As I lay in bed, I kept thinking, *Today is Sunday and I will arrive in Victoria on Thursday.*

I found it incomprehensible. I felt as if I'd been out here forever; and I now felt conflicted at the thought that it would all be over soon.

On the one hand I was excited; on the other I was sad. I felt relieved yet upset, intoxicated yet dissatisfied.

And all these contradictory emotions made it hard to get out of bed the next morning.

Tokens

DAY 64	COMPLETED	REMAINING
106.5 kms in 13:03:57	6759.1 kms	399.9 kms

Another scorcher greeted me as I started my first shuffling steps of the day.

Lana Rae had mentioned that my stride had started to change the past week. What had once been a strong, consistent erect stride now resembled a broken shuffle, and that's exactly how I felt.

The near-paralyzing fear of yesterday's barriered, narrow roads continued today. It wouldn't be until after Chase that the roads would open up a bit as they broke into the flat desert approaching Kamloops. She ran with me on and off all morning. Her love and devotion to me had been obvious during this entire run, and I couldn't wait to return the favour of supporting her in life as we mapped out our future.

Even back at the crew vehicle, she stayed on the phone with me as I darted through narrow sections with limited shoulders, my head on a swivel locating trouble before it got the best of me.

A couple runners joined me, unfamiliar with the dangers of the road, and I tried to share tips on how to stay safe, but when they ignored my advice and got caught up in the excitement of the moment, I decided I just needed to let it go.

As I reached Chase and conditions got a little less insane, I had the privilege of meeting a couple cousins alongside the road. It was great seeing other Proctors, even though they both advised me that I was too skinny.

The road opened to a divided highway shortly thereafter and the shoulders widened for the next 60 kilometres until after Kamloops, where I planned to turn off onto the notorious Coquihalla Highway.

Focused attention on details had been key to the success of this run so far. One of the details that we organized well before this run even started was the concept of permission and sticking to a plan.

Shame has always been a sticking point with me in many places in my life. During the 2018 run, I felt immense shame whenever I caught myself walking. I know, stupid, right? When running across the second largest country in the world one should expect to walk on occasion.

When I brought it up with Erin, she dove into with me to develop a deeper understanding of my hangups, and we came up with a new plan:

Every day, I put six tokens in my pocket. Each token could be used to exchange one kilometre of running for one kilometre of walking.

That meant that if I ran 108 kilometres per day I was really only *running* 102. If my run pace was six minutes per kilometre and my walk pace was ten minutes per kilometre, this would only extend my day by twenty-four minutes, which was very reasonable.

The magic of this approach was that it gave me permission to take a rest if I needed it. It replaced ego with a mature, predetermined plan. Instead of feeling shame about walking, I felt shame only if I didn't follow this new plan.

Most importantly, this plan assured me an easy final three hours of the day, if I played the tokens right and didn't use any during the first eighty kilometres. That way, I had all six to use for the final twenty-five kilometres, allowing me to alternate running four kilometres and walking one for the rest of the day.

Memory is a funny thing. My brain typically didn't remember the first nine hours of the day anyway, but rest assured it always remembered the final three. The confidence that this approach gave me as I recovered each night was invaluable.

The token system had replaced the shame-filled feeling of being weak with an uplifting sensation of being smart and strategic, and the best part was that it was working! Every day I faithfully followed this new plan, and the positive reinforcement instilled confidence for the next day.

As I hit the eighty-kilometre mark today, I broke into a fast walk. I had earned it. Even though a few runners came out to run with me as I approached Kamloops, I didn't care. The plan that Erin created was ironclad and I wasn't about to change it now.

We finished the day's run in Kamloops on the east side of the Great Bear Snow Shed and the Thompson Plateau.

When we got to the hotel that afternoon to settle in for the evening, Lana Rae had a million questions about the route from Hope through Vancouver, heading to Victoria.

When someone has in-depth knowledge from both living and working in an area, it's best to rely on local expertise. My buddy Kevin Barata, a long-standing team leader of the RCMP's

Emergency Response Team, incredible ultrarunner, and the best all around guy I knew had built me the map. I told Lana Rae I hadn't reviewed the map much and trusted that Kevin had chosen the best, safest possible route.

Lana Rae, however, remained laser-focused on control and detail and was intensely triggered by my lack of focus on the topic. We sparred a bit that evening over the whole issue, our differences in approach patently obvious to us both. Neither of us was wrong; rather, we were each right as far as our own roles went. I focused on what I needed to; she focused on what she needed to.

Despite our desire for compromise, we couldn't reconcile my "meh" mindset with Lana Rae's need to have things shipshape going into the final stretch; and we went to bed that night with our backs facing one another—very much in love, yet frustrated as hell.

A Tethered Beast

DAY 65	COMPLETED	REMAINING
106 kms in 13:20:45	6865.1 kms	293.9 kms

When I woke up, Lana Rae's eyes were already wide open, as if she'd been awake for hours. She kissed me deeply as if to say she was sorry. We made up without saying a word.

All morning long, she tried to prepare me for a day we knew was going to be hard as hell. After sixty-five days, it felt like I was now facing cruel punishment for a lifetime of sins.

Today, I'd need to run both summits of the Coquihalla Highway, a fast-and-furious road with limited outcroppings and few pull-offs for a pit stop. The elevation would be by far the greatest of any day during the run. If anything bad was going to happen, it would likely happen today. This section was so tough it could tear my limbs from my torso.

After an extra-large breakfast, we drove a short drive to the start point. It was a cool, brisk morning. A local ultrarunner, Logan, was ready and waiting to run the initial climb with me. From the start, he was a chatty Cathy as we broke into a climb. I understood his excitement and the desire to ask a hundred questions, but my morning mental cobwebs and my fear of what lay ahead made for a one-sided conversation.

Only twenty minutes in, I looked up and saw the exit to Merritt and Highway 5 as I turned left and onto an even steeper climb. Logan kept talking and I'd respond tersely: *Yes. No. Maybe. Over there. I don't know! We'll see. Uh-huh.*

He started labouring as the climb continued, and eventually turned back to his car, leaving me alone to carry on.

Not long after, my phone started ringing. It was Lana Rae telling me to turn back: I had accidentally exited on Highway 5A, instead of our planned Highway 5 route.

After a minute of debate with Lana Rae we concluded that it was best to turn right on a road about two kilometres ahead and zigzag to reconnect with the 5.

Great, we had a plan to correct my mistake.

And what a wonderful mistake it was! Even though the detour elongated the route a bit, these backroads were absolutely amazing. Vera was thrilled to get stunning footage, and Lana Rae was able to navigate the steep dirt roads and support me as needed.

At one point, Lana Rae drove ahead and ran back to pace me for a while, cursing the whole way up the steep pitch as we ran together. I giggled inside, thinking, *Girl, you have no idea.* Yet it also reminded me that I was capable of doing unimaginably hard things and surviving.

As soon as I got to the junction that put me back onto the 5, I immediately missed those back roads. Traffic on the Coquihalla was routinely faster than 140 kms/hr, with a narrow shoulder not designed for pedestrians. Taking a deep breath and reminding myself that I was highly visible and they really could see me, I continued.

A couple hours later at a scheduled pit stop, I noticed a vehicle parked beside Lana Rae's. She often attracted attention from men who would stop to ask her if she needed help. Most no doubt had honourable intentions, but I'm sure there were some nefarious reasons as well.

As I ran up to the pit stop to meet Vera and Lana Rae, I got a strange feeling right away. As I sat on the bumper drinking and eating, the driver of the adjacent car lingered, asking strange questions. I wasn't comfortable leaving the girls alone with him, so I stayed longer than I had planned, hoping that he'd disappear.

Time wore on, and I eventually had to head out. As soon as I left, I tried ringing Lana Rae. No answer.

I called her three times, still no response. I called Vera.

If she didn't pick up, I thought, *I'd circle back to check on them.*

Vera picked up.

We agreed that she'd stay with Lana Rae until either she left or the strange guy left. I Just had a creepy feeling about him.

Vera didn't share my trepidation, but promised to stay. Minutes later I saw Lana Rae drive by, and sighed in relief.

The wind and the heat gradually picked up as I started the long, steep descent into Merritt. My quads took a proper pounding as vehicles whizzed by. Along the valley passing by Merritt, the wind picked up further as a couple local runners showed up to run with me. We struggled to communicate over the noise of the vicious wind.

After Merritt, the giant climb out was accompanied by a brutal headwind.

Again, I thought of all my past sins. At least this was proper punishment, something I could stand if I willed myself to. The six tokens came in handy, and I used them all on that *bitch* of a climb, assisted by the pull of the dragon.

We concluded the day at the top of the plateau, and my legs and soul were properly cooked. I could hardly crawl into the passenger seat.

That night at the motel, Vera stayed with us, as we had gotten a suite. She captured shots of me barely able to walk.

In those videos, I was shirtless, with my ribs and vertebrae poking out. My sinewy skeleton resembled a dying animal, wounded and unable to hunt. My long ratty beard was scraggly in all directions, with bits of food throughout. My face was weatherworn and my voice deep, gravelly and windswept.

I felt like a proper mountain man. The girls said I looked like a proper mess.

While I was in the washroom, I overheard them whispering about whether I'd run tomorrow.

Lana Rae's response was golden: "I've wondered that for awhile now, but every morning Dave takes his first step, doesn't complain, and doesn't stop until the goal is reached. So yeah, he'll run tomorrow."

I hobbled out from the washroom and gave Lana Rae a kiss on the cheek. "Good night girls," I said.

Finding Hope

DAY 66	COMPLETED	REMAINING
107 kms in 12:58:14	6972.1 kms	186.9 kms

Boy, we are getting close, I thought. *Today I run down into Hope, officially clearing the Rocky Mountains and entering the final stretch through the Fraser Valley.*

Lana Rae had to do a scheduled work presentation from the motel room, so Vera agreed to help crew me for the first 50 kilometres.

I gave Lana Rae a kiss and wished her luck as I piled into Vera's Subaru to commute to the start point. I could tell that Vera was nervous and didn't want to screw up. I tried my best to reassure her that even *if* we screwed up, it wasn't the end of the world.

The first forty kilometres of the day's run were rolling climbs with stunning scenery.

The year prior, most of the region had been destroyed by flooding, causing record breaking mudslides. I knew that I would soon be entering a long stretch of construction zones still repairing the damage, and I looked forward to the slowdown in traffic. My legs were fried and my system was thoroughly obliterated. I couldn't have sprinted if I'd tried. The entire day I felt like a deflated tire rolling down the road. Every inch was an effort as I closed out the final stages of the Rockies.

My gnarly beard, once prized as a cool token of this big effort, now annoyed me to no end. The grey, matty mess reminded me of a rotten bird's nest, littered with the refuse of every bite of food that had missed my mouth as I stuffed in calories and kept running. My posture slumped as I began the final push to the top of the Cascade Range.

I kept telling myself over and over again that it was all downhill from here.

Looking ahead, I spotted Lana Rae parked atop the range at the apex of the final climb.

Yes, it *was* all downhill from here!

A small, satisfied smile came over my face, and I stopped briefly to celebrate the feat.

The earth sloped downward under my feet as I started the 37-kilometre descent into Hope.

A constant throughout this run had always been management, management, management, and staying well ahead of problems had served me well. It could be as simple as applying sunscreen, eating on schedule, watching electrolyte consumption, lubing, or managing effort and heart rate. All things done perfectly made for a reasonable day, and things done poorly often resulted in catastrophe.

I am proud to say that I'd had 66 consecutive reasonable days. They'd been hard, yes. But they'd been reasonable. Accordingly, I'd prepared myself to not celebrate too early or let my guard down.

Dave, continue doing all the things that have gotten you this far. Remember, you are still over two hundred kilometres from the finish. A lot of bad shit can still go down. Stay vigilant.

A line-up of traffic heading eastbound behind me and up the hill stared at me impatiently as I entered the construction zone, and I was finally able to take advantage of the slowdown in traffic.

I chuckled to myself as I considered what the passengers were thinking as this sinewy, dark, bearded cowboy looking like Forrest Gump slowly ran by. I waved at the kids as they stared back at me, their mouths hanging open, faces pressed to the windows.

Did I really look so weird as to warrant that attention? I guess I must have. *Well, enjoy the circus, kids. It'll only come this way once.*

The lower I dropped into the Fraser Valley, the hotter it got. I passed the town of Hope with ten kilometres still to go.

At one point I stopped to pee, holding my cowboy hat to the side to shield the view from nearby traffic. Then Vera's video drone buzzed into view, directly in front of me.

I laughed, finished what I was doing and continued on.

Great, I thought sarcastically. *Now I'm a porn star.*

Across the next bridge I saw Vera. She struggled to meet my eyes and as I ran past, all I could really say was "Sorry about that," and hope the shot wouldn't make the final cut.

We finished up the day and made our way back to Hope, where we'd be staying that night.

With limited restaurants, we struggled to find food for our evening meal. Lana Rae was stressed about it, and her anxiety and tone shifted dramatically as I tried to calm her.

Emotion couldn't be met with logic, and logic couldn't be met with emotion. We both knew that, but I kept trying anyway. When my approach was met with further frustration, we met in the middle, silently agreeing to stay quiet about it.

Silence of the Salamander

DAY 67	COMPLETED	REMAINING
107.7 kms in 13:07:27	7079.8 kms	79.3 kms

We were awakened the next morning by a knock on the door.

As Lana Rae answered the door, she was greeted by the face of a handsome man wearing a huge grin. Kevin Barata was a legend. He was a Team Lead with the RCMP Lower Mainland District Integrated Emergency Response Team, The Mounties' version of SWAT. He was also a decorated ultrarunner, the perfect family man, and a man with impeccable ethics and a heart of gold. He looks like a modern-day GI Joe. It was impossible to not love and look up to the guy. Kevin had said that since he had built the route for me and knew the place thoroughly, he'd be running me through Vancouver to make sure I got where I needed to go.

He stepped into the room and immediately gave big bear hugs.

I ate breakfast with Kevin, and before we knew it, we were on our way out to the start point.

Lana Rae seemed relaxed. Perhaps she knew I was in great, capable hands.

Kevin and I ran the north side of the Fraser River, catching up the whole way. We talked about our families, his race plans, and of course this run. He asked specific questions that I knew he had mulled over for weeks.

Boy, I enjoyed hanging with this guy!

And of course a guy like Kevin has lots of friends. Many of Kevin's friends joined for short bits along the way; and it was nice running flats, knowing I wouldn't see another actual mountain again. There was one short section with an 11% grade, but it didn't last long.

We came upon a small town called Deroche that had a general store on the route. Mike Huber and a whole bunch of runners were waiting there to run with me. Seeing all of those warm faces looking back at me made me feel very special; and I did my best to greet each of them. After a group picture, we headed out again.

The roads were getting more congested and the shoulders narrowed as we encroached on the dense city. Runners took turns running at the front or beside me to chat. It was an absolute pleasure getting to know everyone. I later found out that one of the young women had been so inspired that she had committed to running every day for sixty-seven days from this day forward. To have the privilege to inspire others on their journey was something that moved me more than I thought.

The runners gradually started to drop off as we approached Mission, and I thanked each one for being a part of the journey with me; but I could see that the heat was causing some of them to struggle, including Kevin.

At a scheduled pit stop at a gas station, Kevin struggled with his emotions to tell me that he needed to bow out. I think he felt a degree of failure; but what I saw was humility, vulnerability, strength and most importantly, a dear friend who had done everything he could to support his buddy. We hugged it out as he choked back tears and got into the car.

As I angled towards the Mission Bridge and the crossing over the Fraser River, a few more runners dropped, but a few more came on.

It was a party!

Crossing the river, I found my Ditch Find of the Day, an old ratty lawn chair.

I met a larger group of runners just after crossing the bridge. These folks exuded a nervous energy, and among them were Kelly Skoronski and Etienne Durocher, two ultrarunners I'd never met before who were eager as all get-out to help me through their home city.

As you probably know by now, the busier the streets get, the more Lana Rae worries; and as the streets narrowed and the traffic increased, her anxiety grew. She'd drive the arteries not intended for pedestrians with tears in her eyes, all the while whispering prayers.

Truth was I didn't like busy streets either, but sometimes they were the only way to get from point A to point B; and by now I'd developed a battle-worn jadedness that was only rattled by barely avoiding a catastrophe.

With the group shedding members as we progressed, I looked back to see the two smiling faces of Etienne and Kelly tucked behind me.

The wild blackberry and raspberry vines encroached the already dismal shoulder, forcing us into the speeding lane of traffic. I'd wave my arms in the air as we approached a blind curve, hoping that the driver would show a degree of pity by slowing down or giving us a bit of space. This didn't always happen. At one point, a grizzly looking older man driving a Jeep braked dramatically, pointed straight at me, and yelled, "You are fucking crazy!"

And I shouted back, "You have no fucking idea!"

Sufficiently rattled, we exited onto a tamer roadway with sidewalks for the final couple hours of the day, during which we bonded over these shared dangers while talking about pretty much everything. These two had just saved my ass. Instead of one idiot running dangerously down the road, there had been three visible idiots.

Lana Rae's eyes were red from crying throughout the day as she worried about my safety. Every time I met her at a pit stop, I'd give her a hug, telling her I'd try to be safe. Now that we were on tamer roadways, she was noticeably calmer.

Finally, we reached the 108-kilometre point and day's end, placed our pinwheel, and marked the location on Google Maps.

Only one more day to go.

After saying goodbyes and thank yous to the fellas, I climbed into the passenger seat of the SUV and broke down crying. Maybe it was the stress, maybe it was that I was beyond exhausted. OR maybe it was that for the first time in thousands of kilometres, I allowed myself to feel that I might succeed.

Regardless, I cried all the way back to the hotel in Langley.

After showering and eating an enormous platter of sushi, I called my kids. I *so* badly wanted to share my elation with them. I wanted them to know that they could achieve anything if they worked hard enough for it. I had so much to tell them about the day. But as I dialed each one and didn't get an answer, my heart broke just a little and I started to tear up. *Maybe some other time*, I thought.

I went to bed that night feeling a bit strange, knowing that by this time tomorrow, I would, God willing, break the Trans-Canadian speed record, and more importantly, get to do something I hadn't done in so long it felt foreign to me: sleep in.

Flight of the Dragon

DAY 68	COMPLETED	REMAINING
79.3 kms in 9:08:31	7159.1 kms	0 kms

My alarm rang for the final time on Day 68, extra-special early: 2:45a.m.

Our Tsawwassen ferry terminal reservation meant that we needed to be running no later than 3:45 a.m., avoiding any unnecessary delays.

Excitement seeping out from every pore in my body, I sprang out of bed and got to it.

Vera had stayed the night in the suite, so she was busy shooting all the final day action.

I could feel the energy build as we drove out to the starting point. Upon arriving, we noticed that the pinwheel we'd grown attached to for the last sixty-eight days had been stolen. Someone driving by last night must have thought it was cool and just up and took it. Looking back, it's a bit funny to realize that it's probably now in the backyard of someone who has no idea that this cheap dollar- store trinket faithfully staked important landmarks all across Canada.

Lana Rae and I laughed out loud. We saw it as a sign that the run needed to end.

Standing in the dark where the pinwheel had been staked was legendary crosser Andy Sward. Andy had completed numerous crossings of Canada while picking up bottles and trash from the ditches. By my count, only twelve people had ever crossed Canada, so our tribe was incredibly small. We instantly bonded, and Andy entertained me with great stories of his own journeys as I shared my recent stories with him.

Langley is a pretty sketchy area at the best of times. At 3:45 a.m., the streets are crawling with trouble-making zombies tripping out on God knows what, doing all sorts of undesirable things. Andy and I ran in the middle of deserted roads, keeping our distance from anyone we didn't know.

The quicker we got through this place, the better.

To make matters worse, the fog was thick all morning, and my mind kept drifting back to Michael Jackson's *Thriller* music video.

As the morning stretched on, it got a little less trippy, and more and more runners joined in, including my buddies Kevin and Mike. Kevin had me finish off the mainland, running through Mud Bay, where there is a large park with views of the ocean on gravel pathways.

Running along Kevin's section of the route allowed me the opportunity to connect with the guys. Mike was a deep thinker and always had great insight. We shared our thoughts on the last two-plus months of running, his time with me in the prairies, and my thoughts about finishing.

I allowed myself to actually *think* about finishing.

But I found myself getting extremely emotional when I did. Every step closer to the finish, I felt myself riding a strange high. The smells of the ocean filled my nose, while the image of the Ferry terminal in the distance became clearer. Realizing that with my beard now full- grown, I had more than a passing resemblance to Forrest Gump, we decided to re-enact a scene from the movie where he stops in the middle of a desert—and nailed it on the first take!

As we approached the final pit stop, I suddenly saw Lana Rae's Pathfinder surrounded by white police vehicles with lights flashing.

Oh, God, I thought as a rush of panic came over me. *Lana Rae, what did you do now?!*

The boys stayed quiet, but Kevin couldn't hold in his shit-eating grin.

"Dave," he said, "I called in the troops to get you safely to the ferry terminal."

I gave him a one-armed mid run hug as we arrived at the Pathfinder.

A group of enormous men in full combat uniform surrounded us. Lana Rae filled me in later, explaining that she figured Kevin had been up to something as soon as they approached her and asked if she was Dave Proctor's support crew.

These tough characters now stood back as I approached, although a couple of them took videos on their phones, which I thought was funny since it would normally be the other way around.

I got the sense that they deeply respected the accomplishment, and after drinking a quick Coke, we shook hands and I merged onto Highway 17 to run the remaining 7 kilometres to the Tsawwassen Ferry Terminal.

I had run over 7100 kilometres of highway shoulders to this point, but for the remaining 7 kilometres of Canada's mainland, I'd now have an entire lane all to myself. With one armored SUV ahead and one behind, I felt like a frickin' rock star. Two police SUVs would drive ahead to stop traffic at upcoming intersections so I would not need to stop. This was the treatment given to Presidents and Prime Ministers. It felt strange when vehicles were passing us with all passengers hanging out the window videoing me on their cell phones.

I'd wave back as I said to my group, "This is how Mick Jagger must feel."

Kevin, Mike and the fellas were all enjoying themselves.

I was trying to burn the moment into my memory so I would never forget it.

As we got closer to the terminal, I looked up to see two familiar faces, this time with the bikes. It was Jacob and Phil, the two young men cycling across Canada whom I had kept bumping into daily for weeks. They mentioned they wanted to run the 35 kilometres of Vancouver Island with me, but I wasn't sure if that would come to fruition. Regardless, they were happy to jump into the fray of runners and be a part of the moment.

Arriving at the Ferry gates is remarkably different when arriving with an armored police escort. Lana Rae had already arrived and was parked inside the gates, awaiting my arrival and the boarding that would occur 20 minutes from now.

The Emergency Response Team drove right up to the gates and summoned the right people to escort me through. I could tell from the look on people's faces that they couldn't tell what was going on but assumed I must be somebody important. Before making my way through the gate, I gave big hugs to Mike, Kevin and the rest of the runners.

Stopping to take pictures with the ERT fellas, I was escorted through the gates to find Lana Rae in the parking area. After a bit of a search, I found her, jumped into the car, took a deep breath, and tried to hide.

I felt drunk and high to a degree I'd never felt before. It felt like Christmas morning as a child, my first kiss, and the ecstasy of being deeply in love, all rolled into one. Like singing my favorite song out loud, while dancing in the dark and laughing so hard it hurts.

Tears rolled down my face.

Lana Rae cried, but this time they were tears of joy. We sat there, wrapped up in a moment of bliss. I turned to her and said, "Hell, I just completed the mainland of Canada."

Not long after, we were given instructions to drive forward into the loading compartment of the giant ferry.

While on the ferry, my plan was to wait for everyone else to get out of their cars and make their way up to the passenger level. Since I had cooled down a bit, I knew I could only walk at a snail's pace. I also just didn't want to be bombarded by people curious about the hoopla as we had approached the terminal.

Lana Rae smartly suggested I leave the cowboy hat in the car, and she'd grab it just before we arrived on the island. The hat would draw all the attention. Without it, I was just a skinny runner in need of a shave.

Finding a dark corner on the passenger deck, I took my phone out to call my kids. I was worried I might miss them again, just like last night, and I wanted so much to share this moment with them!

My eyes filled with happy tears as their beautiful faces popped up on my screen and I announced that in just five hours, I'd reach Victoria.

That I did it! I had achieved my lifelong goal! The kids were equally as excited and had tons of questions, and while I had hoped they could be at the finish line in Victoria, this was the very best alternative.

Meanwhile, I avoided my fellow passengers, so I could just take in the feelings, soak them up, and *feel* the moment so I'd never forget it.

Normally, I loved talking to anyone who would listen about this wild journey. But just this once, I wanted to be selfish, to build detailed memories of this exact moment that I'll remember when I'm eighty.

As the ferry closed in on Vancouver Island at Swartz Bay, Lana Rae came up with my now very smelly hat. This hat had seen better days; but it only needed to make it through another four hours. Meanwhile, pedestrian passengers had started to assemble close to the doors where the ramp would adjoin once the ferry was docked.

Word had gotten out that I was on the final stages of a record-breaking Trans Canadian run. People started congratulating me, taking pictures, and asking all sorts of questions. Right before departing, the nice people ahead of me in line kindly suggested I leapfrog them to be the first person off the ship. I kept moving forward and thanking those who let me pass until I got to the third position in line to exit.

At that point, one elderly couple remained in front of us, looking determinedly forward, turning for just a second to say, "We got here first."

Some people get worked up about the funniest things. I was totally cool hanging out there. When the gates opened, they walked side-by-side to make sure I couldn't cut in line.

I didn't care. I thought it was funny.

As I was passing through the terminal lobby, a reporter with a camera operator stopped to ask me a few questions. I answered her quickly and promised to answer all of her questions when the run was actually complete, in less than four hours at Mile 0. Until then, there was nothing to celebrate.

Lana Rae told me that the media would be out in full force, as they had relentlessly been calling and texting her. Sixty-seven days with hardly any media, and now they were all showing up for the finale.

I exited the automatic doors of the terminal as memories of 2018 flooded back.

This time I was headed in the opposite direction, in a very different mental space, and 18 pounds lighter.

The Quebec boys pulled in behind me and we were again on our way for the final stretch of the run.

Lana Rae hadn't been kidding about the media. They were lined up one after another. Some shot video from a distance, and some ran alongside me asking questions.

I was reminded of the similar Forrest Gump scene, when he's surrounded by a crowd of reporters. One steps in poop and freaks out, a moment memorialized forever by Forrest's observation that "Shit happens." I waited for the right time to insert something equally witty, but either the time never came or I'm just not very witty.

With so much media attention, I almost forgot that I was to do a final-day podcast recording with Joe Gagnon and Pete Kostelnick at 11 a.m. I jumped onto the audio link that Joe had set up and immediately jumped into a great deep discussion about this final day of running with Joe, a great friend, and Pete, possibly the only other person in the world who could identify with my situation.

They were beyond excited as Pete rolled through some of my stats. 105.3 kilometres per day. A pace that got faster and faster every week over the past 9 weeks. Daily miles that increased day by day. Lower heart rate, with continued endurance.

The man Pete spoke about seemed almost inhuman. That man seemed possessed. He seemed to be able to make the impossible possible.

I was jolted back into reality, and in fact felt a bit scared, when I realized he was talking about me. Those numbers sounded impossible, yet I had just done exactly that.

I think what scared me was that achieving my potential eliminated all the excuses I used to explain why I wasn't great.

Being great comes with vast responsibilities and makes it difficult to hide. It's also burdened by the expectations of others, and perhaps even worse, heightened expectations of myself going forward.

If I'd never achieved anything, I wouldn't have any reason to expect much of myself, and that would make disappointment far less likely.

If safety was what I was searching for, in this run I had found just the opposite.

I hung up the phone to find even more media lining the highway. My running buddies remained a respectful distance behind me, not wanting to pull any attention away from the important moments of these last few hours.

For the first time during the run, Emilio, my Salamander, had nothing to say.

We get so used to negative internal self-talk that when the moment comes that we cannot deny we have accomplished something, the silence of the voices of doubt and self-criticism is unnerving.

Looking for my coyote, I could not see him.

My eagle had disappeared.

As I scanned the distance for my dragon, even he had vanished.

I had gotten used to the daily presence of these characters. For a while, their voices made sense: the salamander spoke of limitations, the coyote of pain; the stoic eagle spoke of goals, and the dragon spoke to my desire to be great.

Now all those voices are silenced.

I continued along the road toward the end of the Trans-Canada Highway and the Terry Fox memorial statue on the west side of Victoria. If I ran any farther, my path would dip into the Pacific Ocean.

As I counted the final steps, I suddenly understood the silence.

My majestic, black, fire-breathing dragon was now inside me, has become part of me. Or perhaps was always part of me, but now is revealed.

And the salamander, the coyote, even the eagle won't approach that place of confidence, accomplishment, and self-actualization.

I broke into tears. I've never before felt anything as strongly

278

and profoundly as I did in that moment, crying and yipping and laughing out loud like a madman.

I could literally taste impending victory. Where tens of thousands of footfalls once lay ahead, few now remained.

And then an unsettling thought crept in.

If this is the best I've ever felt in my life, and I only have another hour to go until I reach Mile 0, there's a good chance I'll never feel this good again.

I slowed my pace to prolong the moment, telling myself to soak every bit of this moment up, that I only had an hour to go and it would all be history.

Then it dawned on me. Who says I need to stop at Mile 0? What if I didn't tell anybody and just circled around the statue and continued running all the way back to St. John's? That way, the high I was on would never end. I could feel this good as long as I wanted to.

This epiphany buoyed me as the fear of losing this high drifted away, and I started dreaming about what it would be like to be laughing and happy 24-7.

Then reality descended.

I've got kids to parent, a romantic relationship I'd like to hold onto, and a job to get back to. There were a million reasons I couldn't and shouldn't continue, only one of which was the damn fractured foot I'd been dragging along since Atlantic Canada.

But the biggest reason, and one I knew I should pay close attention to, was that a high like this made me uncomfortably similar to an addict.

Chasing the dragon to self-destruction was never okay.

I will stop at Mile 0, I tell myself, to make sure I believe it.

No ifs, ands, or buts.

As I approached the busy Victoria downtown on a hot Thursday, the streets were busy with people. Some knew what I was doing; most didn't. My emotions welled up knowing that I had only minutes to go before my journey was complete. Memories of the past sixty-seven days came flooding back, and I basked in each and every painful, gut-wrenching, precious one of them.

I started to think of what I would do when I got to Mile 0. Would I run right into the ocean? Cry at the Terry Fox Memorial?

I would for damn sure press the Stop buttons on my GPS watch and Garmin InReach.

Local runners joined me as we approached the final hill.

The first thing that came into view was the top of the Terry Fox statue.

Seconds later I saw a couple hundred people gathered around his memorial. Some were media, some held signs, and some wore orange Outrun Rare t-shirts that I recognized from 2018. Had it really been that long?

Overwhelming and abundant joy swept over me, and I heard a voice in my head say, *Now you can rest.*

Out of the corner of my eye, I spotted my Uncle George wearing an orange shirt. We high-fived and he astonished me when he exclaimed "I'm running with you!" and kept pace with me in flip-flops, sprinting for the first time in decades.

The last few steps were a blur.

I fell to my knees and wrapped my arms around the foot of Terry's statue as I broke down in tears, tucking my head into the crook of my arm.

The voice in my head returned. *Hello, old friend.*

Then I felt the arms of the woman I love wrap tightly around my back. "You did it, Dave!" Lana Rae whispered.

We paused together for what seemed like forever, finally turning to see my parents standing just feet away. I lurched forward for the greatest hug a man can receive, the embrace of his mother, and pulled my beaming dad in for a big bear hug too.

Dad pulled away with tears in his eyes and shouted, "THAT'S MY BOY!", words every man at every age aches to hear.

I stopped my watch. It displayed 67 days, 10 hours, and 27 minutes.

I had broken Al Howie's record by 5 full days, making this the longest, fastest run in history.

Lana Rae and I embraced, and if I could bottle the way that hug felt, I'd hold onto it for life.

I spent the next hour talking to the media, answering all of the questions they had for me. I really enjoyed it because I felt like I had a lot to say.

One of the final questions was the same one that had been asked in 1991 of Al just after he arrived in Victoria: "Do you believe that this record will ever be broken?"

"Forever is a very long time," I replied. "I hope that one day, someone can string together a hell of a summer and feel the way I feel right now. But if I were a betting man and lucky enough to live another forty years, I'd bet that by the time I turn 80 and am on my deathbed, this record will still stand."

As I stood there in the middle of that grassy field, having just run 7,159 kilometres across the second largest country in the world, averaging 105.3 kilometres a day, through countless challenges, a broken foot, Covid-19, post-concussion symptoms, extreme weather and so much more, little did I know that the real struggle was yet to begin.

CHAPTER 14: THE AFTERMATH

Following the media scrum, Lana Rae and I were the last to depart Mile Zero.

I stood just feet away from the SUV, staring back at the monument. Deep down in my heart I didn't ever want to leave, but I knew I had to.

Lana Rae sprang for a suite at the Marriott only minutes away, and when we arrived, we found champagne on ice and a charcuterie board from our friends Joel and Caelly Campbell.

After a celebratory toast and stuffing ourselves with chocolate-covered strawberries and a selection of fine meats and cheeses, I finally turned my attention to a long-awaited shower.

But first things first: the ratty beard matted with yesterday's lunch had to go, shocking both of us when we saw how thin and sunken my face had become as the kilometres ticked past.

The past 67 days had involved very little of what I wanted to do, and a lot of what I had to do. Suddenly free to do whatever we pleased, we wandered down to the hotel restaurant for a salad and a bracing old-fashioned with a jolt of bourbon. Salads and vegetables hadn't been on the menu in over two months—not enough calories to justify the time it took to eat them—and I had dearly missed both.

No running the next day, of course—and yet, it felt like we were still on the same schedule, with an early wake-up to do live TV interviews.

As we revisited the hotel restaurant for breakfast, other guests started waving the local Victoria Times newspaper at me, astonished to see the face on the front page showing up next to them in the buffet line. Of course it was flattering, and I answered as many questions as I could between bites. We capped off the day with family visits to celebrate the new record and even more importantly, reconnect with my dear Aunt Sandi who's always held a unique and wonderful place in my life.

The next day, we headed back home, stopping for a couple of nights at a lake cabin to decompress. The downtime was restorative—but at the same time, I was desperate to get home to my kids and share my stories with them. And the deep, aching pain in my right foot was a constant reminder of my upcoming visit with my sports medicine specialist, Dr. Robinson.

We got home to the three most wonderful hugs in the world. We talked and laughed until my face hurt. If I could have locked us all in that house forever, I would have. I had missed that love more than anything else and I couldn't get enough of it now that I was back for good.

I gave myself two weeks off before returning to work, and after a few glorious days catching up with friends, family and household chores, my suspicions were confirmed: the MRI of my right leg revealed a non-displaced fracture of the navicular bone, a 9-mm tear in the plantar fascia, a large calcaneal bone spur, and tendonitis in my tibialis posterior tendon.

I was now in an air cast for at least six weeks while it all healed, to be followed by six weeks of plantar fasciitis treatment, so I busied myself with the tremendous task of compiling the data to get this record ratified.

Compiling data from my GPS watch, GPS tracker, cell phone, crew affidavits, photos, videos, and social media posts made Santa's naughty list seem small in comparison. But it was important to me to have two independent, non-biased organizations comb through all the data to verify that the record was real, so I asked FastestKnownTime.com and the Association of Canadian Ultramarathoners to review it all.

Assembling and managing all these records was tedious and exhausting, and I was beyond overjoyed when I received the notification that they had ratified the new Trans Canada record.

Before I could catch my breath, I found myself seeing my patients again.

In 2018, my massage therapy practice had felt like it was on life support after my Trans Canada attempt ended. This time, my practice was thriving. I loved being back at work with familiar faces, and to be honest I never get tired of talking about the run. And although by mid-day I was exhausted and struggling to make it through all my appointments, I chalked that daily fatigue up to the fact that I had just taken 128,000 steps every single day for 67 consecutive days.

Of course I was still recovering, I told myself.

And yet, the exhaustion of the run was a constant presence that could not be dismissed. Every bone in my southern hemisphere felt as if it had been fed through a woodchipper and clumsily pasted back together. An unrelenting ache lived deep inside my body, and it felt like every single bone, joint and muscle in my lower half was bruised and beaten.

The weeks rolled on and the attention died down.

Erin and I spoke weekly to stay on top of the blues so many people had assured me I'd eventually feel. The letdown after an epic accomplishment is a well-known phenomenon in sports. Olympic athletes and other champions often find themselves struggling to smooth the harrowing transition from extreme grandeur to civilian life. Brett Rapkin's documentary, *The Weight of Gold*, narrated by Olympic champion and mental health advocate Michael Phelps, details this letdown.

The key player in this phenomenon is the "feel good" neurotransmitter and hormone dopamine, which sends messages from nerve cells in your brain outward to the rest of the body. It's central to the body's reward system, and lies at the root of the emotional letdown so many elite athletes encounter after great success.

In Dr. Anna Lembke's beautifully-illustrated *Dopamine Nation: Finding Balance in an Age of Indulgence*, she describes the delicate balance between pain and pleasure and their tenuous relationship with motivation and drive as the "teeter-totter effect."

Basically, when we do something rewarding, like eating chocolate, smoking, having sex, or using mood-altering drugs, this "feel good" chemical floods the brain—and the body compensates by releasing other chemicals that offset that rush and restore equilibrium.

As a result, the higher the high, the lower the low. For example, chocolate typically raises dopamine levels 50 percent, and sex causes a 100 percent spike, but amphetamines catapult the pleasure to 1000 percent above baseline, compelling users to administer the drug again to evade the hellish low. No wonder meth is associated with one of the highest relapse rates among drug users.

Erin and I had speculated earlier about the possible effects of my planned run on my body. I knew I'd lose weight, I fully expected injuries—but we also discussed the likely effects on motivation and drive.

Once I learned that dopamine rises with exercise and drops with lack of activity, I understood better how I had been able to crawl out of bed every morning back in 2018 to run, despite excruciating pain. If you're active, dopamine makes it easy to keep going; and if you're inactive, the lack of dopamine makes it easy to stay put on your sofa.

At the same time, our environment, behaviors, and activities can dramatically alter dopamine levels in the moment, and on the fly. Erin had predicted that during *this* run, as I ran from one province to the next, my baseline dopamine would increase steadily, and she couldn't have been more right!

Every morning during the run had felt increasingly euphoric, as if an imaginary doctor had snuck into the hotel at night and shot me up with a miracle stimulant. It was as exhilarating. By the last couple provinces, despite my exhaustion and broken foot, I had never felt so high, and I loved everything about it!

Yet now, this imaginary doctor was gone.

The daily runs that had pushed my dopamine level higher and higher had ended.

Now I had to get through the impending dopamine deficit and its accompanying depression, executive function struggles, low motivation and concentration, memory issues, nightmares, sleep problems, and the constant struggle to find pleasure from things I normally love doing.

As the weeks rolled on, I started to ache for a release that made me feel good again.

I felt like what I needed was a good hard run, to move, to feel my heart pounding—but still in an air cast, I knew that wasn't going to happen, which only made me more anxious, more agitated, more squirrelly. And the rowing machine and weights at the gym were not cutting it.

Every week, I found myself bitching about something different at my appointment with Erin.

Yet when I'd check in with myself, I'd find that I had no rational basis for feeling the way I did. It felt like I was just looking for something or someone to pick on.

Even getting out of the air cast didn't help. It felt good to be able to move more freely, but I still couldn't run. Seven weeks in the air cast had worsened my plantar fascia tear, committing me to as many as eight weeks of shockwave treatments.

Yet going through the treatment protocol was easy compared to my ever-worsening mood swings.

For the first time in my life, I threw things, I broke things, I screamed so loudly my throat burned.

A simple change of tone or innocent comment from Lana Rae would throw me into the deep end. I would find myself immediately limbic, losing all control, fighting relentlessly over some trivial point, refusing to back down or compromise.

During one fight, I blanked out, left the house, and ended up down by the river.

When the mental fog cleared, I didn't remember a thing.

Terrified, I stood there sobbing.

Had I hit Lana Rae? I couldn't remember, but I had this horrible, sick feeling that I might have.

In fact, I hadn't—but I *had* thrown a set of keys so hard it took a chunk out of the drywall.

This was a Dave I didn't know.

For her part, Lana Rae immersed herself in reading, trying to better understand how to help. She spoke with her own psychologist for support, reluctant to breach our privacy by discussing our struggles with friends.

Yet every time she thought she had found answers, I'd throw her a curveball and change the game.

Finally, one week when she was in Toronto and the kids were at Sharon's, my world filled to overflowing with despair. Bawling my eyes out for no reason other than overwhelming sadness, I pulled up to the house after work.

As I parked the car, I stopped crying and sat there staring at the long rope that suspended the kids' tire swing from the sturdy branch of the elm tree in the front yard.

For a moment, I felt a glimmer of hope, anticipating the relief of grabbing a ladder, climbing up to tie a loop at the end of that rope, and simply ending this bottomless pit I was drowning in.

I just wanted it all to stop: the emptiness, the loneliness, the confusion, the drowning sadness that filled my entire being.

But instead, sobbing, I called Lana Rae, not sure if she could understand me through the tears, or whether it was even a good time to call, but knowing that I desperately needed help, I needed to talk to someone, and I needed it to be her.

She heard every word, both the ones I said and the ones I didn't. She tried to talk me out of driving myself to the hospital, instead waiting for Dan to come get me, but I knew I had run out of time to wait.

I put the car in reverse and headed straight to the emergency room.

I guess it must have been the way I was acting or the look on my face, but it didn't take long to be escorted into a private room where I assume all the unhinged patients got locked up. The room looked like all other hospital waiting rooms except that the window was blocked by a dark covering, almost as if sunlight might be too much.

Minutes later, a psychiatrist came in. Radiating caring and concern, she asked bold, intimate questions as casually as if she were discussing the weather: *How long have you been feeling this way? Have you made a plan to end your life? Have you executed activities to end your life?*

After giving her the whole story of my run across Canada, the cascade of feelings thereafter, and my weekly appointments with Erin, she actually looked relieved.

She reassured me that what I was going through was understandable and to be expected, echoing many of Erin's points and suggesting that it might be time for antidepressants to give me increased support while my heart, body and mind rediscovered equilibrium.

I nodded my head immediately, hugely relieved that help was coming my way.

Yet I was equally furious with myself, angry that I had let things get to the point of contemplating such desperate options.

Wake up, Dave, I told myself. *You have three amazing children who need you.*

I imagined their little faces and the pain they would feel if I were gone from their lives forever.

They need you. They love you, your family loves you, Lana Rae loves you, your friends love you. Snap out of it, Dave.

But snapping out of it felt harder than running across Canada.

Leaving the hospital, prescription in hand, I found Dan standing near my car. While I was in the ER, he and Lana Rae had worked like crazy devising a plan of support, and it began with taking me to the drugstore to get my prescription filled and hanging out at the house while Dan searched the internet for things like *how to support a person with depression* and *what to do for a person in a manic episode.*

We both eventually agreed that he'd head home, both bound by my promise to reach out at the first sign of trouble. The rest of the day and night I went to the gym, had a cold shower, threw stones into the river, and meditated—anything and everything to support a good mental state.

And Lana Rae flew back early from Toronto.

The next several weeks I shared how I had been feeling with my friends and family, which was hard; and the support I received in return was spectacular. My parents cared, my brother had my back, and my friends were reaching out.

The low feelings were still there, but their sharp edges were dulling.

The love and support from everyone lifted me up. But at the same time I felt like a burden. I hated that I was a person that needed to be managed; but let's face it, I was.

At home, Lana Rae and I were struggling. Armageddon erupted regularly as my emotions and her frustration would boil over.

At the same time, I heavily relied on her to bring me the joy and happiness I wanted so badly.

Yet I wasn't acting in ways that garnered joy. We stood in a stalemate, each wanting the other to be better and act differently, and to be more present.

Ultimately and unfairly, I wanted her to be the one to take away my pain and come up with a solution for my suffering, a completely unfair ask.

And she didn't hold back, telling me in no uncertain words that I was asking too much, to snap out of it, to stop treating her like shit, and to stop dropping my burdens in her lap.

Meanwhile, the anger and frustration escalated, and our fights continued.

I had started running again, but as I worked my mileage back up, what drove me was need, not desire. I was desperate to recapture the wonderful feelings that running had once brought to my life, yet I felt nothing during and after each run.

I'd lie and tell others it had been great, but it was really just a cover-up, a happy face to hide just how bad I felt.

Increased dosages of my antidepressant weren't helping. I tried cold water immersion to raise my baseline dopamine, taking numerous cold showers and baths every day to no avail. I fought alone against the desire to close down and alienate myself from friends and family. I forced myself to reply to texts and answer phone calls, fighting my deepest impulse to simply ignore them.

Finally, my doctor suggested a different medication that might address my symptoms better, although we wouldn't know for sure for several weeks.

Luckily enough, my job as a massage therapist gave me the entire day to spend talking with patients I'd been treating for years, many of whom I consider friends. I tried to shield my real feelings, but even they were noticing that something was wrong.

I could tell my kids felt the same. I was getting more random hugs than usual, and one day my youngest asked me, "Dad, are you doing okay?"

Kids aren't stupid, and lying to them doesn't serve them. I talked openly about my medications and the sad feelings I was having, reassuring them that these feelings had nothing to do with them, giving them just enough information that they hopefully wouldn't worry needlessly.

But in their hearts, they knew Dad was not okay, and there were many days where some shit or other would hit the fan. I simply could not have my kids see me in such a bad state, and Sharon, Dan or my parents would jump in, pick up the kids and whisk them away to their own homes.

Meanwhile, Lana Rae and I were finding ourselves in deeper and deeper trouble.

Before, we felt secure, as if we had each found our soulmate. Now we struggled to see any future together. My need for her to fix everything for me, and her need for me to figure this out myself, continued to divide us.

Finally, we decided I should move out temporarily while we gave our relationship a break. I packed my bags and drove out to High River, where Mom welcomed me with a hug and Dad poured me a beer. More than anything, I felt deep relief.

Lana Rae had wanted so badly to be what I needed right now; and

I knew that I was better than my recent actions and behaviors, but I was unable to be better right now.

We both desperately wanted the relationship we had once treasured, and this was our last-ditch attempt to get it back.

We remained apart for a few weeks; and even though it was hard, it helped restore calmness to our relationship as we spoke on the phone each night.

I was now on my third antidepressant and felt closer to normal than I'd felt in awhile.

I moved back into our house and we were back together like we hadn't in a long time.

Working through our challenges with a couples psychologist, we found ourselves in a much better place. We were certainly not out of the woods yet, but our arguments were less frequent and less intense. We still had the occasional big dust-up, but through trial and error we had learnt to manage them better, and behind closed doors.

Only once were friends ever an audience to such a conflict: when we braved a public event with another couple. Alcohol fueled a build-up of tension in me through the evening, and in a tantrum of complete frustration and futility I threw a cupcake. It was an ugly and embarrassing scene that stunned and horrified our friends, as they realized just how far down the black hole of depression I had fallen.

As if tossing a cupcake in the air like a toddler weren't bad enough, I spent the rest of the evening digging a hole of despair that only magnified my deplorable behavior. It was almost as if I had constructed the perfect scene to ensure that everyone would despise me as much as I despised myself.

Lana Rae by now recognized my mercurial mood swings, but my friends had no idea. They were shocked and dismayed at my behavior, even suggesting that she leave me.

While I know she considered it, she wanted the man I had once been, and believed I was worth the wait. She knew this wasn't the real me. The real me was kind, generous, and good, and would come back.

And in fact, I did.

About nine months after the run, my body finally started feeling like it was mine again. It's a strange thing when you know that you caused such extreme internal damage that your temperature regulation, digestion, and heart rhythms stay cockeyed for months. But finally, my bones, muscles, and joints started to feel normal again.

And gradually, my state of mind returned to normal(ish). I no longer needed antidepressants and began trying to repair damaged relationships with my family and friends.

The damage of the last year still occasionally spills over into conflict with Lana Rae, and only time will tell how it has affected our relationship; but no matter what comes next, our time together across Canada's vast spaces has made an indelible impression on my life.

As I rediscover my own equilibrium, my kids, now teenagers with teenage problems, have recovered theirs, and all were in good places in their lives. I love them with all my heart and will always be there for them as long as they'll have me.

They adore their dad and we treasure our time together. Even when I tell my legendary dad jokes, they pretend not to like them. Yet I see their joy in their faces when they hear them.

My family and so many friends stuck with me and extended so much grace during this year. I am and will forever be grateful. I stand committed to extend them the same love they've shown me when times get tough.

For some, the turmoil and pain of this period were just too much. Some relationships will never be the same and I need to accept that. If you're one of those people and you're reading this now,

I want you to know that I'm truly sorry. My intent was never to hurt anyone—but that said, hurt is what I did.

I returned to racing a year after breaking the Trans Canada speed record. Counting on the fitness and single-mindedness I forged running across Canada, I signed up in September 2023 for the stunningly beautiful Divide 200-Mile Race in the Canadian Rockies, planning to set a course record.

Yet I struggled to find the fire. I pretended I was enjoying racing for 120 miles.

Then I pulled the plug and dropped out.

But this time I wasn't overcome with sadness.

This time, peace and clarity filled my soul.

The simplicity of running in the woods with friends rather than racing overcame my desire to win.

Maybe I'm through with racing, I thought. *Maybe racing will take a back seat in my life, at least for a while.*

Yet while I'm not sure what the future holds for me, I'm certain of the path that brought me here. And for now, I'm content to wander and see where the road takes me.

My mental health continues to be a work in progress, and maybe it always will be; but now, I'm equipped with healthy tools to help me stay on track, and an abundant supply of support and love around me.

Pleasure and pain, risk and reward work in tandem throughout our lives.

You can't have one without the other.

In the summer of 2022, I aimed high, risking it all—and succeeded.

For a brief exhilarating moment, for a glorious instant, I was a majestic, black fire-breathing dragon.

And untethered at last, I flew.

ACKNOWLEDGMENTS

Writing a book is hard. Running across Canada is harder. Believing in myself was the hardest.

I'm eternally grateful to Lana Rae Ledene for not only believing in me but teaching me to believe in myself. Through patience, compassion, giving and trust you have shown me what true love is.

To my mom, I owe everything. Aside from this gift of life you have lit a path of dignity and grace. You've taught me the way to live with an open heart. Your love has lifted me when I needed it the most. You always have been and will forever be the greatest person I have ever known.

To my dad, I owe my strength and resilience. Your silent stoicism and obstinacy continue to teach us the extreme power of decision. Hard work, determination, patience, and discipline heard repeatedly four decades ago now serve as my north star.

My big brother Dan has always had my back. You have always defended, protected, and wanted the best for me. I know I'm a real pain in the ass sometimes—but you continue loving me in spite of myself.

To my former wife Sharon, I extend heartfelt thanks. We met

young, and matured together. You've raised three amazing humans who share your many strengths. I am forever grateful for the support and love you bestowed on me.

To my crew members during the run across Canada—thank you isn't enough. Wayne Gaudet, you brighten my life. You are a dear friend and I hope to look half as good as you when I'm 67. Myron Tetreault, you've always been there for me and continue to be my loudest cheerleader. Matt " Shep" Shepard, you exude love, gratitude, and joy like no one I've met and for that reason you can count me in for any journey you have in mind. Joel Campbell, your spirit and giving ways are magnetic and I will forever be indebted for the support you gifted me. Last, I want to thank Mike Huber for teaching me how to lean forward and live with integrity and purpose. What would a runner be without his pose?

Thank you to my 67-day shadow Vera Neverkevich Hill, the filmmaker who expertly captured every step and reported her story from her unique front-row seat. She has at all times been the perfect professional and dear friend, and her documentary of this adventure is evidence that I didn't dream it.

I extend my deepest thanks for laser-like focus and guidance to my publicist Stephanie Gillis-Paulgaard. Your support and friendship have meant the world to me. To my spectacular editors Don Muchow and Leslie Nolen from Radial Group, thank you for your careful eye , literary expertise, and making me read sober.

Finally, I thank the sponsors who have stuck with me and made this run possible: Altra Running, G2G Protein Bars, Coros, Performance Tea, Stoked Oats, Swiftwick Socks, and UltrAspire.

And most importantly, I want to extend a huge shout-out to Bryan from Aspenleaf Energy Limited for believing in me throughout the best of times and the worst of times.

PHOTO GALLERY

Words cannot express how grateful I am to those who quietly, faithfully, and diligently recorded the everyday images I now forever treasure, and for their generosity in letting me use them here. Every picture, whether a quick cellphone shot or a wonderfully composed high-resolution image, brings back the memories, makes them real again, and reminds me that once upon a time when the magic was happening, I was there.

It's difficult to preserve the raw memory of what it was like to be out there putting one foot in front of the other for over two months. In the moment, it was intense; but looking back, some of the memories have grown grainy and indistinct, like an old documentary shot on decaying film; and recapturing the true sense of what it was like seems almost impossible.

Nevertheless, certain moments really stand out. The kindness of strangers. The hordes of well-wishers and running buddies, crazy ditch finds, impossibly delicious pastries, and most of all, the time spent with loved ones who cheered me on and helped me keep body and soul together.

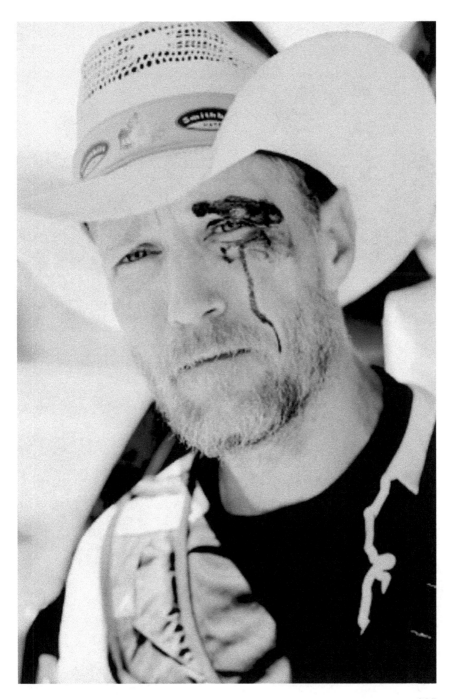

DOUG MIT

Photo Credits

Page 298 – Starting at St. John's Harbour with Lana Rae

Page 299 – The 12 pairs of shoes I wore out over 7159.1 km

Page 300 –Newfoundland (credit: Vera Neverkevich Hill) and The Moose

Page 301– Nova Scotia (credit: Vera Neverkevich Hill)

Page 302 – A quick snack in Novia Scotia, and better weather

Page 303 – New Brunswick and the infamous Theragun

Page 304 – Quebec with Myron, and with Wayne Gaudet

Page 305 – West of Thunder Bay, Ontario, after the fall

Page 306 – With Matt "Shep" Shepard in Manitoba (credit: Vera Neverkevich Hill), and in Saskatchewan with Mike Huber and Joel Campbell

Page 307 – Running with Mike Huber in Saskatchewan

Page 308 – Saskatchewan with cyclists Phil & Jacob, and Alberta

Pages 309–310 – Ditch finds, and a brief rest in British Columbia

Page 311 – British Columbia and running buddies

Page 312 – Final steps and my ERT escort team

Page 313 – Finish line and interviews (credit: Doug Mitchell)

Page 314 – With Mom & Dad (credit: Doug Mitchell)

Page 315 – With Lana Rae Ledene (credit: Doug Mitchell)

Printed in the USA
CPSIA information can be obtained
at www.ICGtesting.com
LVHW020005231223
767244LV00014B/1083